ABOUT THIS BOOK
The objective of this guide is to give collectors the accurate market values of British coins in Great Britain, as sold by most dealers. For details of how condition affects prices, turn to p43.

Consultant Editor
Mark Rasmussen

Art Editor
Alexandra Bourdelon

Advertising Manager
Jay Jones

Advertising Production
Nik Harber

Illustrations supplied by
Mark Rasmussen

Chief Executive
Owen Davies

Chairman
Peter Harkness

Published by
MyTimeMedia Ltd.
ISBN 978 1 916159 1 2
www.mytimemedia.co.uk

Distributed to the news trade by:
Seymour Distribution Ltd,
2 East Poultry Avenue,
London EC14 9PT.

Distributed to the book trade by:
Booksource, 50 Cambuslang Rd,
Cambuslang, Glasgow G32 8NB

Printed by
William Gibbons & Sons Ltd,
26 Planetary Road, Willenhall,
West Midlands WV13 3XT.

Every care has been taken in compiling this guide: the publishers do not accept any responsibility for errors and omissions and their consequences.

© 2021 MyTimeMedia Ltd.
All rights reserved.

CONTI

SPECIAL FEATURES

The year in coins: market trends 6
Collecting tips 18
Keeping your coins 24
Books to read 28
Britain's museums 34
Avoiding forgeries 38
Coin grading 43
Abbreviations and terminology 45

ABOVE: Baldwin's of St James's sold Part 1 of the Comber collection, including a superb pattern half pound for £70,680

LATEST MARKET PRICES

Celtic Coinage	**49**
Hammered Gold	**56**
Hammered Silver	**64**
Royal and Rose Farthings	**84**
Milled Coinage	**86**
Cromwell Gold Patterns	86
Five Guineas	86
Two Guineas	87
Broads	87
Guineas	87
Half Guineas	89
Third Guineas	89
Quarter Guineas	89
Five Pounds	89
Two Pounds	91
Sovereigns	91
Half Sovereigns	95
Crowns	97
Double Florins	100
Three Shilling Bank Tokens	100
Halfcrowns	100
Florins	104
Eighteenpence Bank Tokens	106
Shillings	106
Sixpences	112

Groats	116
Silver Threepences	116
Small Silver for Colonies	118
Nickel–brass Threepences	118
Copper Twopences	119
Copper Pennies	119
Bronze Pennies	119
Copper Halfpennies	122
Bronze Halfpennies	124
Copper Farthings	126
Bronze Farthings	128
Fractions of Farthings	129
Maundy Sets	**132**
Decimal Coinage	**134**
Proof and Specimen Sets	**142**
Scottish Coins	**145**
Irish Coins	**154**
The Anglo–Gallic Series	**164**
Island Coinages	**169**
Guernsey	169
Jersey	170
Isle of Man	171
British Paper Money	**174**

BRITISH COINS MARKET VALUES 2022 3

St. James's Auctions

We are now seeking consignments for our forthcoming auctions

0% Commission for lots that sell for over £1000

There are no hidden costs, you get the entire hammer price!
Photography and insurance free of charge

Generous advances available

For more information please contact:

St. James's Auctions Ltd.
10 Charles II Street, London SW1Y 4AA
Phone: +44 (0)20 7930 7888
Fax: +44 (0)20 7839 5500
Email: info@stjauctions.com
www.stjauctions.com

Mark Rasmussen Numismatist

Specialising in Coins of Great Britain, Scotland, Ireland and the Islands

A small selection of notable coins handled in recent years

Twenty Pound Piece of James VI of Scotland

Sovereign of Henry VII

Sovereign of Henry VIII

Ryal of Elizabeth I

Triple Unite of Charles I

Five Guineas of Charles II

Counstermarked U.S. Dollar of George III

Proof Gold Penny of George III

1933 Penny of George V

1935 Proof Crown in Gold

1937 Penny of Edward VIII

1819 Sovereign of George III

1952 Penny of George VI

1937 Threepence of Edward VIII

P. O. Box 42, Betchworth, Surrey RH3 7YR
Telephone/Fax: 01306 884 880
Mobile: 07798 611006
e-mail: mark.rasmussen@rascoins.com www.rascoins.com

BNTA

THE YEAR IN COINS

Discover the biggest sellers at auction in the last 12 months and the latest state of the British coin market

MARKET TRENDS

The world has significantly changed since the last *British Coins Market Values* in 2020. With Covid-19 consuming the globe, hobbies could have been put aside. However, the demand for coins has never been stronger. The price of gold bullion increased to over £1,500 per ounce in 2020, a record. Bullion and tangible items like coins have historically been a safe haven in times of uncertainty. As coin fairs were unable to go ahead, auctions took over. Dealers who produce lists also experienced a surge in demand. Once again top quality examples fetched record prices around the world. Even lesser grade coins have seen significant increase in prices.

Demand continued throughout 2020 and into 2021 when a series of high profile auctions set new records. No matter where coins are sold the most desired material is breaking records. As collectors are seeing these new record prices, more collections are coming to the market. Elusive coins that have remained off the market for many years are now appearing for sale, whether it is by auction or fixed price list by dealers. However, you will have to dig deep in your pockets to acquire rarities.

There have been a number of highlights since 2020. A sensational 1937 Edward VIII five pound sold for a staggering $1.9 million in 2021. This is a record price for an English coin but there have been many other outstanding collections and prices. Baldwins of St James sold part one of the superb Comber collection, one of the finest group of Elizabeth I coins ever formed by a collector. Spink sold part one of Tony Abramson's collection of Dark Age coins. Other outstanding prices include an exceptional group of high grade English coins which was sold by MDC Monaco auctions in October 2020. In this sale an 1839 Una and the Lion five pound, encapsulated by NGC, PR66 and cameo, hammered at €820,000. This was an outstanding price for this popular and beautiful coin.

The demand for the finest gold, silver, copper and bronze coins remains stronger than ever. If one compares the prices of English coins to US coins, where examples fetch millions of dollars on a regular basis, the former still seem very reasonably priced in comparison. It could be this factor that is driving the record prices being achieved by dealers and auctions around the world.

In addition, English, Scottish and Irish coins have some of the most beautiful engraving of any coins. If you compare the enchanting Elizabeth I ship ryal which shows the Queen standing in a ship holding an orb, to the siege pieces of Charles I, through to the superbly engraved Gothic crown of Victoria. Their beauty along with many other issues makes them treasured by collectors in all spheres around the world.

Dealers have been struggling to find new material due to Covid-19 movement restrictions. They are a key part of the coin collecting world and it is important to support them. Remember most dealers started as coin collectors before full-time dealing so they fully understand the collector mindset. Most offer free advice to collectors so it's a good way to obtain assistance and advice. Mark Rasmussen, Colin Cooke, Roderick Richardson, AMR and Lloyd Bennett to name just a few, continue to produce fixed price lists.

As always, we recommend that when buying coins for your collection, look for the highest grade in your budget. Avoid cleaned or damaged coins and look for naturally toned examples. In taking time and care choosing the best coins for your collection, you will have many years of enjoyment ahead.

As of writing this article Covid-19 is coming under control with the help of vaccines. Gold bullion has decreased to £1,260 per ounce reflecting more certainty in the world. Coin fairs will resume in later in 2021. This will see a less frantic marketplace. We can all then resume our hobby and start to enjoy life again.

CELTIC COINAGE

In the last year there has been little to report, with exception of a magnificent collection formed by John Follows, sold in three parts by Chris Rudd. There was a total of 146 coins over auctions 169, 170 and 171 in March, May and July 2020. Final sale price (inc. premium plus VAT) was £532,222 against an estimate of £296,600.

ABOVE: Chris Rudd sold a unique Caratacus gold stater for £88,040

WORLD & ANCIENT COINS

World Records Set at Heritage Auctions
The Two Most Valuable British Coins Ever Sold at Auction

Edward VIII gold Proof Pattern 5 Pounds 1937
PR67 Ultra Cameo NGC

Highest Price Realised for a British Coin in History – March 2021

Realised $2,280,000

Victoria gold Proof "Una and the Lion" 5 Pounds 1839
PR66★ Ultra Cameo NGC

Second-Highest Price Realised – August 2021

Realised $1,440,000

Accepting consignments year-round to tailored events presented to a global audience of more than 1.5 million bidder-members. Generous cash advances and purchase offers available upon request.

Inquiries: Cole Schenewerk | Managing Director, Heritage London
+44 (0)207 493 0498 | UK@HA.com

HERITAGE
AUCTIONS
THE WORLD'S LARGEST NUMISMATIC AUCTIONEER

DALLAS | NEW YORK | BEVERLY HILLS | SAN FRANCISCO | CHICAGO | PALM BEACH
LONDON | PARIS | GENEVA | AMSTERDAM | HONG KONG

BP 20%; see HA.com 62199

The highlight for this series was a superb stater, thought to be the first gold coin of Caratacus, an impressive coin depicting a naked warrior on a stallion, holding a javelin and a shield, currently thought be unique. It realised and deserved its £88,040. It sold in Chris Rudd's auction 173 in November 2020 against an estimate of £30,000.

This market is supported by a strong coterie of dedicated collectors and has avoided becoming over-commercialised.

HAMMERED GOLD

LEFT: The Tony Abraham collection sold by Spink achieved £42,000 for a Eadbald gold shilling

ABOVE & RIGHT: Part 1 of the Comber collection of coins of Elizabeth I, sold by Baldwin's of St James's included a superb pattern half pound for £70,680

Spink sold part one of the Tony Abramson collection of Anglo-Saxon coinage. This collection had been on display at the Ashmolean Museum for many years.

Among the highlights was a Kent Eadbald gold shilling, which attained £42,000 against a pre-sale estimate of £25,000. Strong prices continued with a Bishops of York (620–655 AD) gold shilling selling for £31,000 against an estimate of £10,000 and a Crondall type gold shilling (630–655 AD) sold for £36,000 against a estimate of £7,000.

The demand for these small pieces of history was strong from the US, and bidding enthusiastic. There are several more parts of this collection coming to the market over the next year.

The demand for quality hammered gold has never been stronger. As collectors worldwide increasingly appreciate the beauty of these pieces, prices have increased accordingly. Even lower grade pieces have shown growth as demand has been so strong. While this article highlights more expensive prices there has been a lot more interest in all grades and areas.

Heritage Auctions sold a magnificent rarity and important piece of English history. The coin was the famous Henry III gold penny of twenty pence. The provenance traces back to 1830 and it has graced the cabinets of some great collections over the centuries. There are only seven known examples, most of which are in museums. This rarity was fought over by collectors and sold for an outstanding $712,000.

DNW also had some attractive and rare coins in 2020. Of particular note was a high grade Henry IV noble, 'heavy coinage' type, described as extremely fine, extremely rare. This sold for just over £28,000 hammer against an estimate of £20,000–£24,000.

Baldwins of St James sold part one of the 'Comber' collection. There were many highlights in the sale with global interest in all the lots being offered. An outstanding and elusive first issue fine sovereign in very fine sold for £47,000, against a presale estimate of £30,000–£40,000; a superb pattern half pound, described as 'practically as struck', sold for £70,680, estimate was £40,000–£50,000. A further superb coin from this illustrious collection was an Elizabeth I sovereign, sixth issue, mint mark crescent, described as extremely fine/practically as struck and the finest known. The coin sold for £93,000 against an estimate of £40,000–£60,000.

While these prices were strong, it would be difficult to try and buy these great coins again. Quality finds its level and prices are set accordingly.

HAMMERED SILVER

Hammered coins incorporate a vast age range in English coinage. From crude early Anglo-Saxon issues, to the sophisticated Eloye Mestrelle coinage of Elizabeth I, and the superbly engraved pieces by Nicholas Briot for Charles I. All these issues show how coinage has evolved over the centuries. These pieces can still be purchased for relatively small amounts

MARKET TRENDS

ABOVE & RIGHT: The Comber sale also sold a delightful 'proof-like' milled shilling for £41,540

of money in lower grades. They form the backbone of English numismatics and give a perspective to history and the events surrounding it.

Baldwin of St James sold the 'Comber' collection, including a superb Elizabeth I milled issue shilling, described as 'proof-like'. The coin sold for £41,540 against a pre-sale estimate of £8,000–£12,000, surely a record. In the same sale was an extremely rare Elizabeth I halfcrown, mint mark 2, probably the finest known. It sold for £48,620 hammer price against a pre-sale estimate of £20,000–£25,000. The sale was a huge success and achieved some record prices.

DNW sold the North Yorkshire Moors collection part four on the 21 January 2021. There were some high grade rarities on offer. Highlights were a 1651 pattern shilling by Ramage; provenance included the Duke of Devonshire collection sold in 1844. This coin hammered at £77,280 against a presale estimate of £15,000–£20,000. Another rarity was a Charles II half crown, first issue, very fine, at £10,300 against a presale estimate of £3,000–£4,000.

MILLED GOLD

Perhaps the strongest area of growth in English numismatics has been milled gold. This area has consistently shown growth with interest in all areas. In particular five guineas continue to exceed all expectations in top grades. Other areas that continue to be in strong demand are 1839 Una and the Lion five pounds. These beautiful coins designed by William Wyon have always been prized by collectors. Over the last year both five guineas and 1839 Una and Lion coins have realised some exceptional prices at auction for superlative examples.

Heritage Auctions sold the 'Paramount' collection of world coins on March 2021. This sale included many outstanding English coins.

The highlight was the 1937 Edward VIII five pounds mentioned in the introduction. Others include a magnificent 1662 Charles II pattern crown in gold by Jan Roettiers, the provenance dating back to the 18th century with only four known examples. The coin was graded PR63 cameo and sold for $780,000. Another rarity from this sale was 1773 pattern five guineas by Tanner, graded PR64 cameo. This superb coin sold for $750,000.

In January 2021 DNW sold a 1656 Oliver Cromwell fifty shillings for £489,440, a great rarity with only a dozen known examples. In October 2020 MDC Monaco

ABOVE & RIGHT: DNW sold part 4 of The North Yorkshire Moors collection, attaining £77,280 for a pattern 1651 pattern shilling by Ramage

ABOVE: In January 2021 DNW sold a 1656 Oliver Cromwell Fifty Shillings for £489,440

BRITISH COINS MARKET VALUES 2022 **11**

DNW
Dix Noonan Webb Mayfair

London Specialist Auctioneers
Coins Banknotes Medals Jewellery

THE COLLECTORS' AUCTIONEERS

SPECIALISTS IN THE SALE OF
Coins, Tokens, Historical and Art Medals, Numismatic Books, Banknotes, Orders, Decorations, Medals, Militaria, Jewellery, Watches, Objects of Vertu and Antiquities

Sold for £471,200

Sold for £62,000

Sold for £27,200

Sold for £248,000

If you wish to sell a single item or a collection in our London saleroom please contact our friendly team

COINS	Peter Preston-Morley	coins@dnw.co.uk
BANKNOTES	Andrew Pattinson or Thomasina Smith	banknotes@dnw.co.uk
MEDALS & MILITARIA	Oliver Pepys	medals@dnw.co.uk
JEWELLERY	Frances Noble	jewellery@dnw.co.uk

Dix Noonan Webb Ltd   www.dnw.co.uk

16 Bolton Street Mayfair London W1J 8BQ   T. 020 7016 1700

BNTA

MARKET TRENDS

auctions sold an 1826 proof five pound, encapsulated PR66*, for €421,600. These prices show the demand for the very best is stronger than ever.

Five guineas continue to be as popular as ever, a number of examples appeared on the market in high grades. Morton and Eden sold a 1701 five guineas 'fine work' graded MS63, it made £198,000. MDC Monaco auctions in October 2020 sold a magnificent 1693 five guineas, graded MS65, at €570,000. This particular example had been sold by a London auction house only a few years earlier.

A superb 1817 George III pattern 'Incorrupta' crown in gold, graded PR65 ultra cameo, sold for €595,000 against an estimate of €300,000. The crown is a magnificent example in breathtaking condition. In the same sale the finest known 1831 five pounds by Wyon, graded PR66*, hammered at €1,016,800 against an estimate of €500,000.

Spink auctioned the Stratos collection of gold coins on September 15, 2020. It was a sale which included several collections amalgamated into one. There were some great rarities alongside higher grade pieces. Highlights include an extremely rare 1819 sovereign which was described as fine with mount attached; this coin hammered at £37,200 against an estimate of £20,000. Had the coin not had a mount attached it would have sold for a much higher price. Also in this sale was a very attractive Oliver Cromwell broad. Encapsulated as MS63, it was sold for £58,280 against a presale estimate of £10,000. Another lot was a charming 1821 proof half sovereign. Described as 'much as struck' it made £7,800 against a pre-sale estimate of £2,500. The sale was a success with most lots selling substantially over the lower estimates.

MILLED SILVER

Milled silver covers an enormous area of numismatics from Charles II to Elizabeth II. Collectors can form collections by type, denomination or year. All budgets are catered for and the scope is endless in collecting terms.

Quality milled silver has always been in demand and for some time undervalued. Proof issues In particular have seen a surge in interest from the Far East. Prices have exceeded all expectations as collectors compete for the finest examples. Also, key dates such as the 1905 halfcrown and the 1853 crown all keep increasing in price as demand increases.

At MDC Monaco Auctions in October 2020 a superb 1839 proof crown, encapsulated PR66 and cameo, attained a staggering €136,400, far exceeding the estimate.

An outstanding 1687 proof half crown was sold by

ABOVE & RIGHT: MDC Monaco Auctions in October 2020 sold a William IV proof crown in gold for a record price of €1,016,800

ABOVE & RIGHT: An outstanding 1687 proof half crown from the Waterbird collection sold by Spink for £42,160

Spink as part of the 'Waterbird' collection, it hammered at £42,160. This example had an excellent provenance, forming part of the Dr Carter collection and more

BRITISH COINS MARKET VALUES 2022 **13**

recently the Noad collection sold by Mark Rasmussen in his fixed price list.

DNW had a number of choice silver coins in its North Yorkshire Moors sale, one particular rarity being a 1656 Oliver Cromwell halfcrown. This date is extremely rare in any grade. This example was described as almost extremely fine, and sold for £17,360 against a pre-sale estimate of £8,000–£10,000.

Heritage Auctions included some choice silver coins in its 'Paramount' collection. A beautiful George III Three Graces crown slabbed PR65 went for $312,000. This superbly engraved issue has always been greatly desired. This sale also included the legendary 1663 'Petition' crown by Thomas Simon. This example was graded XF40, and sold for $260,000.

COPPER AND BRONZE

This area in numismatics has always been more affordable. Once again due to a lack of high-profile sales there has been little movement in this section. The 'Waterbird' collection sold by Spink in 2019, however, contained an iconic coin. The 1937 Edward VIII penny sold for £114,200 including buyers premium. The demand for superb rarities is always strong.

The DNW North Yorkshire Moors collection, sold in January 2021, included a group of rarely seen Oliver Cromwell farthings. The highlight of the group was a Cromwell pattern farthing from the famous Virgil Brand collection. This example was described as extremely fine. It fetched a staggering £41,000 against a pre-sale estimate of £10,000–£15,000.

SCOTTISH

ABOVE & RIGHT: DNW sold a very rare high grade Cromwell farthing in its January 2021 sale for £41,000

Demand for Scottish coins has increased and consequently prices have strengthened in the last few years. There is greater demand especially for those elusive pieces and coins of high quality, Mark Rasmussen's list 34 had a good section devoted to coins of Scotland.

ABOVE & RIGHT: Mark Rasmussen sold an extremely fine Scotland Charles II 1682 dollar for £4500

An almost extremely fine Mary 1557 ryal was sold for £3,000 and a high grade Charles II dollar 1682, described as possibly one of the finest, sold for £4500.

IRELAND

Coins of Ireland have a strong collector base and rare pieces are highly contested. There have been no major collections on offer in the last 18 months.

DNW 's sale 187, February 2021, had a rare George III pattern 1813 penny by Thomas Wyon. It sold for £5,456 against an estimate of £4,000–£5,000. The Irish market remains strong, but the demand for rare pieces far exceeds supply.

ANGLO GALLIC

Anglo-Gallic coinage is supported by an elite group of collectors. It is a complex and historically interesting

14 BRITISH COINS MARKET VALUES 2022

MARKET TRENDS

series, extending from the reign of Henry II to Henry VI.

The gold coins are in many cases very well executed and of attractive intricate design. One such coin, an Edward the Black Prince, pavillion d'or from the first issue, struck at the La Rochelle mint, was recently sold for £12,400 by DNW in its February 2021 sale. This magnificent piece portrays the crowned Prince berobed, sword in hand standing beneath an ornate portico, its reverse has an elaborate cross with leopards in the angles. In the current strong market this series looks a little under appreciated.

ABOVE: in February 2021 DNW sold an Anglo-Gallic Edward the Black Prince pavillion d'or for £10,000

For all the best and latest GB news read Stamp Magazine

DORSET COIN COMPANY

We buy bullion & collectable coins, general collections & accumulations of British & foreign coin.

01202 739606
193 Ashley Rd, Upper Parkstone
Poole, Dorset BH14 9DL

sales@dorsetcoincompany.co.uk

Est. DEALER TO TRADE & PUBLIC
FOR OVER 35 YEARS.
WE GUARANTEE TO OFFER ON ANY ITEMS
BOUGHT IN TO US REGARDLESS OF
CONDITION & QUANTITY.

Open Monday to Friday 9am until 3.30pm

---

b&g coins

We are actively buying:
- Pre 1947/1920 silver coins
- Bullion Sovereigns
- Single coins and collections
- Single medals and collections
- Local house visits arranged (further for large collections)
- Immediate payment arranged

Numismatic consultants, offering services to auctioneers and charities, and quality coins and medals to all

PO Box 1219, Spalding, PE11 9FY
info@bandgcoins.com
07950 287349 or 01406 408123

www.bandgcoins.co.uk

BRITISH COINS MARKET VALUES 2022

NORTH AMERICAN SPECIALISTS IN BRITISH COINS, TOKENS, AND MEDALS

Davissons Ltd.

- Select Annual Auctions •
- Bi-monthly E-Auctions •

All online, and in high quality print catalogs

No Buyer's Fees

www.davcoin.com

Allan, Marnie, & Lief Davisson
PO Box 323
Cold Spring, MN 56320 USA
(001) 320-685-3835
info@davcoin.com

THE LONDON COIN FAIR

L&M LONDON AND MIDLAND COIN FAIRS

THE MIDLAND COIN FAIR

2 of the biggest UK Numismatic shows
Specialist Dealers in Ancient and Modern Coins, Paper Money, Medals, Tokens, Books and Antiquities

HOLIDAY INN
LONDON BLOOMSBURY

Coram Street, WC1N 1HT
2 minutes from Russell Square Tube, Piccadilly line

- 6th November 2021
- 5th February 2022
- 4th June 2022
- 3rd September 2022
- 5th November 2022

NATIONAL MOTORCYCLE MUSEUM

Bickenhill, Birmingham, B92 0EJ
(Opposite NEC on the M42/45 Junction)

14th November 2021	12 June 2022
12th December 2021	10th July 2022
9th January 2022	14th August 2022
13th February 2022	11th September 2022
13th March 2022	9th October 2022
10th April 2022	13th November 2022
8th May 2022	11th December 2022

LONDON COIN FAIR
Admission £5.00
(concessions £3.00)

For more information contact Lu Veissid
• 01694 731781 • 07826 550410
l.veissid@btinternet.com
www.coinfairs.co.uk

MIDLAND COIN FAIR
Admission £3.00

R. INGRAM COINS

2 Avonborne Way, Eastleigh, SO53 1TF
023 80275079 & 07730 782810

info@ringramcoins.com   www.ringramcoins.com

The biggest and best list of British and foreign coins issued anywhere in the UK. We sell:

English Gold, Silver, Copper and Bronze coins, Maundy sets and odds, Roman and Hammered coins, Silver proofs, Proof and uncirculated sets, Irish, Scottish, US and Foreign Gold and Silver. We also stock a big selection of lots and a large number of banknotes.

We still issue catalogues and have been doing so for 23 years. We don't charge for it, it is entirely free. We issue 6 a year. Each one contains 76 pages and about 13,000 coins.

To obtain our catalogue, just send us your contact details and we will send it to you. You can telephone, e-mail, write or message us on Facebook. Most of our buyers have been with us for a long time, some for decades, we hope you join them. Get the UK's most extensive list.

Twitter: @ringramcoins
Facebook: R. Ingram Coins

www.ringramcoins.com

TIPS FOR COLLECTING

If you are new to the hobby, here is some advice to get you started and put you in touch with the experts

HOW MUCH IS IT WORTH?

There was a time when newcomers to coin collecting would ask "What is it?" Nowadays, the most common question dealers hear is "What is it worth?"

The aim of *British Coins Market Values* is to try to place a value on all the coins in the British Isles, in other words England, Wales, Scotland, Ireland and the Channel Islands as well as the Anglo-Gallic series and British banknotes.

This is a difficult task because many items don't turn up in auctions or lists every year, even though they are not really rare. However, we can estimate a figure so you have an idea of what you will have to pay.

HOW TO SELL AT AUCTION

Potential sellers have considerable choice when it comes to auction houses. In London alone there are several: Spink & Son Ltd, St James's, Dix Noonan Webb, Morton & Eden and Bonhams. There are also smaller companies up and down the country, such as Croydon Coin Auctions and London Coins.

The best approach for the seller is to compare the auction houses' catalogues and to attend the auctions so that you can see how well they are conducted.

Talk over your collection with the specialist, as you may find that one of the firms will look after your needs better than the others.

A well-known coin requires little expertise and will probably sell at a certain price in most auctions. However, if you require cataloguing of a specialist collection of a more academic nature, for example early Medieval coinages, then you need to know what a company is capable of before you discuss a job rate.

Remember that, while it is not complicated to sell by auction, and a good auction house will guide you through the process, you may have to wait three or four months from the time you consign the coins to the auctioneers before you receive any money.

There are times when items at auction manage to achieve very high prices, and other times when, for some reason, they fail to reach even a modest reserve.

Finally, auctioneers will usually charge you at least 10% of the knock-down price, and will charge the buyer a premium of up to 22.5% plus VAT.

HOW TO TRADE WITH DEALERS

The British coin market is very much dependent upon and benefits from the support of a strong network of

18 BRITISH COINS MARKET VALUES 2022

HOW TO COLLECT

dealers, with their professional numismatic expertise and long experience of the business. Fortunately, the needs of the collector, at any level, are eminently well served by them.

Most offer a large and varied stock of coins for sale at marked prices. And all dealers will provide advice and guidance on any aspect of collecting or disposal free of charge. When selling to a dealer, it is true that they generally prefer to obtain fresh material.

A proportion of dealers also offer to sell on a commission basis. In this instance the retail prices would be discussed in advance, allowing the collector a degree of control and a far more active role in the dispersal of their collection. Accordingly, the dealer offers a valuable and unique personal service and it is this relationship which has been responsible for helping to form some of our greatest numismatic collections.

BULLION COINS

Bullion coins can be priced simply by looking at the price of gold, which is fixed twice daily by a group of leading banks. Most newspapers carry this information in their financial pages.

Anyone can buy bullion coins (investment gold), such as sovereigns or Krugerrands, and they are not subject to VAT.

Normally, when you sell a bullion coin you should expect the coin dealer to make a few pounds profit on each coin. For mounted or damaged coins do not expect more than their intrinsic value.

HOW TO COLLECT COINS

You should obviously purchase your coins from a reputable dealer or auction house.

You can be sure of some protection if you choose a member of the British Numismatic Trade Association or the International Association of Professional Numismatists.

Membership lists, detailing dealers' main interests, can be obtained from the respective secretaries:
■ Christel Swan, 3 Unwin Mansions, Queen's Club Gardens, London W14 9TH. Tel: 07799 662 181. Email: secretary@bnta.net. Website: www.bnta.net
■ Jean-Luc Van Der Schueren, 14 Rue de la Bourse, B 1000 Brussels, Belgium. Tel: +32 2 513 3400. www.iapn-coins.org

HOW TO COLLECT

However, many are not members of either organisation, but it does not mean that they are not honest and professional. The best approach is to find one who will unconditionally guarantee that the coins you buy from him are genuine and accurately graded.

As a general rule, you should only buy coins in the best condition available, which is normally considered to be Extremely Fine or better. This applies particularly to the milled (post-1600) series, which is more commercial and therefore has a bigger emphasis on condition.

Hammered coins should be clear, legible and struck in good metal, with Very Fine being perfectly acceptable. One can obtain specimens in higher grade but they are much more difficult to get than their milled counterparts.

Collectors should be prepared that in some series and in the case of great rarities, they might have to make do with a coin that is only Fine or even Poor. It very much depends on factors such as type, reign and rarity and of course affordability, so try to be realistic.

It is worth taking out subscriptions with auction houses so that you regularly receive their catalogues, because this is an excellent way to keep up with current market prices and trends, as well as the collections that are being offered. Arguably, just as important are dealers' fixed price lists, where coins can be chosen and purchased at leisure by mail order or alternatively from the internet.

A good cross-section of other dealers, who produce excellent retail lists, either for mail order or online, in alphabetical order, follows:

■ A H Baldwin & Sons, 399 Strand, London, WC2R 0LX. Hammered and milled.
■ AMR Coins, PO Box 352, Leeds, LS19 9GG. Hammered and milled.
■ Lloyd Bennett, PO Box 2, Monmouth, Gwent NP25 3YR. Hammered, milled, tokens.
■ Classical Numismatics Group (Seaby Coins), 20 Bloomsbury Street, London, WC1B 3QA. Hammered, some milled.
■ Coinage of England, 11, 1 Sloane Court East, Chelsea, SW3 4TQ.
■ Dorset Coin Company, 193 Ashley Road, Parkstone, Poole, Dorset BH14 9DL. All coins and banknotes.
■ Format, Unit K, Burlington Court 2nd Floor, 18 Lower Temple Street, Birmingham B2 4JD. All British.
■ K B Coins, PO Box 499, Stevenage, Hertfordshire, SG1 9JT. Hammered, milled.
■ Timothy Millet, PO Box 20851, London SE22 0YN. Medallions.
■ Simon Monks, PO Box 299, Lowestoft. NR32 9GD. Medallions, tokens, hammered, milled.
■ Peter Morris, PO Box 223, Bromley, Kent BR1 4EQ. Hammered, milled, tokens.
■ Mark Rasmussen, PO Box 42, Betchworth, Surrey RH3 7YR. Hammered, milled, medallions, tokens.
■ Roderick Richardson, The Old Granary Antiques Centre, King's Staithe Lane, King's Lynn, Norfolk PE30 1LZ. Hammered and milled.
■ Chris Rudd, PO Box 222, Aylsham, Norfolk NR11 6TY. Celtic.
■ Simmons Gallery, PO Box 104, Leytonstone, London E11 1ND. Medallions, tokens.
■ Sovereign Rarities Ltd, 32, St. George Street, Mayfair, London, W1S 2EA. Greek, Roman and Byzantine periods, British and World coins, Indian and Islamic coins, commemorative medals, and numismatic books.
■ Studio Coins, 1, Studio 111, 80, High Street, Winchester, Hampshire, SO23 9AT. Hammered.
■ Mike Vosper, PO Box 32, Hockwold, Brandon IP26

SOVEREIGN RARITIES LTD

MORE THAN A CENTURY *of* COLLECTIVE EXPERIENCE *in the* HIGHEST QUALITY NUMISMATICS

We are dealers and auctioneers of coins of exceptional quality and rarity, encompassing the Greek, Roman and Byzantine periods, British and World coins, Islamic coins, and Commemorative Medals. Our dedicated team of specialists are passionate about their respective subjects, and welcome enquiries from anyone wishing to buy, sell or auction a single coin or group, or asking advice about numismatics. Our aim is simple: to offer our collectors the highest quality material available, to provide professional advice and a bespoke personal service, and our experienced team of specialists are on hand to answer your enquiries. Our extensive stock includes classic collectibles and great rarities from some 2500 years of world history right up to the most exciting of today's new issues. We're based in Mayfair in central London, where you are welcome to come and view our stock by appointment. We're always keen to buy either single numismatic items or whole collections, and are able to offer you direct purchase, auction, or sale by private treaty. Our terms are very favourable. We can make competitive offers or offer helpful advice and we're happy to do both. We look forward to hearing from you.

17-19 MADDOX STREET, LONDON, W1S 2QH

INFO@SOVR.CO.UK   TEL: +44 (0)20 3019 1185

WWW.SOVR.CO.UK

HOW TO COLLECT

4HX. Ancient, Celtic, hammered.

SOCIETIES

Consider joining your local numismatic society, of which there are over 50 across the UK. To find if there is one near you, get in touch with the present Secretary of the British Association of Numismatic Societies (BANS), William Pugsley, 0777 1764 200. Email: bill.pugsley@pugsley.bz

BANS organises annual congresses and seminars, and it is a good idea for the serious collector to consider attending these. Details are published in the numismatic press or available via their website.

Collectors who wish to go further can apply for membership of the British Numismatic Society. The Society holds ten meetings each year at the Warburg Institute, Woburn Square, London, WC1H 0AB, in addition to out-of-town lecture days. As a member, you receive a copy of the *British Numismatic Journal*, which has details of current research, articles and book reviews.

The current Secretary of the Society is Peter Preston-Morley, c/o The Warburg Institute, Woburn Square, London, WC1H 0AB. Email: secretary@britnumsoc.org

COIN FAIRS

While it's important to see coins in museums, it's worth remembering that there's a fine array on show at coin fairs, and most dealers don't mind showing coins to would-be collectors, even if they can't afford to buy them on the spot.

The UK's premier international numismatic show, the BNTA Coinex show, is held in late September every year. For more information call the BNTA Secretary, Christel Swan, Tel: 07799 662 181. Email: secretary@bnta.net. Website: www.bnta.net

Mike and Lu Veissid run the London Coin Fairs at the Holiday Inn, Bloomsbury, London on the first Saturday in February, June September and November. For all enquiries contact Lu Veissid. Tel: 01694 731781. Email: l.veissid@btinternet.com

The Bloomsbury Coin Fair is held seven times a year at the Royal National Hotel, 38-52, Bedford Way, London, WC1H 0DG. Contact John & Sophie Philpotts. Tel: 01242 898107. Email: bloomsburycoinfair.com. Website: info.bloomsburycoinfair.com

The monthly Midland Coin Fair, is on the second Sunday of every month at the National Motorcycle Museum in Birmingham. For further details, contact Lu Veissid. Tel: 01694 731781 or visit: www.coinfairs.co.uk. Email: l.veissid@btinternet.com

For the Harrogate Coin Show, Old Swan Hotel, Harrogate, in April, contact John & Sophie Philpotts. Tel: 01242 898107. Email: info@harrogatecoinfair.com

There are also biannual coin and stamp fairs at York racecourse in January and July. These are coordinated by Kate Puleston and Chris Rainey. Tel: 01425 656459 or 0208 946 4489. Or visit: www.stampshows.net

---

Keep up with all the latest Post & Go news in the pages of Stamp Magazine

philateliheritage.co.uk

PH Philateli Heritage

Whether you prefer to browse our website or pop into our beautiful shop, you will always find friendly, knowledgeable and professional staff and we are ever ready to advise and assist in anyway we can. You can see our online presence at www.philateliheritage.co.uk or you can swing by the shop in the beautiful market town of Hungerford for a chat and to see some of our ever evolving stock.

WE ARE VERY KEEN TO BUY!
We are paying record prices for the following:-
Stamp Collections, Coin Collections, inc Royal Mint, London Mint Office, Westminster Collection etc etc, Gold Sovereigns & Half Sovereigns, Pre-1947 & Pre 1920 Silver Coins, War Medals, Campaign Medals, Medallions, Scrap Gold and Silver (even if damaged & broken), Proof Sets in boxes, Maundy Money Sets, Banknotes etc.

Scan me with your camera phone!

Coin & Stamp Centre, 35a High Street,
Hungerford, Berkshire, RG17 0NF - 01488 684008
philateliheritage@gmx.com

COIN ACCESSORIES

STORING YOUR COINS

Here are some helpful hints, along with some of the best accessories on the market, to help you keep your collection in good condition

ABOVE: One of Peter Nichols' handmade wooden cabinets

Store coins carefully, as a collection which is carelessly or inadequately housed can suffer irreparable damage.

Water vapour causes corrosion and therefore coins should not be stored in damp attics or spare bedrooms but, where possible, in evenly-heated warm rooms.

One must be careful only to pick up coins by the edges, as sweaty fingerprints contain corrosive salt.

WOODEN CABINETS

A collection carefully laid out in a wooden cabinet looks very impressive.

Unfortunately, custom-built wooden cabinets are not cheap.

Their main advantages are the choice of tray and hole sizes but also, more importantly, they are manufactured from untreated well-matured wood, ideally mahogany, which has historically proven to be the perfect material for the long-term storage of coins.

Peter Nichols' handmade mahogany coin and medal cabinets can be made to order.
Tel: 0115 922 4149. www.coincabinets.com

Cabinets are also manufactured by Rob Davis in Ticknall, Derbyshire. Tel: 01332 862755. www.robdaviscoincabinets.co.uk

If you cannot afford a new cabinet, then a second-hand one may be the answer.

These can sometimes be purchased at coin auctions

ABOVE: Attaché cases are available from the Duncannon Partnership

or from dealers but it can be hard to find one with tray hole sizes to suit your coins.

Do-it-yourself cabinet-makers should be careful not to use new wood, which will contain corrosive moisture.

ALBUMS, PLASTIC CASES AND CARRYING CASES

There are many of these on the market, some both handsome and inexpensive.

There are also attractive Italian and German-made carrying cases for collectors.

These can be obtained from a number of dealers such as Token Publishing. Tel: 01404 46972. www.tokenpublishing.com

Coin albums, where the coins are contained in cards with crystal-clear film windows, claim to prevent oxidisation. The cards slide into pages in the album, which is a convenient method of storage, especially for new collectors.

Lindner Publications, Unit 3A, Hayle Industrial Park, Hayle, Cornwall TR27 5JR, supplies useful coin and collecting boxes, as well as albums. Tel: 01736 751910. Fax: 01736 751911. www.prinz.co.uk

An extended range of Lighthouse coin accessories, including presentation and carrying cases, is available from the Duncannon Partnership, 4 Beaufort Road, Reigate, Surrey RH2 9DJ. Tel: 01737 244222. www.duncannon.co.uk

Crystalair Compression packs or membrane boxes immobilise items between two layers of clear, inert, polyurethane film that moulds to the object placed between it. They are perfect for storing and transporting valuable and delicate items that also need to be viewed.

For details contact Lane Packaging, Headley Park 8, Headley Road East, Woodley, Reading, Berkshire RG5 4SA. Tel: 0118 944 2425. www.lanepackaging.com

ENVELOPES

Transparent plastic envelopes are very useful for exhibitions, but not recommended for long-term storage purposes.

They tend to make the coins 'sweat' which can lead to corrosion.

Manila envelopes are much more suitable since the paper is dry. Most collectors use them with a cardboard box, a simple, unobtrusive and inexpensive method of storing a collection.

The best article on coin and medal storage is

ABOVE: Another type of attaché case

COIN ACCESSORIES

ABOVE: Lindner supply coin albums

by L R Green, who is Higher Conservation Officer at the Department of Coins and Medals at the British Museum. It appeared in the May 1991 issue of *Spink's Numismatic Circular*.

CLEANING COINS

Every week, coin dealers examine coins that someone has unwittingly ruined by cleaning.

Never clean coins unless they are very dirty or corroded. 'Dirt' does not mean oxide, which on silver coins can give a pleasing bluish tone favoured by collectors.

Do not clean extremely corroded coins found in the ground, because if they are important, they will be handed over to a museum conservationist.

GOLD COINS

Gold should cause collectors few problems, since it is subject to corrosion only in extreme conditions such as a long spell in the sea.

A bath in methylated spirits will usually improve a dirty gold coin. But it is vital that gold coins are not rubbed in any way.

SILVER COINS

Silver coins discolour easily, and are susceptible to damp or chemicals in the atmosphere. Gentle brushing with a soft, non-nylon, bristle brush will clear loose dirt. If the dirt is deep and greasy, a dip in ammonia and careful drying on cotton wool should work. There is no need to clean a coin that has a darkish tone.

COPPER AND BRONZE COINS

There is no safe method of cleaning copper or bronze coins without harming them. Use only a non-nylon, pure bristle brush to deal with dirt.

There is no way of curing verdigris (green spots) or bronze disease (blackish spots) permanently, so do not buy pieces with these problems, unless they are very inexpensive.

Remember that looking after your coins could make you money in the future!

ABOVE: Coin cases are also available from Lindner

BRITISH COINS MARKET VALUES 2022

COLIN COOKE

P.O. Box 602, Altrincham WA14 5UN
Telephone: 0161 927 9524   Fax: 0161 927 9540
website: www.colincooke.com   email: coins@colincooke.com

Complimentary List available on request
Coins to sell? Please get in touch

www.colincooke.com

Colin Cooke Coins is founded on long-established traditions of honesty, integrity and accurate grading of merchandise, always dedicated to total customer satisfaction.

BNTA

READING MATERIAL

Our directory of suggested books has a range of essential and specialist titles for all aspects of the hobby

We have included the prices you can expect to pay, but some of the books are long out of print and can only be obtained secondhand, indicated by SH

■ Abdy, R, with P Mittag, *Roman Imperial Coinage II.3: From AD 117 to AD 138 – Hadrian*. Hardback, jacketed, 608pp. £150
■ Abramson, T, *SCBI: 69 – The Abramson Collection: Coins of Early Anglo Saxon England and the North Sea Area*. Hardback, jacketed, 294pp, £50
■ Abramson, T, *The Sceatta List*, 2012. 280pp. A comprehensive, illustrated, catalogue of early Anglo-Saxon silver coinage. £25
■ Allen, M, *The Durham Mint*, British Numismatic Society Special Publication No.4, 2003. 222pp, £45
■ Bateson, J D, *Coinage in Scotland*, 1997. 175pp, well illustrated. The most up-to-date narrative account of Scottish coins in print. £25
■ Bateson, J D, *Scottish Coins*, Shire Publications number 189, 1987. 32pp, illustrated. A useful little introduction to the subject. The Shire publications are always good value. £2.95
■ Besly, E, *Coins and Medals of the English Civil War, Second edition – completely revised and updated*, 2019, 260pp, illustrated, £40
■ Besly, E, *Loose Change, a Guide to Common Coins and Medals*, 1997. 57pp, £6.95
■ Bland, R, Besly, E and Burnett, A, *The Cunetio and Normanby Hoards*, with notes to aid identification by Moorhead, S, 304pp, hardback, two of the largest Roman coin hoards from Britain newly available in one volume, £60
■ Blackburn, M, *Viking Coinage and Currency in the British Isles*, British Numismatic Special Publication number 7, 2011. 416 pp. £29
■ Blunt, C E, Stewart, B H I H, Lyon, C S S, *Coinage in 10th Century England*, 1989. 372pp, 27 plates. £50
■ Buck, I, *Medieval English Groats*, 2000. 66pp, illustrated. £15
■ Bull, M, *The Half-Crowns of Charles I 1625–1649*, Volume 1–5, 2009. Highly detailed and illustrative analysis of the series. £85
■ Byatt, D, *Promises to Pay: The First Three Hundred Years of Bank of England Notes*, 1994. 246pp, beautifully illustrated. SH
■ British Academy, publisher, *Sylloge of Coins of the British Isles*. 50 volumes, many still in print
■ Brooke, G C, *English Coins*, reprinted 1966. 300pp, 72 plates. An important one-volume guide to English coinage. SH
■ Carroll, J and Parsons, D N, *Anglo-Saxon Mint Names, volume 1: Axbridge-Hythe*, 2007. £25
■ Challis, C, *A New History of the Royal Mint*, 1992. 806pp, 70 figures and maps. £95
■ Cheek, J, *Monarchy, Money and Medals: Coins Banknotes and Medals from the Collection of Her Majesty The Queen, 2018*. 184pp, colour illustrations throughout. £40
■ Chick, D, *The Coinage of Offa*, British Numismatic Society Special Publication number 6, 2010. 232 pp, illustrated. £40
■ C.H.V. and Carson, R.A.G., *Roman Imperial Coinage*

BOOKSHELF BASICS

Vol. I: From 31 BC to AD, hardback, jacketed, 360pp, reprinted to 2018, £150
■ Clancy, K, *A History of the Sovereign, Chief Coin of the World*. The Royal Mint, 2015. Full-colour illustrations throughout, 112pp. £25
■ Clancy, K, *Objects of War: Currency in a Time of Conflict, 2018*, 136pp. Softcover, colour illustrations throughout. £25
■ Coincraft, publisher, *Standard Catalogue of English and UK Coins*, 1999. 741pp, fully illustrated. £19.50
■ Coincraft, publisher, *Standard Catalogue of the Coins of Scotland, Ireland, Channel Islands and Isle of Man*, 1999. 439pp, illustrated. £34.50
■ Colman, F, *Royal Cabinet Stockholm, SCBI 54, Anglo-Saxon Coins, Edward the Confessor and Harold II*. £60
■ Cooper, D, *Coins and Minting*, Shire Publications number 106, 1996. 32pp, illustrated. An excellent account of minting. £2.25
■ Davies, P, *British Silver Coins Since 1816*, 1982. Still a useful reference for varieties in this area. £22
■ Dolley, M, *Viking Coins in the Danelaw and Dublin*, 1965. 32pp, 16 plates. Excellent introductory handbook. SH
■ Dolley, M, *Anglo-Saxon Pennies*, reprint, 1970. 32pp, 16 plates. SH
■ Dolley, M, *The Norman Conquest and English Coinage*, 1966. 40pp, illustrated. SH
■ Dowle, A, and Finn, P, *The Guide Book to the Coinage of Ireland*, 1969. First standard catalogue of Irish, still useful, good bibliography. SH
■ Dyer, G P, editor, *Royal Sovereign 1489–1989*, 1989. 99pp, fully illustrated. £30
■ Elias, E R D, *The Anglo-Gallic Coins*, 1984. 262pp, fully illustrated. Essential for collectors of this series. £30
■ Freeman, A, *The Moneyer and Mint in the Reign of Edward the Confessor 1042–1066*. Two parts, 1985. £40. A complete survey of the coinage of the reign.
■ Freeman, M, *The Bronze Coinage of Great Britain*. Reprinted with updated values 2006. 256 pp, illustrated. Extremely useful handbook for the varieties on the bronze coinage. £35
■ Frey, A R, *Dictionary of Numismatic Names*, reprinted 1973. 405pp. The best numismatic dictionary; search for a secondhand copy. SH
■ Giodarno, J S, *Portraits of a Prince: Coins, Medals and Banknotes of Edward VIII*, 2009. 704pp, fully illustrated, values in US$. £49.50
■ Greenhalgh, D, *Medieval Half Groats, Edward III–Richard III*, 2010. 174 pp, illustrated. £45
■ Grinsell, L V, *The History and Coinage of the Bristol Mint*, 1986. 60pp, illustrated. £5
■ Grüber, H A, *Handbook of the Coins of Great Britain and Ireland*, revised edition, 1970. 272pp, 64 plates. A superb book. SH
■ Hobbs, R, *British Iron Age Coins in the British Museum*, 1996. 246pp, 137 plates. Invaluable. Lists over 4,500 pieces. £40
■ Holmes, R, *Scottish Coins, a History of Small Change in Scotland*, 1998. An invaluable guide to historic small change. 112pp, illustrated. £5.99
■ Holmes, N M McQ, SCBI 58, *Scottish Coins in the Museums of Scotland*, Part 1, 1526–1603, 2006. 58pp,

BRITISH COINS MARKET VALUES 2022 29

99 plates. £55
■ Kent, J P C and Carson, R A G, *Roman Imperial Coinage Vol. X: The Divided Empire and the Fall of the Western Parts 395–491*, hardback, jacketed, 856pp, reprinted for 2018, £195
■ de Jersey, P, *Celtic Coinage in Britain*, Shire Publications, 1996. 56pp, illustrated. £4.99
■ Linecar, H W A, *British Coin Designs and Designers*, 1977. 146pp, fully illustrated. SH
■ Linecar, H W A, *The Crown Pieces of Great Britain and the Commonwealth of Nations*, 1969. 102pp, fully illustrated. The only book dealing solely with all British crowns. SH
■ Linecar, H W A, editor, *The Milled Coinage of England 1662–1946*, reprinted 1976. 146pp, illustrated. Useful with degrees of rarity. SH
■ Linecar, H W A, and Stone, A G, *English Proof and Pattern Crown-Size Pieces, 1658–1960*, 1968. 116pp, fully illustrated. SH
■ Manville, H E, and Robertson, T J, *Encyclopedia of British Numismatics, volume 1: British Numismatic Auction Catalogues from 1710 to the Present*, 1986. 420pp, illustrated. £40
■ Manville, H E, *Encyclopedia of British Numismatics, volume 2.1: Numismatic Guide to British and Irish Periodicals, 1731–1991*, 1993. 570pp, illustrated. £60
■ Manville, H E, *Encyclopedia of British Numismatics, volume 2.2: Numismatic Guide to British and Irish Periodicals, 1836–1995*, 1997. 634pp, 31 illustrations. An important reference. £60
■ Manville, H E, *Encyclopedia of British Numismatics volume 2.3: Numismatic Guide to British and Irish Printed Books, 1600–2004*, 2005. 291pp. £60
■ Manville, H E, *Encyclopaedia of British Numismatics volume 2.4: Biographical Dictionary of British Numismatics*, Spink, 2009. 358pp. £60
■ Manville, H E, *Tokens of the Industrial Revolution: Foreign Silver Coins Countermarked for Use in Great Britain, c1787–1828*. 308pp, 50 plates. A highly important work. £40
■ Marsh, M A, *The Gold Sovereign*, Jubilee edition,

2002. 136pp. £16.95
■ Marsh, M A, *The Gold Half-Sovereign*, 2nd edition, 2004. 119pp, 54 plates. £18.50
■ Martin, S F, *The Hibernia Coinage of William Wood, 1722–1724*, 2007. 492pp, illustrated. £60
■ Mass, J P, *The J P Mass Collection: English Short Cross Coins, 1180–1247*, 2001. 2,200 specimens from the author's collection. £50
■ McCammon, A L T, *Currencies of the Anglo-Norman Isles*, 1984. 2 volumes, 358pp, fully illustrated. Essential for students and collectors.
■ Mucha, M, *Hermitage Museum, St Petersburg, Part IV: English, Irish and Scottish Coins, 1066–1485*, 2005. 23 plates. £40
■ Naismith, R, *The Coinage of Southern England 796–865*, British Numismatic Society Special Publication number 8, 2011. 2 volumes. 588 pp, 104 plates. £90
■ North, J J, *English Hammered Coins, volume 1: Early Anglo-Saxon to Henry III, cAD600–1272*, 1994. 320pp, 20 plates. A great reference for collectors. £45
■ North, J J, *English Hammered Coins, volume 2: Edward I–Charles II, 1272–1662*, 1993. 224pp, 11 plates. A great reference for collectors. £45
■ North, JJ, *English Hammered Coinage Volume I*, 320pp, hardback, newly reissued for 2018, £50
■ North, JJ, *English Hammered Coinage Volume II*, 256pp, hardback, newly reissued for 2018, £50
■ North, J J, and Preston-Morley, P J, *The John G Brooker Collection: Coins of Charles I*, 1984. £25

BOOKSHELF BASICS

■ Naismith, R, *Sylloge of Coins of the British Isles 67 – British Museum, Anglo-Saxon Coins II: Southern English Coinage from Offa to Alfred C. 760–880*, 2016. 272pp. £50

■ O'Sullivan, W, *The Earliest Irish Coinage*, 1981. 47pp, 4 plates. Hiberno–Norse coinage. SH

■ O'Sullivan, W, *The Earliest Anglo–Irish Coinage*, 1964. 88pp, 10 plates. Deals with coinage from 1185–1216. SH. Reprint available at £5

■ Peck, C W, *English Copper, Tin and Bronze Coins in the British Museum*, 1558–1958, 1960. 648pp, 50 plates. Essential. The seminal work on the subject. SH

■ Pudill, R, and Eyre, C, *The Tribes and Coins of Celtic Britain*, 2005. 81pp, fully illustrated, price list inc. £15

■ Rayner, P A, *English Silver Coins since 1649*, 1992. 254pp, 3rd edition. Essential. 3,000 coins listed, 400 illustrated. Covers varieties, rarities, patterns and proofs and mintage figures. £25

■ Robinson, B, *Silver Pennies and Linen Towels: The Story of the Royal Maundy*, 1992. 274pp, 118 illustrations. A very important work on the subject, entertaining. £29.95

■ SCBI, Vol. 64. Grosvenor Museum, Chester, Pt. II. Anglo-Saxon Coins and Post-Conquest Coins to 1180, by Hugh Pagan. British Academy. 2012. 156 pp. 34 plates. £50

■ SCBI, Vol. 65. Norwegian Collections, Pt. I, Anglo-Saxon Coins to 1016, by Elina Screen. British Academy. 2012. 426 pp. 34 plates. £90.

■ SCBI, Vol. 66. Norwegian Collections, Pt. II, Anglo-Saxon and Later Coins, 1015–1279, by Elina Screen. British Academy. 2015. 426 pp. 34 plates. £90.

■ SCBI, Vol. 68. The Lyon Collection of Anglo-Saxon Coins, by Stewart Lyon, British Academy. 2017. 326 pp. 42 plates. £90.

■ Spink, publisher, Standard Catalogue of British Coins, 2006. 42nd edition. Fully illustrated. Still the first point of reference for collectors.

■ Spink, publisher, Coins of Scotland, Ireland and the Islands, 2015. 3rd edition. Illustrated. An important addition to one's library. £40

■ Spink, publisher, by Bull, M, *English Silver Coinage*. VI Edition, July 2015, Spink and Son Ltd

■ Spink, publisher, SCBI 61, *The Herbert Schneider Collection, volume 3: Anglo-Gallic, Flemish and Brabantine Gold Coins 1330–1794*. Cataloguing and illustrating 348 coins with transcriptions of legends and details of classification and die-linking. £60

■ Spink, publisher, *English Gold Coinage 1649–1816* (Volume I), 2020. 680pp, with colour illustrations throughout. Brand new comprehensive guide covering every type of English gold coin up to 1816. £50

■ Spink, publisher, *Coins of Scotland, Ireland and the Islands* (4th Edition), 2020. 312pp, colour illustrations throughout. An essential guide for collectors in this area with new information and current prices. £40

■ Spink, publisher, *English Silver Coinage Since 1649*, 2020. 620pp, with black and white illustrations throughout. Complete update with new varieties, corrections and rarity values. £50

■ Stewart, I H, *The Scottish Coinage*, 1967. 2nd edition. 215pp, 22 plates. Long out of print, but still essential for the serious collector. SH

■ Stewartby, Lord, *English Coins 1180–1551*, 2009. 624 pp, illustrated. An indispensable overview of English medieval coins. £45

BRITISH COINS MARKET VALUES 2022   31

BOOKSHELF BASICS

- Sutherland, C H V, *English Coinage, 600–1900*, 1973. 232pp, 108 plates. Beautifully written and the best narrative account of coinage. SH
- Thompson, J D A, *Inventory of British Coin Hoards*, AD 600–1500, 1956. 165pp, 24 plates. SH
- Van Arsdell, R D, *Celtic Coinage of Britain*, 1989. 584pp, 54 plates. A pioneering, controversial work; important for the images alone. SH
- Williams, J, *Money, A History*, 1997. 256pp, fully illustrated. Accompanies the British Museum's HSBC Money Gallery. £20
- Wilson, A and Rasmussen, M, *English Pattern Trial and Proof Coins in Gold*, 1547–1968, 2000. 537pp, illustrated. Covers a fascinating series. £85
- Withers, P and B, *British Coin Weights*, 1993. A corpus of the coin-weights made for use in England, Scotland and Ireland. 366pp, illustrated. For the serious student. £95
- Withers, P and B, *Farthings and Halfpennies, Edward I & II*, 2005. 60pp, illustrated. Helpful series guide. £12
- Withers, P and B, *Farthings and Halfpennies, Edward III & Richard II*, 2002. 56 pp, illustrated. £12
- Withers, P and B, *Halfpennies and Farthings, Henry IV, V & VI*, 2003. 68pp, illustrated. £12
- Withers, P and B, *Halfpennies and Farthings, Edward IV–Henry VII*, 2004. 56pp, illustrated. £12
- Withers, P and B, *Small Silver, Henry VIII–the Commonwealth*, 2004. 56pp, illustrated. £12
- Withers, P and B, *Irish Small Silver, John–Edward VI*, 2004. 56pp, illustrated. £12
- Withers, P and B, *The Galata Guide to the Pennies of Edward I & Edward II and the Coins of the Mint of Berwick-upon-Tweed*, 2006. 64pp, fully illustrated. £20
- Withers, P and B, and Ford, S, *Anglo-Gallic Coins/Monnaies Anglo-Francaises*, 2015. Well-illustrated in English and occasional French. 200pp. £55
- Woodhead, P, *The Herbert Schneider Collection of English Gold Coins, Part 1: Henry III–Elizabeth I*, 1996. 466pp, 83 plates. A great catalogue of the best collection in private hands. £60
- Woodhead, P, *The Herbert Schneider Collection of English Gold Coins, Part 2: 1603–20th Century*, 2002. 58 plates. Essential, describes and illustrates 674 coins. £60
- Wren, CR, *The Voided Long-Cross Coinage 1247–1279*, 88pp, paperback, newly reissued for 2018, £20
- Wren, CR, *The Short-Cross Coinage 1180–1247*, 96pp, paperback, newly reissued for 2018, £20
- Wren, CR, *The English Long-Cross Pennies 1279–1489*, 200pp, paperback, newly reissued for 2018, £25

AMR COINS

Specialists in rare British Coins

BNTA

British Coins

Bought and Sold

Wanted: Full collections or quality single items

- Coins purchased outright
- Coins sold for clients on a commission basis
- Fine selection of quality coins always in stock
- Auction viewing and bidding service
- Valuations
- Wants lists managed

View our regularly updated stock at

www.amrcoins.com

e-mail: info@amrcoins.com   tel: +44(0)7527 569308   P.O. Box 352, Leeds, LS19 9GG

MUSEUM COLLECTIONS

Here is a round-up of the best places to see coins on display in the British Isles

ABOVE: The Ryther Hoard, found in 1992 consists of 812 silver coins from Edward I to Henry VI, is on display at the York Museum.

LONDON, THE BRITISH MUSEUM

The Department of Coins and Medals at the British Museum boasts the country's premier numismatic collection, a selection of which is on permanent display including the unique Anglo-Saxon gold penny of King Offa. The Money Gallery in Room 68 chronicles the development and use of money throughout the world.

The collection also contains significant hoards such as the Alton hoard of Celtic gold staters and the Appledore hoard of 11th century pennies. The latest major hoard acquisition is the Vale of York hoard, jointly owned with The Yorkshire Museum, which provides a valuable insight into the Viking world.

The museum has two or three temporary exhibitions a year. Collectors can access to the reserve collections in the departmental study room by appointment.

The Money and Medals Network has been continuing in its key aims to support UK museums with numismatic collections, adapting its activity due to pandemic restrictions. Its database of UK collections has continued to expand, and a handful of site visits have taken place between lockdowns. Its training programme has recently transferred to online events via Zoom, attracting large audiences of people

COINS ON DISPLAY

working and volunteering with numismatic collections in museums all over the world, helping to spread best practice in numismatic collections care and curatorial subjects. Active since 2008, the Network is winding down its activity, reverting to just its website, where the database of UK numismatic holdings can be found, and thrice-yearly newsletter.

Jane Portal, Keeper of Asia, is managing the Coins and Medals Department for the time being. Dept. Coins and Medals, British Museum, Great Russell Street, London WC1B 3DG
- Tel: 0207 323 8607
- www.britishmuseum.org
- Email: coins@thebritishmuseum.org

EDINBURGH, NATIONAL MUSEUM OF SCOTLAND

The Museum of Scotland has the most important collection of Scottish coins in the country. Highlights include one of the two known specimens of the Henry and Mary ryal of 1565, acquired in 2002. A selection of coins is on display alongside other exhibits.

For all enquiries, contact the National Museum of Scotland, Chambers Street, Edinburgh EH1 1JF.
- www.nms.ac.uk

GLASGOW, HUNTERIAN MUSEUM

The Hunterian has an extensive collection of Roman, Anglo-Saxon, Medieval and later coinages. It has an exhibition showcase; the display is changed regularly.

The Curator of Numismatics is Jesper Ericsson, Hunterian Museum, University of Glasgow, Glasgow G12 8QQ.
- Tel: 0141 330 4221.
- www.gla.ac.uk/hunterian
- Email: Jesper.Ericsson@glasgow.ac.uk

CARDIFF, NATIONAL MUSEUM

The numismatic collection comprises coins, tokens, medals and related objects. It ranges widely, from ancient times to the present, with five main areas of strength: Celtic coins; Greek and Roman coins; coins of England and the British Isles; tokens, banknotes and 'paranumismatica', primarily Welsh; and commemorative medals and awards, especially relating to Wales and the exploits of Welsh people. There are also small comparative collections of European, British Colonial and world coins.

The collections includes numerous hoards, archaeological site finds and single coin finds from the Roman period onwards. Coins found in or relating to Wales remain an important element of current collecting. Occasional Welsh finds of treasure, such as the English Civil War hoard from Tregwynt, Pembrokeshire (buried around 1648 and rediscovered in 1996), provide spectacular individual acquisitions.

Visitors are welcome by appointment.

Curator of coins is Edward Besly. Department of Archaeology and Numismatics, National Museum Cardiff, Cathays Park, Cardiff CF10 3NP.
- Tel: 029 2057 3291.
- www.museumwales.ac.uk

BIRMINGHAM, MUSEUM AND ART GALLERY

Birmingham Museum has one of the largest regional collections in England, with important Celtic, Saxon, Norman and Medieval coins. Some items can be viewed online but visits are by appointment only.

The Staffordshire Hoard, the largest hoard of Anglo-Saxon gold artefacts ever found, discovered in July 2009, has been safely secured and there is a permanent display of items from the find.

The Curator of Antiquities and Numismatics is Dr David Symons, Birmingham Museum and Art Gallery, Chamberlain Square, Birmingham B3 3DH.
- Tel: 0121 348 8000.
- www.bmag.org.uk

CAMBRIDGE, THE FITZWILLIAM MUSEUM

The Department of Coins and Medals has an internationally important numismatic collection, many of which are on permanent display. Coins on display include an outstanding selection of ancient and Medieval coins, such as a gold penny of Henry III and the 14th century hoard found at Chesterton Lane Corner in Cambridge.

A major strength is the museum's Anglo-Saxon and Norman coins, with many pieces from the Christopher Blunt and William Conte collections. Acquisitions in recent years include the Lester Watson collection of military medals, with two Victoria Crosses and other rarities. These medals and other items from the collection can be viewed on the Department's website.

Visitors are welcome by appointment. The Keeper of Coins and Medals is Dr Adrian Popescu,

COINS ON DISPLAY

Fitzwilliam Museum, Trumpington Street, Cambridge CB2 1RB.
■ Tel: 01223 332900.
■ www.fitzmuseum.cam.ac.uk/dept/coins

OXFORD, THE ASHMOLEAN MUSEUM
The museum's Heberden Coin Room contains a wide range of Roman, Celtic and Medieval coins.

Highlights include a magnificent 1645 'Oxford crown' of Charles I and a selection of Anglo-Saxon gold thrymsas from the Crondall Hoard of 1828.

Since the museum re-opened in late 2009, the Coin Room now has a major new Money Gallery where many of the coins and related numismatic items are on show in a superb thematic exhibition.

A recent acquisition is the spectacular Asthall Tudor hoard of 210 gold angels and half-angels.

The Keeper of the Heberden Coin Room is Professor Chris Howgego, Ashmolean Museum, Beaumont Street, Oxford OX1 2PH.
■ Tel: 01865 278058.
■ www.ashmolean.org/departments/heberdencoinroom/coinroom@ashmus.ox.ac.uk

YORK, YORKSHIRE MUSEUM
The Vale of York Viking Hoard is jointly owned with British Museum. It is the most significant Viking treasure to be found in Britain in over 150 years. Since its 2007 discovery it has been shown in Berlin, Copenhagen and is now on display at the British Museum as part of the exhibition "Vikings: Life and Legend".

The Yorkshire museum is strong on Roman coinage, Northumbrian stycas, English hammered silver coins and trade tokens. Hoards such as the 4th century Heslington hoard and single finds from Yorkshire are well represented, as well as Roman, Viking and medieval artefacts. The Ryther Hoard is on display, it consists of 812 silver groats, half-groats and pennies from Edward I to Henry VII contained in a Humber ware jug, It was found by a metal detectorist in North Yorkshire in 1992.

The Curator of Numismatics is Dr Andy Woods, Yorkshire Museum, Museum Gardens, York YO1 7FR.
■ Tel: 01904 687227.
■ www.yorkshiremuseum.org.uk

BELFAST, ULSTER MUSEUM
The museum houses the best collection of banknotes in Ireland. A representative array of coins is now incorporated into a narrative exhibition of Irish history since 1550 to recent times. The main collection is accessible by arrangement.

For all enquiries contact the Ulster Museum, Botanic Gardens, Belfast BT9 5AB.
■ Tel: 028 9044 0000.
■ www.nmi.com/um/Collections/History/Coins-and-Medals

DUBLIN, NATIONAL MUSEUM OF IRELAND
The museum has a permanent exhibition telling the story of coins and money in Ireland from the 10th Century. Highlights are seven of the eleven known specimens of the exceedingly rare Ormonde gold pistoles.

There is currently no Curator of Coins. Enquiries should be addressed to the Duty Officer, Art and Industrial Division, National Museum of Ireland, Collins Barracks, Benburb Street, Dublin 7, Ireland.
■ Tel: +353 1677 7444.
■ www.museum.ie

OTHER IMPORTANT UK MUSEUMS
Other museums with good collections include:
■ Blackburn Museum & Art Gallery, Museum Street, Blackburn, Lancashire BB1 7AJ.
Tel: 01254 667130. museum@blackburn.gov.uk
■ City Museum, Queen's Road, Bristol BS8 1RL.
Tel: 01179 223571.
■ The Leeds Museum Discovery Centre, Carlisle Road, Leeds, West Yorkshire LS10 1LB.
Tel: 0113 378 2100.
■ Manchester Museum, The University of Manchester, Oxford Road, Manchester M13 9PL.
Tel: 0161 275 2634.
■ Manx Museum, Douglas, Isle of Man IM1 3LY.
Tel: 01624 648000.
■ Reading Museum, Town Hall, Blagrave Street, Reading, Berkshire RG1 1QH. Tel: 0118 937 3400.
■ Royal Albert Memorial Museum, Queen Street, Exeter, Devon EX4 3RX. Tel: 01392 265858.

Keep up with all the latest GB news with Stamp Magazine

PROTECT, ORGANISE AND DISPLAY

12.5% OFF YOUR FIRST ORDER*
ARCHIVAL STORAGE AND PRESENTATION SOLUTIONS FOR ALL YOUR NEEDS

FREE From Chemical Softners

Over 100 Stamp, Coin, Postcard & Collectable Archival Pocket Sheets from Arrowfile, Grande, Folio, Kanzlei, Optima, Vario, Numis PLUS a wide selection of binder albums to choose from.

arrowfile — For all your Coin Storage Needs with great brands such as:- **Lighthouse**, **SVAR**, **SAFE**

- Banknote Albums
- Binder Albums
- Coin Wallets
- Coin Trays
- Coin Drawers & Cases
- Coin Holdes & Capsules
- Coin Scales
- Coin Accessories
- Coin Ultrasonic Cleaner

100% Money Back Guarantee

*Please quote ref: **BCM0122** to claim your discount off your first order. Cannot not be used in conjunction with any other offers/discounts

Photos | CD/DVDs | Scrapbooking | Collectables | Genealogy | Portfolios & much more

SHOP ONLINE WWW.ARROWFILE.COM/BCM0122
CALL OUR FREEPHONE HOTLINE 0800 027 0636

COUNTERFEIT COINS

Forgeries have always been a problem. Here is some advice on the most commonly counterfeited coins

ABOVE: 'Fantasy' Celtic stater

There have been forgeries since the earliest days of coin production, so, of course, new forgeries appear on the scene every year. There is always someone willing to try to deceive the collector and the dealer.

However, nowadays few forgers end up making much money.

As a result of the diligence and ongoing monitoring of the situation by the British Numismatic Trade Association and the International Association of Professional Numismatists, the trade is now more informed about the latest forgeries before they have had a chance to be a serious menace.

It has recently come to light that there are forgeries of British coins on the market, allegedly emanating from China. They include forgeries of modern British silver and copper coins in lower grades, including common coins. Two or more identical coins show the same defects, or purported 'damage', revealing them as fakes. It seems that the counterfeiters sell on the internet, picking up clients in various countries who are then set up as distributors. At the moment there is not a full list available.

ABOVE: Dennington Edward III noble

Examples reported are: George III half crowns, 1763 'Northumberland' Shilling, the rare 1816 Bank Token three shillings, George V 'wreath' crowns and Victoria 'old head' half crowns. There is also a convincing 1826 penny, with a die-axis deviation to 7mm off-centre and a weight of 18.04g instead of 18.8g; a 1854 penny with a die-axis deviation to 3mm off-centre, weighing 19.02g instead of 18.8.g and an Isle of Man 1813 penny with a die-axis deviation to 3mm off-centre, weight 19.11g instead of 20.3g–20.6g.

They can easily deceive as they appear to have signs of circulation and are toned, and are therefore not easily detectable.

Two hammered gold coins, apparently from the same source, have also been deemed forgeries. They are an Edward VI third period half-sovereign and an Elizabeth I angel.

As always, collectors should buy with caution and from reputable dealers.

ABOVE: A new forgery of the 1826 penny

Forgeries were last a matter of major concern in the late 1960s and early 1970s. A considerable number of forged 1887 £5 and £2 pieces, early sovereigns and some silver pieces, in particular the 'Gothic' crown, thought to be manufactured in Beirut, came on to the market.

Also in the early 1970s, the Dennington forgeries

ABOVE: Ceolwulf penny forgery

38 BRITISH COINS MARKET VALUES 2022

FORGERIES

could have made a serious impact on the English hammered gold market, but luckily they were detected early on. Fortunately, only a few of these are still in circulation.

In the late 1970s a crop of forgeries of ancient British coins came to light, causing a panic in academic and trade circles.

This caused a lack of confidence in the trade and it took a number of years for the confidence to return.

A spate of copies of Anglo-Saxon coins from the West Country were being sold as replicas in the early 1990s, but they are still deceptive in the wrong hands.

Bob Forrest compiled a list of them and it was published in the IAPN *Bulletin of Forgeries* in 1995–96, volume 20, number 2.

ABOVE: A copy of an Apollo Ambiani stater

THE DIFFERENT TYPES OF FORGERY

Forgeries can be divided into two main groups: contemporary forgeries which are intended to be used as face-value money and forgeries which are intended to deceive collectors.

The following five methods of reproduction have been used for coins which attempt to deceive collectors:

■ Electrotyping. These could deceive an expert.
■ Casting. Old casts are easily recognisable, as they have marks made by air bubbles on the surface, and showing a generally 'fuzzy' effect. Modern cast copies are much more of a problem. They are produced by sophisticated pressure-casting, which can be extremely difficult to distinguish from the originals.
■ The fabrication of false dies. With hammered coins, counterfeits are not difficult for an expert to detect. However, the sophisticated die-production techniques used in Beirut have resulted in good forgeries of modern gold and silver coins.
■ The use of genuine dies put to illegal use, such as re-striking.

■ Alteration of a genuine coin, most commonly a George V penny. The 1933 is extremely rare, so other years are often altered to provide the rarer date.

COUNTERFEIT COIN CLUB

There is a Counterfeit Coin Club that produces a small quarterly journal. For membership details write to its President: Ken Peters, 8 Kings Road, Biggin Hill, Kent TN16 3XU.
E-mail: kenvoy@hotmail.co.uk

DENNINGTON FORGERIES

A man called Anthony Dennington was tried at the Central Criminal Court in the 1970s and found guilty of six charges of 'causing persons to pay money by falsely pretending that they were buying genuine antique coins'.

A small number of these pieces are still in the trade, and since they have deceived some collectors and dealers, we have recorded them here, as they appeared in the *International Bureau for the Suppression of Counterfeit Coins Bulletin* in August 1976.

These copies are generally very good and you must beware of them. The following points may be useful guidelines:

■ The coins are usually slightly 'shiny' in appearance, and the edges are not good, because they have been filed down and polished.
■ They are usually very 'hard' to touch, whereas there is a certain amount of 'spring' in the genuine articles.
■ They usually, but not always, feel slightly thick. They do not quite feel like an electrotype but are certainly thicker than normal.
■ Although the Mary fine sovereign reproduction is heavier, at 16.1986g, these pieces are usually lighter in weight than the originals.

MODERN COINS

As far as forgeries of modern coins are concerned, the most worrying aspect has been

ABOVE: A Dennington Mary fine sovereign of 1553

BRITISH COINS MARKET VALUES 2022 **39**

the enormous increase in well-produced forgeries in the last 25 years.

They are so well produced that it is often impossible for the naked eye to detect the difference, and it has therefore become the job of the scientist and metallurgist.

Many of these pieces have deceived dealers and collectors, but they do not seem to have caused a crisis of confidence.

This increase in the number of modern counterfeits has been due to the massive rise in coin values since the 1960s.

The vast majority of these forgeries emanate from the Middle East, where it is not illegal to produce counterfeits of other countries' coins. But the coin trade is alert and reports are circulated quickly whenever a new forgery is spotted.

But with the profits available to the forger, no one should be complacent. At the time of writing, it only

ABOVE: A forged 1832 sovereign

ABOVE: A copy of an Una and Lion 1839 five pounds

takes about £950 worth of gold to make an 1887-dated five pound piece of correct composition, valued at approximately £1,650.

Detecting forgeries requires specialist knowledge, so we can only point out to you which coins are commonly counterfeited. In the catalogue section of *British Coins Market Values*, we have placed F beside a number of coins which have been counterfeited and which frequently turn up.

Watch out for sovereigns, in particular, of which there are forgeries of every date from 1900 to 1932 and even recent dates such as 1957 and 1976.

Pieces you should be particularly careful about, especially if they are being offered below the normal catalogue value, are listed in the boxes.

Most modern forgeries of, for example, Gothic crowns, are offered at prices that are 10% or 20% below the current market price.

The moral is: if something looks too good to be true, it probably is!

DENNINGTON FORGERIES STILL IN THE TRADE

- Henry III gold penny
- Edward III Treaty period noble
- Edward III Treaty period noble with saltire before King's name
- Henry IV heavy coinage noble
- Henry V noble, Class C, mullet at King's sword arm
- Henry VI mule noble
- Henry VI noble, annulet issue, London
- Edward IV royal, Norwich
- Edward IV royal, York
- Elizabeth I angel
- Mary fine sovereign 1553
- James I unite, mintmark mullet
- James I rose royal, third coinage, mint mark lis
- James I third coinage laurel
- Commonwealth unite 1651
- Commonwealth half-unite 1651
- Charles II touch piece

ABOVE: A forged 1820 £5

ABOVE: A copy of a 1847 Gothic Crown, edge UNDECIMO

FORGERIES

ABOVE: A forged 1913 sovereign

OTHER SAFEGUARDS
The best protection against purchasing forgeries is to buy from a reputable dealer or auctioneer who is a member of the BNTA or the IAPN, or one who will unconditionally guarantee all his coins are genuine.

Legal tender coins, which include £5 and £2 pieces, sovereigns, half sovereigns and crowns, are protected by the Forgery and Counterfeiting Act. Contact the police if you believe this Act may have been contravened.

If your dealer is unhelpful over a non-legal tender item which you have purchased, and which you think has been falsely described, you can take legal action under the Trades Description Act 1968. This is a long and difficult process. Contact your local Trading Standards Office or Consumer Protection department.

If in doubt always seek advice from a member of the BNTA or the IAPN.

ABOVE: A counterfeit 1822 sovereign

ABOVE: A forged 1827 sovereign

LITERATURE ON FORGERY
The back issues of *Spink's Numismatic Circular* and *Seaby's Coin & Medal Bulletin* are useful sources of information on the forgeries that have been recorded over the years.

The ISBCC also produced a series of forgery bulletins, mainly on modern coins, which can now only be found secondhand.

The most useful work on hammered coins is by L A Lawrence in the *British Numismatic Journal* back in 1905!

ABOVE: A copy of a Mary ryal

COMMONLY FORGED COINS

- 1738, 1739 two guineas
- 1793, 1798 guineas, there could also be other dates
- 1820 pattern five pounds
- 1820 pattern two pounds
- 1839 five pounds, plain edge variety
- 1887 five pounds
- 1887 two pounds, many forgeries in circulation
- 1893 five pounds, two pounds
- 1902 five pounds, two pounds
- 1911 five pounds, two pounds
- 1817, 1819 (altered date), 1822, 1825, 1827, 1832, 1887, 1889, 1892, 1892M, 1908C, 1913C sovereigns; 1900–1932 inclusive, plus 1957, 1959, 1963, 1966, 1967, 1974, 1976
- 1847 Gothic crowns
- 1905 half crowns

RECENT FORGERIES

- George III half crowns
- George III 1763 'Northumberland' shilling
- George III 1816 Bank Token three shillings
- George V 'wreath' crowns
- Victoria 'old head' half crowns
- Edward VI third period half-sovereign
- Elizabeth I angel

BRITISH COINS MARKET VALUES 2022 41

HWI

For your numismatic insurance requirements, contact H W Wood Limited, the preferred insurance broker for coin collectors and dealers Worldwide.

Whether you require insurance at home, at a business premises, at exhibition and/or in transit* give us a call, we have a range of flexible insurance plans that we consider are sure to offer you the coverage you need.

Telephone: +44 (0)20 7398 9000
Email: finearts@hwint.com
Visit us online at www.hwiuk.com

European based clients are looked after by HWI Europe, a branch of HWI France, based in the UK.
Email: fineart@hwieurope.com

H W Wood Limited is authorised and regulated by the Financial Conduct Authority (FCA).
FCA register number 309408. For confirmation of our regulatory status please visit the FCA website www.fca.org.uk
HWI Europe, with the registered address of The Baltic Exchange, 38 St Marys Axe, London, EC3A 8BH, is the trading name for HWI France in the UK.
Company Registration Number BR021326.
HWI France is registered with Orias and regulated in the UK by the Financial Conduct Authority, financial reference number 844225

COIN GRADING

The basics of grading and details of the different conditions

It is important that newcomers to collecting should get to know the different grades of condition before buying or selling coins.

The system of grading most commonly used in Britain recognises the following main classes in descending order of quality: Brilliant Uncirculated (B Unc, BU), Uncirculated (Unc), Extremely Fine (EF), Very Fine (VF), Fine (F), Fair, Poor.

Beginners often get confused when they first encounter these grades.

The word 'fine' implies a coin of high quality, yet this grade is near the bottom of the scale. Fine is, in fact, about the lowest grade acceptable to most collectors of modern coinage in Britain.

But, to some extent, the grade 'is in the eye of the beholder', and there are always likely to be differences of opinion as to the exact grade of a coin.

Some collectors and dealers have tried to make the existing scale of definitions more exact by adding letters such as N (Nearly), G (Good, meaning slightly better than the grade), A (About or Almost) and so on. In cases where a coin wears more on one side than the other, two grades are shown, the first for the obverse, the second for the reverse such as: GVF/EF.

Any major faults not apparent from the use of a particular grade are often described separately. These include dents and noticeable scratches, discoloration, areas of corrosion, edge knocks and holes.

SPECIAL TERMS
Full mint lustre
There are two schools of thought on the use of the terms Brilliant Uncirculated and Uncirculated. The former is often considered to be the most useful and descriptive term for coins of copper, bronze, nickel-brass or other base metals, which display what is known as 'full mint lustre'.

When this term is being used it is often necessary to employ the grade Uncirculated to describe coins which have never been circulated but have lost the original lustre of a newly minted coin.

However, some dealers and collectors tend to classify as Uncirculated all coins which have not circulated, whether they are brilliant or toned, and do not use the term Brilliant Uncirculated.

Fleur de coin
Sometimes FDC (fleur de coin) is used to define top-grade coins, but it really only applies to pieces in perfect mint state with no flaws or surface scratches.

With modern methods of minting, slight damage to the surface is inevitable, except in the case of proofs, and therefore Brilliant Uncirculated or Uncirculated best describe the highest grade of modern coins.

The word 'proof' should not be used to denote a coin's condition. Proofs are pieces struck on specially prepared blanks from highly polished dies and usually have a mirror-like finish.

Fair and Poor
Fair is applied to very worn coins which still have the main parts of the design distinguished and Poor denotes a grade in which the design and rim are worn almost flat and few details are discernible.

AMERICAN GRADING
The American grading system is quite different to the British one. It purports to be a lot more accurate, but is actually much more prone, in our opinion, to be abused, and we prefer the British dealers' more conservative methods of grading.

American dealers use many more terms, ranging from Mint State to About Good. The latter could be described as 'very heavily worn, with portions of lettering, date and legend worn smooth. The date may be partially legible'. In Britain we would simply say 'Poor'.

There is also a numerical method of describing coins, often used in the United States. For example, an MS–65 coin would be Mint State and a 65 would mean 'an above average Uncirculated coin which may be brilliant or lightly toned but has some surface marks'.

The MS system seemed to be acceptable at first but there are two schools of thought in the United States and you will quite frequently see coins graded in the more traditional manner in sale catalogues.

GRADING EXAMPLES

It would be impossible to show every coin in different grades. We show instead representative examples from three different periods in the British series, to illustrate the middle range of coin conditions.

Each coin is shown in Extremely Fine, Very Fine and Fine condition.

Extremely Fine
This describes coins which have been put into circulation, but have received only the minimum amount of damage since. There may be a few slight marks or minute scratches in the field, – the flat area around the main design – but otherwise the coin should show little sign of having been in circulation.

Very Fine
Coins in very fine condition show some wear on the raised surfaces, but all other detail is very clear. Here, all three coins have had a little wear which can be seen in the details of the hair and face. But they are still in attractive condition from the collector's viewpoint.

Fine
In this grade coins show noticeable wear on the raised parts of the design; most other details should still be clear.

GRADES OF COIN

EXTREMELY FINE (EF)

VERY FINE (VF)

FINE (F)

44 BRITISH COINS MARKET VALUES 2022

ABBREVIATIONS & TERMS

These are the abbreviations and terms used in the price guide section

* Asterisks against some dates indicate that no firm prices were available at the time of going to press.
2mm The P of PENNY is 2mm from the trident on some 1895 pennies. Otherwise, the gap is 1mm
AE numismatic symbol for copper or copper alloys
Arabic 1 or Roman I varieties of the 1 in 1887
arcs decorative border of arcs which vary in number
B on William III coins, minted at Bristol
BB beaded border
BBITANNIAR lettering error
Bank of England issued overstruck Spanish dollars for currency use in Britain 1804–1811
black farthings 1897–1918, artificially darkened to avoid confusion with half sovereigns
brilit lettering error
B Unc, BU Brilliant Uncirculated condition
BV bullion value
C on milled gold coins, minted at Ottawa, Canada
C on William III coins, minted at Chester
close colon colon close to DEF
crosslet 4 having upper and lower serifs on the horizontal bar of the 4 (compare plain 4)
cu-ni cupro-nickel
debased in 1920 the silver fineness in British coins was debased from .925 to .500
'Dorrien and Magens' issue of shillings by a group of bankers, which was suppressed on the day of issue
DRITANNIAR lettering error
E minted at Exeter on William III coins
E, E* on Queen Anne coins, minted at Edinburgh
Edin Edinburgh
EEC European Economic Community
EF over price column Extremely Fine condition

ABOVE: E.I.C. initials

ABOVE: English shilling, 1937–46

E.I.C. East India Co, supplier of metal
Eleph, eleph & castle elephant or elephant and castle provenance mark, below the bust. Taken from the badge of the African ('Guinea') Company, which imported the metal for the coins
Eng English shilling. In 1937, English and Scottish versions of the shilling were introduced. English designs have a lion standing on a crown between 1937–1951 and three leopards on a shield between 1953–66
exergue segment below main design, usually containing the date
Ext extremely
F face value only
F over price column Fine condition
F forgeries exist of these pieces. In some cases the forgeries are complete fakes. In others where a particular date is rare, the date of a common coin has been altered. Be very cautious when buying any of these coins
Fair rather worn condition
fantasies non-currency items, often just produced for the benefit of collectors
far colon colon further from DEF than in close colon variety
FDC fleur de coin. A term used to describe coins in perfect mint condition, with no flaws, scratches or other marks
fillet hair band
flan blank for a coin or medal
GEOE lettering error
Gothic Victorian coins featuring Gothic-style portrait and lettering
guinea-head die used for obverse of guinea

ABOVE: Victoria Gothic florin

ABOVE: The Jubilee Head was introduced in 1887 to mark Victoria's Golden Jubilee

ABOVE: KN mintmark

BRITISH COINS MARKET VALUES 2022 **45**

TERMINOLOGY

H mintmark of The Mint, Birmingham
hd head
hp, harp for example early, ordinary varieties of the Irish harp on reverse
hearts motif in top right-hand corner of Hanoverian shield on reverse
im initial mark
inc incised, sunk in
inv inverted
JH Jubilee Head
KN mintmark of the Kings Norton Metal Company
L.C.W. Initials of Leonard Charles Wyon, engraver
LIMA coins bearing this word were struck from bullion captured from vessels carrying South American treasure, which may have come from Lima, Peru
low horizon on normal coins the horizon meets the point where Britannia's left leg crosses behind the right. On this variety the horizon is lower
LVIII etc regnal year in Roman numerals on the edge
matt type of proof without a mirror-like finish
M on gold coins minted at Melbourne, Australia
'military' popular name for the 1813 guinea struck for the payment of troops fighting in the Napoleonic Wars
mm mintmark
mod eff modified effigy of George V
mule coin struck from wrongly paired dies
N on William III coins, minted at Norwich
obv obverse, usually the 'head' side of a coin
OH Old Head
OT ornamental trident
P on gold coins, minted at Perth, Australia
pattern trial piece not issued for currency
piedfort a coin which has been specially struck on a thicker than normal blank. In France, where the term originates, the kings seem to have issued them as presentation pieces from the 12th century onwards. In Britain, Medieval and Tudor examples are known, and their issue has been reintroduced by the Royal Mint, starting with the twenty pence piedfort of 1982
plain on silver coins, no provenance marks in angles between shields on reverse
plain 4 with upper serif only to horizontal bar of 4
plumes symbol denoting Welsh mines as the source of the metal

ABOVE: 'Military' guinea, reverse

ABOVE: Plumes provenance mark

proof coin specially struck from highly polished dies. Usually has a mirror-like surface
prov a provenance mark on a coin, such as a rose, plume or elephant, which indicates the supplier of the bullion from which the coin was struck
PT plain trident
raised in relief, not incuse
RB round beads in border
rev reverse, 'tail' side of coin
r & p roses and plumes
rose symbol denoting west of England mines as the source of the metal
PRITANNIAR lettering error
QVARTO fourth regnal year, on edge
QVINTO fifth regnal year, on edge
rsd raised
S on gold coins minted at Sydney, Australia
SA on gold coins mined at Pretoria, South Africa
Scot Scottish shilling. In 1937, English and Scottish versions of the shilling were introduced. Scottish designs have a lion seated on crown, holding a sword and sceptre between 1937–51 and a lion rampant on a shield between 1953–66
SS C South Sea Company, the source of the metal
SECUNDO second regnal year, on edge
SEPTIMO seventh regnal year, on edge
Slabbed a term referring to a coin that has been graded and encapsulated.
'spade' the spade-like shape of the shield on George III gold coins
TB toothed beads in border
TERTIO third regnal year, on edge
trnctn base of head or bust where the neck or shoulders terminate
Unc Uncirculated condition
var variety
VF above price column Very Fine condition
VIGO struck from bullion captured in Vigo Bay, Spain
VIP 'very important person'. The so-called VIP crowns were the true proofs for the years of issue. Probably most of the limited number struck would have been presented to high-ranking officials
W.C.C. Welsh Copper Company, indicating the supplier of the metal
wire type figure of value in thin wire-like script
W.W., ww initials of William Wyon, engraver
xxri lettering error
y, Y on William III coins minted in York
YH Young Head

ABOVE: 1723 halfcrown with W.C.C. initials

46 BRITISH COINS MARKET VALUES 2022

St. James's Auctions

Auctioneers of Rare Coins

George V, sovereign, 1920S
Sold for £525,000
The only UK auctioneer to have sold
two different 1920S sovereigns

0% Commission for lots that sell for over £1000
There are no hidden costs, you get the entire hammer price!

St. James's Auctions Ltd.
10 Charles II Street, St. James's, London SW1Y 4AA
Phone: +44 (0)20 7930 7888
Fax: +44 (0)20 7839 5500
Email: info@stjauctions.com
www.stjauctions.com

BNTA

PAUL DAVIES
– WE BUY –

WORLD GOLD COINS
MODERN BRITISH GOLD AND SILVER PROOF COINS
WORLD GOLD AND SILVER PROOF SETS

PLEASE CONTACT US IF YOU HAVE ANYTHING TO SELL

PAUL DAVIES
PO BOX 17, ILKLEY
WEST YORKSHIRE LS29 8TZ, ENGLAND
PHONE: 01943 603116
EMAIL: paul@pauldaviesltd.co.uk

ANA LIFE MEMBER

BNTA

PETER MORRIS
Dealer in Coins & Medals

BNTA

Retail: **1 STATION CONCOURSE, BROMLEY NORTH BR STATION, KENT**
Postal: **P.O. BOX 233, BROMLEY, KENT BR1 4EQ**

Buying and Selling
COINS, MEDALS, BANKNOTES, TOKENS AND ANTIQUITIES

Shop Hours: Mon-Fri 10am-6pm, Sat 9am-2pm Closed Wed

Send for list - ask for one of our six - coins/tokens/medals/notes or ancients.

Tel: 020-8313 3410   Fax: 020-8466 8502
Visit our Web Site: www.petermorris.co.uk   Email: info@petermorris.co.uk

MARKET PRICES

CELTIC COINAGE

The early British series is the hardest to price, as the market has developed considerably since the publication of R D Van Arsdell's *Celtic Coinage of Britain* in 1989, an essential book for collectors.

A number of forgeries of this series exist, some of relatively recent production, and numerous items from undeclared hoards are also on the market. It is therefore essential to buy from a reputable dealer.

We are very grateful for the help of Robert Van Arsdell who produced the synopsis of the material we have used.

We have kept this very basic, and linked it for easy reference with *The Coinage of Ancient Britain* by R P Mack, third edition (now out of print), and with the *British Museum Catalogue of British Iron Age Coins* by R Hobbs, where possible.

In the listings, Mack types are indicated by 'M' and BMC types by 'B'. The V numbers relate to the Van Arsdell catalogue. The existence of forgeries is indicated by F.

The map on the right shows the distribution of the tribes in Britain based on the map in *The Coinage of Ancient Britain*, by R P Mack, published by Spink and B A Seaby Ltd.

KEY TO TOWNS:
1. Calleva Atrebatum (Silchester)
2. Verulamium (St Albans)
3. Camulodunum (Colchester)

■ GOLD STATERS WITHOUT LEGENDS

AMBIANI	F	VF
Large flan type M1, 3, V10, 12	£2500	£6250
Defaced die type M5, 7, V30, 33	£700	£2250
Abstract type M26, 30, V44, 46	£325	£950
Gallic War type M27, a, V50, 52 F	£200	£475

ABOVE: Gallo-Belgic Stater

SUESSIONES		
Abstract type M34a, V85	£575	£1950

VE MONOGRAM		
M82, a, b, V87 F	£395	£1250

WESTERHAM	F	VF
M28, 29, V200, 202, B1–24	£275	£685

ABOVE: Chute Gold Stater

CHUTE		
M32, V1205, B35–76 F	£225	£495

CLACTON		
Type I M47, V1458, B137–144	£525	£1675
Type II M46, a, V30, 1455, B145–179	£375	£1325

CORIELTAUVI		
Scyphate type M–, V–, B3187–93	£225	£525

CORIELTAUVI (N E COAST TYPE)		
Type I M50–M51a, V800, B182–191	£225	£600
Type II M52–57, S27, V804	£265	£650

CELTIC COINAGE

	F	VF
NORFOLK Wolf type M49, a, b, V610, B212–278	£385	£1375
CORIELTAUVI South Ferriby Kite & Domino type, M449–450a, V811, B3146–3186	£300	£750

ABOVE: Corieltauvi (South Ferriby) Stater

	F	VF
WHADDON CHASE M133–138, V1470–1478, B279–350 F	£250	£700
Middle, Late Whaddon Chase V1485–1509	£300	£850
WONERSH M147, 148, V1522, B351–56	£550	£1750
WEALD M84, 229, V144, 150, B2466–68	£1100	£3650
ICENI Freckenham Type I M397–399, 403b, V620, B3384–95	£475	£1100
Freckenham Type II M401, 2, 3a, 3c, V626, B3396–3419	£475	£1250
Snettisham Type M–, V–, B3353–83	£700	£2000
ATREBATIC M58–61, V210–216, B445–76	£295	£825
SAVERNAKE FOREST M62, V1526, B359–64	£225	£650
DOBUNNIC M374, V1005, B2937–40	£750	£2500

ABOVE: Iceni Stater

■ GOLD QUARTER STATERS WITHOUT LEGENDS

	F	VF
AMBIANI Large flan type M2, 4, V15, 20 F	£425	£1100
Defaced die type M6, 8, V35, 37	£395	£950
GEOMETRIC M37, 39, 41, 41A, 42, V65, 146, 69, 67	£170	£475
SUSSEX M40, 43–45, V143, 1225–1229	£100	£250
VE MONOGRAM M83, V87 F	£165	£425
ATREBATIC M63–6, 69–75, V220–256, B478–546	£165	£450
KENTISH Caesar's Trophy type V145	£165	£450

■ GOLD STATERS WITH LEGENDS

	F	VF
COMMIUS M92, V350, B724–730	£485	£1000
TINCOMARUS M93, 94,93, V362, 363, B761–74	£875	£2650
VERICA Equestrian type M121, V500, B1143–58	£400	£1100
Vine leaf type M125, V520, B1159–76	£425	£1375
EPATICCUS M262, V575, B2021–23	£1350	£3950
CARATACUS Warrior CCI 20.0001 (this coin)	Ext. rare	
DUBNOVELLANUS In Kent M283, V176, B2492–98	£475	£1425
In Essex M275, V1650, B2425–40	£365	£1050
EPPILLUS In Kent M300–1, V430, B1125–28	£3000	£8250
ADDEDOMAROS M266, 7, V1605, B2390–94 F Three types	£395	£1200
TASCIOVANUS Bucranium M149, V1680, B1591–1607 F	£500	£1650
Equestrian M154–7, V1730–1736, B1608–13	£400	£1200
TASCIO/RICON M184, V1780, B1625–36	£800	£2350
SEGO M194, V1845, B1625–27	£2650	£7000

CELTIC COINAGE

ANDOCO
M197, V1860, B2011–14 £900 £2650

ABOVE: Tasciovanus 'Celtic Warrior' Stater

ABOVE: Cunobeline Stater

CUNOBELINE	F	VF
Two horses M201, V1910, B1769–71	£925	£2650
Corn ear M203 etc V2010, B1772–1835 F	£425	£975

ANTED of the Dobunni
M385–6, V1062–1066, B3023–27 F £750 £1950

EISU
M388, V1105, B3039–42 F £825 £2500

INAM
M390, V1140, B3056 F £1750 £5750

CATTI
M391, V1130, B3057–60 F £685 £1850

COMUX
M392, V1092, B3061–63 F £1750 £5000

CORIO
M393, V1035, B3064–3133 £785 £2000

BODVOC
M395, V1052, B3135–42 F £1350 £3000

ABOVE: Volisios Dumnocoveros Stater

AVN COST
ABC 1929; V.910; BMC 3258 £400 £1500

ESVP RASV
ABC 1917; V. 920; BMC 3269 £400 £1200

VEP
ABC 1851; V.905; BMC3274–75 £450 £1625

VEP CORF
M549–460, V940, 930, B3296–3304 F £400 £1100

DUMNOC TIGIR SENO
M461, V972, B3325–27 £725 £2650

VOLISIOS DUMNOCOVEROS
M463, V978, B3330–36 £485 £1625

VOLISIOS CARTIVEL £1250 £4500
VA 933
LAT ISON
ABC 1956 Ext. rare
ECEN
ABC 1651, V.725, BMC 4032 £900 £2750

ABOVE: Cunobeline Quarter Stater

■ GOLD QUARTER STATERS WITH LEGENDS

TINCOMARUS
Abstract type M95, V365 £185 £500
Medusa head type M97, V378, B811–26 £485 £1500
Tablet type M101–4, V387–390, B825–79 £165 £485

EPPILLUS
Calleva M107, V407, B986–1015 £195 £525

VERICA
Horse type M111–114, V465–468, B1143–46 £195 £525

TASCIOVANUS
Horse type M152–3, V1690, 1692, B1641–1650 £200 £525

CUNOBELINE
Various types, B1836–55 from £195 £500

■ SILVER COINS WITHOUT LEGENDS

DUROTRIGES
Silver Stater M317, V1235, B2525–2731 F £90 £275
Geometric type M319, V1242, B2734–79 £35 £100
Starfish type M320, V1270, B2780–81 £65 £235

DOBUNNIC

BRITISH COINS MARKET VALUES 2022 51

CELTIC COINAGE

Face M374a, b, 5, 6, 8, V1020,
B2950–3000 £50 £170
Abstract M378a–384d, V1042, F VF
B3012–22 £55 £185

CORIELTAUVI
Boar type M405a, V855, B3194–3250 £60 £200
South Ferriby M410 etc, V875 £45 £125

ICENI Boar type
M407–9, V655–659,
B3440–3511 £30 £125
Wreath type M414, 5, 440, V679,
675, B3763–74 £35 £125
Face type M412–413e, V665, B3536–55 £90 £350

QUEEN BOUDICA
Face type M413, 413D, V790, 792,
B3556–3759 £55 £195

COMMIUS
Head left M446b, V355, 357, B731–58 £55 £195

■ SILVER COINS WITH LEGENDS

EPPILLUS
Calleva type M108, V415, B1016–1115 £50 £250

EPATICCUS
Eagle type M263, V580, B2024–2289 £35 £120
Victory type M263a, V581, B2294–2328 £45 £150

VERICA
Lim type M123, V505, B1332–59 £50 £200

CARATACUS
Eagle Type M265, V593,
B2376–2384 F £185 £585

TASCIOVANUS
Equestrian M158, V1745, B1667–68 £90 £350
VER type M161, V1699, B1670–73 £90 £300

CUNOBELINE
Equestrian M216–8, 6, V1951
1983, 2047, B1862 £90 £350
Bust right M236, VA2055, B1871–73 £80 £300

ABOVE: Anted, silver Unit

ANTED of the Dobunni
M387, V1082, B3032–38 £40 £180

	F	VF
EISU M389, V1110, B3043–55	£45	£185
BODVOC M396, V1057, B3143–45 F	£150	£465
ANTED of the Iceni M419–421, V710, 711, 715 B3791–4025	£35	£100
ECEN M424, V730, B4033–4215	£30	£85
EDNAM M423, 425b, V740, 734, B4219–4281	£30	£85
ECE M425a, 426, 7, 8, V761, 764, 762, 766, B4348–4538	£30	£75
AESU M432, V775, B4558–72	£50	£150
PRASUTAGUS King of the Iceni (husband of Boudica) B4577–4580	£750	£2750
ESUP ASU M4566, VA924, B3272	£65	£250
VEP CORF M460b, 464, V394, 950, B3277–3382, B3305–3314	£45	£120
DUMNOC TIGIR SENO M462, V974, 980, B3339	£165	£550
VOLISIOS DUMNOCOVEROS	£185	£625
ALE SCA M469, V996	£175	£800

■ BRONZE, BASE METAL COINS WITHOUT LEGENDS

POTIN
Experimental type M22a, V104 £30 £75
Class I M9–22, V122–131 £20 £70
Class II M23–25, V136–139 £20 £70
Thurrock Types V1402–1442 £25 £80

ARMORICAN
Billon stater £50 £200
Billon quarter stater £65 £285

DUROTRIGES
Bronze stater M318, V1290 £25 £65
Cast type M332–370,
V1322–1370 £35 £135

CELTIC COINAGE

	F	VF
NORTH THAMES		
M273, 274, 281, V1646, 1615, 1669	£35	£135
NORTH KENT		
M295, 296, V154	£55	£225

■ BRONZE COINS WITH LEGENDS

	F	VF
DUBNOVELLANUS in Essex		
M277, 8, V1665, 1667	£60	£200
TASCIOVANUS		
Head, beard M168, 9, V1707	£50	£165
VERLAMIO	F	VF
M172, V1808	£50	£165
Head, VER M177, V1816	£45	£165
Boar, VER M179, V1713	£50	£165
Equestrian M190, V1892	£65	£300
Centaur M192, V1882	£75	£350

	F	VF
ANDOCOV		
M200, V1871	£60	£225
CUNOBELINE		
Victory, TASC M221, V1971	£50	£165
Victory, CUN M22, a, V1973	£55	£175
Winged animal, M225, V2081	£50	£165
Head, beard, M226, 9, V2131, 2085	£50	£165
Panel, sphinx, M230, V1977	£45	£175
Winged beast, M231, V1979	£45	£175
Centaur, M242, V2089	£45	£175
Sow, M243, V2091	£35	£145
Warrior, M244, V2093	£35	£130
Boar, TASC, M245, V1983	£50	£165
Bull, TASC M246, V2095	£50	£165
Metal worker, M248, V2097	£35	£175
Pegasus, M249, V2099	£35	£135
Horse, CAMV, M250, V2101	£45	£165
Jupiter, horse, M251, V2103	£45	£175
Janus head, M252, V2105	£50	£165
Jupiter, lion, M253, V1207	£40	£140
Sphinx, fig, M260, a, V2109	£50	£175

BRITISH COINS MARKET VALUES 2022 **53**

STAMP
MAGAZINE™

OFFER ENDS 30TH SEPT 2022

SPECIAL OFFER FOR BCMV READERS!

MyTimeMedia Ltd reserves the right to withdraw this offer at any time without prior notice.
**Terms & conditions apply - visit www.mytimemedia.co.uk/terms for full terms & conditions.
FOR PRINT & PRINT + DIGITAL SUBSCRIPTIONS PLEASE VISIT
WWW.STAMPMAGAZINE.CO.UK/SUBSCRIBE

6 ISSUES FOR JUST £20!

SAVE £10!

As Britain's longest-running independent philatelic magazine, Stamp Magazine offers a wide range of news, features and opinion to interest, entertain and inform you, whatever you collect.

SUBSCRIBE TODAY!
http://stamp.secureorder.co.uk/STP/BCMV21
or call 0344 243 9023 and quote ref BCMV21

LINES OPEN MON - FRI - 9.00AM - 5.00PM GMT & SAT - 9.30AM - 3.30PM GMT.

Calls are charged at the same rate as standard UK landlines and are included as part of any inclusive or free minutes allowances.
There are no additional charges with this number. Overseas calls will cost more.

HAMMERED GOLD 1344–1662

Prices in this section are approximately what collectors can expect to pay for the commonest types of the coins listed. For most other types prices will range upwards from these amounts.

Precise valuations cannot be given since they vary from dealer to dealer and have to be determined by a number of factors such as a coin's condition, which is of prime importance in deciding its value.

For more detailed information, look at *English Hammered Coins, Volumes 1 and 2,* by J J North (Spink, 1994, 1992).

Serious collectors should also obtain *The Herbert Schneider Collection, Volume 1: English Gold Coins 1257–1603* (Spink, 1996) and *Volume 2: English Coins 1603–20th Century* (Spink, 2002).

■ THE PLANTAGENET KINGS

HENRY III 1216–1272	F	VF
Gold penny		£500000

One sold for $712,500 (including buyer's premium) in the US in 2021

ABOVE: Edward III Treaty Quarter-noble

EDWARD III 1327–77
Third coinage
First period

		F	VF
Double-florins or Double Leopards			ext. rare
Florins or leopards			ext. rare
Half-florins or helms		£80000	*

Second period

Nobles	from	£50000	£130000
Half-nobles	from	£9000	£50000
Quarter-nobles	from	£3700	£11000

Third period

Nobles	from	£3250	£9750
Half-nobles	from	£3000	£9000
Quarter-nobles	from	£500	£1400

Fourth coinage
Pre-treaty period with France (before 1315)
With French title

Nobles	£1300	£2750
Half-nobles	£725	£1950
Quarter-nobles	£400	£700

Transitional treaty period, 1361
Aquitaine title added

Nobles	£1300	£3850
Half-nobles	£800	£1950
Quarter-nobles	£400	£800

ABOVE: Edward III Transitional Treaty Half-noble

Treaty period 1361–9
Omits FRANC

	F	VF
Nobles, London	£1300	£3000
Nobles, Calais (C in centre of reverse)	£1300	£3000
Half-nobles, London	£900	£2000
Half-nobles, Calais	£950	£2950
Quarter-nobles, London	£400	£700
Quarter-nobles, Calais	£400	£700

Post-treaty period 1369–77
French title resumed

Nobles, London	£1300	£3750
Nobles, Calais (flag at stern or C in centre)	£1300	£3750
Half-nobles, London	£2700	£5750
Half-nobles, Calais	£2700	£5750

There are many other issues and varieties in this reign. These prices relate to the commoner pieces.

ABOVE: Richard II Calais Noble

RICHARD II 1377–99

Nobles, London	£1850	£4000
Nobles, Calais (flag at stern)	£2000	£4250
Half-nobles, London	£1950	£4750
Half-nobles, Calais (flag at stern)	£2250	£5250
Quarter-nobles, London	£750	£1700

There are many different varieties and different styles of lettering.

ABOVE: Henry IV heavy coinage London Noble

HENRY IV 1399–1413   F   VF
Heavy coinage
Nobles (120g) London   £8500   £20000
Nobles, Calais (flag at stern)   £9000   £23500
Half-nobles, London   £6250   *
Half-nobles, Calais   £7500   *
Quarter-nobles, London   £2000   £4000
Quarter-nobles, Calais   £2000   £5750

Light coinage
Nobles (108g)   £2000   £5750
Half-nobles   £2850   £7500
Quarter-nobles   £700   £2000

ABOVE: Henry V Noble

HENRY V 1413–22
Nobles, many varieties   from   £1500   £4200
Half-nobles   £1000   £3200
Quarter-nobles   £450   £800

This reign sees an increase in the use of privy marks to differentiate issues.

ABOVE: Henry V annulet London Noble

HENRY VI 1422–61   F   VF
Annulet issue, 1422–27
Nobles, London   £1350   £3000
Nobles, Calais (flag at stern)   £1650   £3750
Nobles, York   £1650   £4750
Half-nobles, London   £775   £2000
Half-nobles, Calais   £2000   £4750
Half-nobles, York   £2250   £4850
Quarter-nobles, London   £375   £625
Quarter-nobles, Calais   £400   £950
Quarter-nobles, York   £400   £900

Rosette-mascle issue 1427–30
Nobles, London   £2250   £6850
Nobles, Calais   £2850   £8000
Half-nobles, London   £2950   £8750
Half-nobles, Calais   £3850   £11000
Quarter-nobles, London   £1100   £3000
Quarter-nobles, Calais   £1250   £3250

ABOVE: Henry VI rosette-mascle Calais Noble

Pinecone-mascle issue 1430–4
Nobles, London   £2250   £6850
Half-nobles, London   £3850   £11000
Quarter-nobles   £1200   £3500

Leaf-mascle issue 1434–5
Nobles, London   £4500   £13750
Half-nobles, London   £3850   £11500
Quarter-nobles   £1200   £3950

BRITISH COINS MARKET VALUES 2022

HAMMERED GOLD

Leaf-trefoil issue 1435–8	F	VF
Nobles	£3750	£10250
Half-nobles	£3750	£11000
Quarter-noble	£1200	£3950

Trefoil issue 1438–43		
Nobles	£3950	£10500

ABOVE: Henry VI Pinecone-mascle Noble

Leaf-pellet issue 1445–54		
Nobles	£4000	£12250
Cross pellet issue 1454–60		
Nobles	£4750	£15000

EDWARD IV 1st reign 1461–70
Heavy coinage 1461–65

	F	VF
Nobles (108g)	£7000	£18000
Quarter-noble	£1950	£5750

Light coinage 1464–70

Ryals or rose-nobles (120g) London	£975	£2350
Flemish copy	£750	£1750

Edward IV Light coinage Norwich Ryal

	F	VF
Ryals, Bristol (B in waves)	£1750	£4850
Ryals, Coventry (C in waves)	£2500	£6500
Ryals, Norwich (N in waves)	£2650	£7000
Ryals, York (E in waves)	£1200	£3500
Half-ryals, London	£700	£1925
Half-ryals, Bristol (B in waves)	£1750	£5000
Half-ryals, Coventry (C in waves)	£6750	£16000
Half-ryals, Norwich (N in waves)	£4250	£13500
Half-ryals, York (E in waves)	£1350	£3000
Quarter-ryals	£425	£1000
Angels	£16500	£47500

HENRY VI restored 1470–71

Angels, London	£2000	£5000
Angels, Bristol (B in waves)	£3500	£8750
Half-angels, London	£6500	£15000
Half-angels, Bristol (B in waves)	£7500	*

EDWARD IV 2nd reign 1471–83

Angels, London	£750	£2500
Angels, Bristol (B in waves)	£5000	£11000
Half-angels, some varieties	£875	£2000

EDWARD IV or V 1483
im halved sun and rose

Angels	£7000	£15850
Half-angels	£7000	*

RICHARD III 1483–85
Angels, reading EDWARD, im
boar's head on obverse, halved sun
and rose on reverse £9750 £26500
Angels, reading RICHARD or RICAD £6250 £17000
Half-angels £10500 *

ABOVE: Edward IV second reign Angel

■ THE TUDOR MONARCHS

HENRY VII 1485–1509
Sovereigns of 20 shillings
(all extremely rare) from £27500 £90000
Ryals ext. rare
Angels, varieties, different ims from £1000 £2500
Half-angels £1000 £2000

58 BRITISH COINS MARKET VALUES 2022

HAMMERED GOLD

ABOVE: Henry VIII Third coinage type I Sovereign

ABOVE: Henry VIII first coinage Angel, im portcullis

	F	VF
Angels	£1200	£2500
Half-angels	£750	£2000
Quarter-angels	£800	£2250
Crowns, HENRIC 8, London	£750	£2250
Crowns, Southwark	£875	£2500
Crowns, Bristol	£750	£2250
Halfcrowns, London	£600	£1650
Halfcrowns, Southwark	£700	£1850
Halfcrowns, Bristol	£800	£2500

HENRY VIII 1509–47

		F	VF
First coinage 1509–26			
Sovereigns of 20 shillings im crowned portcullis only		£12500	£37500
Ryal			ext. rare
Angels (6s 8d)	from	£825	£2000
Half-angels		£675	£1700
Second coinage 1526–44			
Sovereigns of 22s 6d, various ims	from	£13000	£32500
Angels (7s 6d)	from	£1500	£4500
Half-angels im lis		£1250	£4500
George-nobles im rose		£16000	£35000
Half-George-noble		£15000	*
Crowns of the rose im rose		£15000	*
Crowns of the double rose			ext. rare
HK (Henry and Katherine of Aragon)		£1200	£3000
HA (Henry and Anne Boleyn)		£3500	£8000
HI (Henry and Jane Seymour)		£1200	£3000
HR (HENRICUS REX)		£1000	£2500
Halfcrowns of the double-rose			
HK		£700	£2250
HI		£900	£2500
HR		£1050	£3000
Third coinage 1544–47			
Sovereigns of 20s, London	from	£7250	£20000
Sovereigns of 20s, Southwark		£7250	£20000
Sovereigns of 20s, Bristol	from	£13500	£39500
Half-sovereigns, London		£1200	£3250
Half-sovereigns, Southwark		£1300	£3500
Half-sovereigns, Bristol		£2500	£6750

EDWARD VI 1547–53
Posthumous coinage in the name of Henry VIII, 1547–51

		F	VF
Sovereigns, London	from	£8500	£27500
Sovereigns, Bristol		£13500	£38500
Half-sovereigns, London		£1000	£2750
Half-sovereigns, Southwark		£1000	£2750
Crowns, London		£725	£2000
Crowns, Southwark		£825	£2500
Halfcrowns, London		£650	£2000
Halfcrowns, Southwark		£650	£2000

Coinage in Edward's own name
First period 1547–49

	F	VF
Half-sovereigns, Tower, reads EDWARD 6	£3000	£8500

ABOVE: Edward VI second period Sovereign im arrow

BRITISH COINS MARKET VALUES 2022 **59**

HAMMERED GOLD

	F	VF
Half-sovereigns, Southwark	£2500	£6750
Crowns	£3500	£8500
Halfcrowns	£2750	£5750

Second period 1549-50
Sovereigns	£8250	£21500
Half-sovereign, uncrowned bust, London	£4250	£12000
Half-sovereigns, SCUTUM on obverse	£2250	£7250
Half-sovereigns, Durham House MDXLVII	£10000	*
Half-sovereigns, crowned bust, London	£1875	£6500
Half-sovereigns, half-length bust, Durham House	£9500	*
Crowns, uncrowned bust	£2750	£8000
Crowns, crowned bust	£2500	£6750
Halfcrowns, uncrowned bust	£2500	£6850
Halfcrowns, crowned bust	£2250	£6000

ABOVE: Mary 1553 Sovereign

PHILIP AND MARY 1554–8

	F	VF
Angels, im lis	£7750	£20000
Half-angels	£15000	*

ABOVE: Edward VI third period Sovereign im tun

ABOVE: Elizabeth I sixth issue Ryal

Third period 1550–53
'Fine' sovereigns of 30s, king enthroned	£50000	£135000
Sovereigns of 20s, half length figure	£7000	£19000
Half-sovereigns, similar to last	£3000	£7250
Crowns, similar but SCUTUM on reverse	£2950	£7250
Halfcrowns, similar	£2250	£7000
Angels	£18500	£42500
Half-angels	£18500	*

ELIZABETH I 1558–1603
Hammered issues

	F	VF
'Fine' Sovereigns of 30s, different issues from	£8250	£20000
Ryals	£20000	£57500
Angels, different issues	£1500	£3750
Half-angels	£1100	£3250
Quarter-angels	£1000	£2850

MARY 1553–4
Sovereigns, different dates, some undated, im pomegranate or half rose	£10000	£26500
Ryals, dated MDLIII (1553)	£47500	£95000
Angels, im pomegranate	£3250	£7500
Half-angels	£8000	*

ABOVE: Elizabeth I second issue Quarter-angel

60 BRITISH COINS MARKET VALUES 2022

	F	VF
Pounds of 20s, different ims from	£4000	£12000
Half-pounds, different issues	£3500	£7500
Crowns	£2000	£6250
Halfcrowns	£1500	£4000

ABOVE: Elizabeth I sixth issue Crown

Milled issues

	F	VF
Half-pounds, one issue but different marks	£5000	£11500
Crowns	£2950	£8000
Halfcrowns	£4750	£11000

	F	VF
Britain crowns	£385	£750
Halfcrowns	£285	£600
Thistle crowns, varieties	£325	£700

ABOVE: James I third coinage Rose-ryal

■ THE STUART KINGS

ABOVE: James I third coinage Spur-ryal

ABOVE: James I third coinage Laurel

JAMES I 1603–25
First coinage 1603–4

	F	VF
Sovereigns of 20s, two busts	£3850	£11000
Half-sovereigns	£4875	£15000
Crowns	£2850	£7750
Halfcrowns	£925	£3250

Second coinage 1604–19

	F	VF
Rose-ryals of 30s	£3750	£11000
Spur-ryals of 15s	£9250	£25000
Angels	£2000	£5250
Half-angels	£4850	£12750
Unites, different busts	£1000	£2000
Double crowns	£500	£1250

Third coinage 1619–25

	F	VF
Rose-ryals, varieties	£5000	£13850
Spur-ryals	£9250	£26000
Angels	£2750	£6000
Laurels, different busts	£1000	£2200
Half-laurels	£650	£1450
Quarter-laurels	£400	£750

CHARLES I 1625–49
Tower mint 1625–42
Initial marks: lis, cross-calvary, negro's head, castle, anchor, heart, plume, rose, harp, portcullis, bell, crown, tun, triangle, star, triangle-in-circle.

BRITISH COINS MARKET VALUES 2022 **61**

HAMMERED GOLD

HAMMERED GOLD

ABOVE: Charles I Tower mint Unite, im heart

	F	VF
Angels, varieties from	£5000	£12500
Angels, pierced as touchpieces	£1350	£2850
Unites	£950	£2250
Double-crowns	£600	£1500
Crowns	£400	£700

ABOVE: Charles I Tower mint Double-crown, im heart

Tower mint under Parliament 1642-9
Ims: (P), (R), eye, sun, sceptre

	F	VF
Unites, varieties	£1850	£5750
Double-crowns	£1100	£2750
Crowns	£425	£1000

Briot's milled issues 1631-2
Ims: anemone and B, daisy and B, B

	F	VF
Angels	£10000	£40000
Unites	£4950	£13500
Double-crowns	£3500	£8250
Crowns	£5000	£14500

Briot's hammered issues 1638-9

	F	VF
Unite	£8000	*
Double-crowns	£3500	£8750
Crowns	£1250	£3750

Coins of provincial mints
Bristol 1645

Unites		ext. rare
Half-unites		ext. rare

Chester 1644

Unites		ext. rare

Exeter 1643-44

Unites		ext. rare

Oxford 1642-46

Triple unites	from	£22500	£42500
Unites	from	£4250	£9750
Half-unites	from	£2850	£6250

Truro 1642-43 — F — VF

Half-unites		ext. rare

Shrewsbury 1644

Triple unites and unites	ext. rare

Worcester 1643-44

Unites	ext. rare

ABOVE: Charles I 1643 Oxford Triple unite

Siege pieces 1645-49
Pontefract 1648-49

Unites F		ext. rare

ABOVE: Commonwealth 1651 Unite

COMMONWEALTH 1649-60

	F	VF
Unites im sun	£3500	£7000
im anchor	£9500	£20000
Double-crowns im sun	£2750	£5950
im anchor	£6500	£14500
Crowns, im sun	£1500	£3750
im anchor	£4850	£14000

ABOVE: Commonwealth 1650 Crown

CHARLES II 1660–85
Hammered Coinage 1660–62

ABOVE: Charles II hammered coinage Unite

		F	VF
Unites, two issues	from	£2750	£6750
Double-crowns		£1500	£4250
Crowns		£1850	£5750

CHARLES RILEY
COINS & MEDALS
Professional Numismatist since 1990

www.charlesriley.co.uk
PO Box 733, Aylesbury,
HP22 9AX
Tel: 01296 747598
email: charlesrileycoins@gmail.com
BNTA

We pay the BEST prices for all COINS; British, European and World, gold, silver and copper, war medals and badges, medallions, masonic pre - '47 silver; gold and silver articles, jewellery, pocket and wrist watches, scrap precious metals, bric-a-brac, antiques, cig. cards, banknotes, postcards, etc. etc. We deal courteously with dealers and collectors alike and will travel to purchase worthwhile collections.

Collectors' Forum

at Nicholas James
16 Rowallan Parade
Green Lane
Dagenham, Essex

020 8597 6267
Freephone: 0500 778878

HAMMERED GOLD

BRITISH COINS MARKET VALUES 2022   63

HAMMERED SILVER

In this section, coins are mainly valued in Fine or Very Fine condition. Prices are based on coins of good metal that are not chipped or cracked.

However, pennies of the early Plantagenets, where higher-grade coins are seldom available, are valued in Fair or Fine condition.

Again it should be noted that prices are for the commonest types only, and are the amounts collectors can expect to pay, rather than dealers' buying prices.

Prices for the Saxon and Norman series are based on common mint towns. Rarer mints command higher premiums.

Descriptions such as 'cross/moneyer's name' indicate that a cross appears on the obverse and the moneyer's name on the reverse. For more details see *Standard Catalogue of British Coins* (Spink, annual), and *English Hammered Coins*, volumes 1 and 2 by J J North, Spink (1991, 1994).

■ ANGLO-SAXON SCEATS AND STYCAS

ABOVE: Examples of Sceats

		F	VF
EARLY PERIOD c600–750			
Silver Sceats	from	£95	£265
Large numbers of types and varieties.			
NORTHUMBRIAN KINGS c737–867			
Silver Sceats c737–796	from	£165	£475
Copper Stycas c 810–867	from	£25	£60

Struck for many kings. Numerous moneyers and different varieties. The copper Styca is the commonest coin in the Anglo-Saxon series.

		F	VF
ARCHBISHOPS OF YORK c732–900			
Silver Sceats	from	£175	£485
Copper Stycas	from	£20	£60

■ KINGS OF KENT

HEABERHT c764
Pennies monogram/cross — ext. rare
One moneyer (Eoba).

	F	VF
ECGBERHT c765–780		
Pennies monogram/cross	£1750	£5750
Two moneyers (Babba and Udd).		
EADBERHT PRAEN 797–798		
Pennies EADBERHT REX/moneyer	£1750	£5500
Three moneyers.		
CUTHRED 789–807		
Pennies non-portrait, various designs from	£850	£2950
Bust right	£1250	£4000
Different moneyers and varieties.		
BALDRED c825		
Pennies bust right	£1850	£5750
Cross/cross	£1000	£3250
Different types and moneyers.		
ANONYMOUS		
Pennies bust right	£1250	£4000
Different types and moneyers.		

■ ARCHBISHOPS OF CANTERBURY

		F	VF
JAENBERHT 766–792			
Pennies various types non-portrait	from	£1200	£4750
AETHELHEARD 793–805			
Pennies various types non-portrait	from	£1200	£50
WULFRED 805–832			
Pennies various groups portrait types	from	£1200	£3750
CEOLNOTH 833–870			
Pennies various groups, portrait types	from	£1500	£4000
AETHELRED			
Pennies, portrait		£3850	£12000
non portrait		£1500	£5250
PLEGMUND 890–914			
Pennies various types, non-portrait	from	£950	£3000

ABOVE: step portrait Penny

■ KINGS OF MERCIA

		F	VF
OFFA 757–796			
Pennies non-portrait	from	£850	£2000
Portrait	from	£1650	£5000

HAMMERED SILVER

CYNETHRYTH (wife of Offa)		F	VF
Pennies portrait		£4650	£11000
Non-portrait		£1750	£5000

COENWULF 796–821
Pennies various types, portrait, non-portrait	from	£1200 £725	£3250 £1850

ABOVE: Coenwulf portrait Penny

CEOLWULF 821–823
Pennies various types, portrait	£1850	£5750

BEORNWULF 823–825
Pennies various types, portrait	£1500	£5750

LUCIDA 825–827
Pennies two types, portrait F	£8500	£26500

WIGLAF 827–829, 830–840
Pennies portrait	£4000	£13000
Non-portrait	£3000	£8500

BERHTWULF 840–852
Pennies portrait	£3000	£8500
non-portrait	£3750	£9500

BURGRED 852–874
Pennies one type portrait, five variants from	£275	£600

CEOLWULF II 874–c 877
Pennies two types portrait	£2650	£6750

■ KINGS OF EAST ANGLIA

BEONNA c758
Silver Sceat	£950	£2750

ALBERHT (749–?)
Penny, non-portrait type	£4500	£17500

AETHELBERHT died 794
Pennies, portrait type F	£6000	£18500

EADWALD c796
Pennies, non-portrait types	£1300	£4850

AETHELSTAN I c850
Pennies various types, portrait, non-portrait,	from from	£1500 £600	£5750 £1650

AETHELWEARD c 850		F	VF
Pennies, non-portrait types		£825	£2850

EADMUND 855–870
Pennies, non-portrait types	£400	£1000

■ VIKING INVADERS 878–954

ALFRED
Imitations of portrait, different types,
Pennies	from	£2850	£7500
Halfpennies	from	£975	£3000

Non-portrait, different types,
Pennies	from	£650	£2000
Halfpennies	from	£750	£2000

Danish East Anglia, c885–954

AETHELSTAN II 878–890/1
Pennies cross/moneyer	£1950	£7000

OSWALD
Pennies A/cross	£3000	£9750

ST EADMUND
Pennies memorial coinage,
various legends	£200	£425

Many moneyers.
Halfpennies	£600	£2000

Many moneyers.

ABOVE: St Eadmund memorial Penny

ST MARTIN OF LINCOLN c917
Pennies sword/cross	£4500	£14250

AETHELRED I c870
Pennies temple/cross	£2250	£6850

York
SIEVERT–SIEFRED–CNUT c897
Crosslet/small cross from	£225	£525

Many different groups and varieties.
Halfpennies	£895	£2250

Many different groups and varieties.

EARL SIHTRIC unknown
Pennies non-portrait	£5250	£16500

REGNALD c 910
Pennies various types, some blundered	from	£3750	£12500

BRITISH COINS MARKET VALUES 2022 **65**

HAMMERED SILVER

	F	VF
SIHTRIC I 921–926/7		
Pennies sword/cross	£3000	£10000
ANLAF GUTHFRITHSSON 939–941		
Pennies raven/cross	£3500	£8000
Cross/cross	£3250	£9500
Flower/cross	£5000	£15000
OLAF SIHTRICSSON 941–944, 948–952		
Pennies various types	£2850	£7250
SIHTRIC II c941–943		
Pennies shield/standard	£3000	£8750
REGNALD II c941–943		
Pennies cross/cross	£4250	£13750
Shield/standard	£4000	£12000
ERIC BLOODAXE 948, 952–954		
Pennies cross/moneyer	£7750	£25000
Sword/cross	£10000	£40000
ST PETER OF YORK c905–925			
Pennies various types	from	£400	£1375
Halfpennies, various types	from	£875	£2500

■ KINGS OF WESSEX

BEORHTRIC 786–802
Two types, non-portrait — ext. rare

ECGBERHT 802–839
Pennies four groups,
portrait, non-portrait — £1500 £4500
Mints of Canterbury, London, Rochester, Winchester

AETHELWULF 839–858
Pennies four phases, portrait, non-portrait — £750 £2250
from mints of Canterbury, Rochester

AETHELBERHT 858–866
Pennies two types portrait from £1250 £3250
Many moneyers.

AETHELRED I 865–871
Pennies portrait types from £925 £3250
Many moneyers.

ALFRED THE GREAT 871–899
Pennies portrait in style of Aethelred I — £1500 £4000
Four other portrait types, commonest
has the London monogram reverse — £3400 £8750
Halfpennies — £1750 £5000
Pennies non-portrait types from — £800 £1750
Many different styles of lettering.
Halfpennies — £875 £2250

EDWARD THE ELDER 899–924
Non-portrait types

	F	VF
Pennies cross/moneyer's name in two lines	£275	£700
Halfpennies cross/moneyer's name in two lines	£1500	£3500

ABOVE: Edward the Elder, non-portrait Penny

Portrait types
Pennies bust/moneyer's name £1250 £3850
Many types, varieties and moneyers.
Pennies design has buildings,
floral designs and others £3500 £9500
Many types, varieties and moneyers.

■ KINGS OF ALL ENGLAND

AETHELSTAN 924–39
Non-portrait types
Pennies cross/moneyer's name in two lines £375 £875
Cross/cross £385 £1100

Portrait types
Pennies bust/moneyer's name in two lines £1100 £4000
Bust/small cross £1000 £3500
Many other issues, some featuring buildings. There are also different mints and moneyer's names.

EADMUND 939–46
Non-portrait types
Pennies cross or rosette/moneyer's
name in two lines £325 £850
Halfpennies, cross or rosette/moneyer's
name in two lines £925 £2750

Portrait types
Pennies crowned bust/small cross £1000 £3850
Helmeted bust/cross crosslet £1250 £5000
Many other issues and varieties, different mint names and moneyers.

EADRED 946–55
Non-portrait types
Pennies cross/moneyer's
name in two lines £300 £750
Halfpennies cross/moneyer's
name in two lines £1250 £2500
Pennies rosette/moneyer's name £485 £1500

Portrait types
Pennies crowned bust/small cross £875 £3250
Many variations and mint names and moneyers.

66 BRITISH COINS MARKET VALUES 2022

SOUTH AFRICA
WANTED
Gold Coins 1874–1902

TOP PRICES PAID

ROYAL GOLD
Established 1979

PO Box 123, Saxonwold,
Johannesburg 2132,
South Africa
Tel: +27 11 483 0161
Fax: +27 11 483 0440
Email: info@royalgold.co.za

Authorised Partner of the South Africa Mint

www.royalgold.co.za

HAMMERED SILVER

HOWEL DDA King of Wales, died c948   F   VF
Pennies small cross/moneyer's
name in two lines (Gillys)   ext. rare

EADWIG 955–59
Non-portrait types
Pennies cross/moneyer's name   from   £650   £1850
Many variations, some rare.
Halfpennies, non portrait types
cross/moneyer's name   £1950   £4750

Portrait types
Pennies bust/cross   from   £8500   £26500

EADGAR 959–75
Non-portrait types
Pennies cross/moneyer's name   from   £295   £700
Cross/cross from   £295   £700
Rosette/rosette from   £300   £785
Halfpennies   from   £1250   £4850

ABOVE: Eadgar, non-portrait Penny

Portrait types
Pennies pre-reform, bust right   £1500   £4850
Halfpennies, diademed
bust/London monogram   £1750   £4750
Pennies reform (c972), bust left   £1750   £5000
Many other varieties.

EDWARD THE MARTYR 975–78
Portrait types
Pennies bust left/small cross   £2500   £6500
Many different mints and moneyers.

AETHELRED II 978–1016

ABOVE: Aethelred II last small cross type Penny

Pennies first small cross type   from   £825   £2650
First hand type   from   £190   £450
Second hand type   from   £180   £425
Benediction hand type   from   £1250   £4000

                                            F   VF
CRUX type   from   £140   £315

ABOVE: Aethelred II CRUX type Penny

ABOVE: Aethelred II long cross type Penny

Long cross type   £155   £350
Helmet type   £165   £375
Agnus Dei type   £10000   *
Other issues and varieties, many mints and moneyers.

CNUT 1016–35
Pennies quatrefoil type   from   £165   £300

ABOVE: Cnut quatrefoil type Penny

Pointed helmet type   from   £140   £300

ABOVE: Cnut pointed helmet type Penny

Short cross type   from   £140   £300
Jewel cross type   from   £700   £2250
Other types, and many different mints and moneyers.

HAROLD I 1035–40
Pennies Short cross type   from   £1000   £3250
Jewel cross type   from   £325   £825
Long cross type with trefoils   from   £315   £800
Long cross type with fleurs-de-lis   £300   £750
Many different mint names and moneyers.

68 BRITISH COINS MARKET VALUES 2022

HAMMERED SILVER

HARTHACNUT 1035–42

	F	VF
Pennies jewel cross type, bust left	£1650	£4250
Bust right	£1450	£4000
Arm and sceptre type	£1350	£3750
Different mint names and moneyers.		
Pennies Scandinavian types struck at Lund	£350	£800

EDWARD THE CONFESSOR 1042–66

	F	VF
Pennies PACX type from	£260	£650
Radiate crown/small cross type	£185	£365
Trefoil quadrilateral type	£175	£350
Small flan type	£150	£300
Expanding cross type	£175	£400

ABOVE: Edward the Confessor transitional pyramids type Penny

Pointed helmet type	£180	£425
Sovereign/eagles type	£185	£450
Hammer cross type	£145	£365

ABOVE: Edward the Confessor hammer cross type Penny

Bust facing/small cross type	£150	£350
Pyramids type	£165	£385
Transitional pyramids type	£1750	£5250

Other issues, including a unique gold penny; many different mints and moneyers.

ABOVE: Harold II Pax type Penny, bust left, without sceptre

HAROLD II 1066

Pennies Pax type, crowned head left,		
with sceptre	£1750	£4250
without sceptre	£1950	£4650

	F	VF
Pennies Pax type crowned head right, with sceptre	£3950	£9250

■ THE NORMAN KINGS

WILLIAM I 1066–87

Pennies profile left/cross fleury type	from	£500	£1495
Bonnet type	from	£350	£950
Canopy type	from	£500	£1600
Two sceptres type	from	£425	£975
Two stars type	from	£350	£800
Sword type	from	£600	£1450

ABOVE: William I profile/cross fleury type Penny

Profile right/cross and trefoils type	from	£685	£1975
PAXS type	from	£265	£575

WILLIAM II 1087–1100

ABOVE: William II cross voided type Penny

Pennies profile right type	from	£825	£2750
Cross in quatrefoil type	from	£750	£2250
Cross voided type	from	£750	£2250
Cross pattée over fleury type	from	£800	£2500
Cross fleury and piles type	from	£800	£2500

ABOVE: Henry I large bust/cross and annulets type Penny

BRITISH COINS MARKET VALUES 2022 **69**

HAMMERED SILVER

HENRY I 1100–1135

		F	VF
Pennies annulets type	from	£550	£1600
Profile/cross fleury type	from	£385	£1000
PAXS type	from	£350	£950
Annulets and piles type	from	£385	£1150
Voided cross and fleurs type	from	£850	£2850
Pointing bust and stars type	from	£1600	£5000
Facing bust/quatrefoil and piles type	from	£375	£975
Large profile/cross and annulets type	from	£1500	£4750
Facing bust/cross in quatrefoil type	from	£775	£2500
Full bust/cross fleury type		£285	£785
Double inscription type		£685	£1850
Small profile/cross and annulets type		£525	£1400
Star in lozenge fleury type		£500	£1300
Pellets in quatrefoil type		£260	£685
Quadrilateral on cross fleury type		£215	£550
Halfpennies		£2500	£6500

STEPHEN 1135–54

		F	VF
Pennies cross moline (Watford) type	from	£275	£725

ABOVE: Stephen 'Watford' Penny

	F	VF
Similar, reads PERERIC	£875	£2500
Voided cross and mullets type	£315	£800
Cross and piles type	£425	£1300
Cross pommée (Awbridge) type	£345	£800

There are also a number of irregular issues produced during the civil war, all of which are very rare. These include several extremely rare and attractive pieces bearing the names of Empress Matilda and barons, such as Eustace Fitzjohn and Robert de Stuteville.

■ THE PLANTAGENET KINGS

HENRY II 1154–89

ABOVE: Henry II cross and crosslets (Tealby) Penny

	F	VF
Pennies cross and crosslets ('Tealby' coinage)	£125	£350

The issue is classified by bust variants into six groups, struck at 32 mints.

		F	VF
Pennies short cross	from	£80	£185

The 'short cross' coinage was introduced in 1180 and continued through successive reigns until Henry III brought about a change in 1247. HENRICVS REX appears on all these coins but they can be classified into reigns by the styles of the busts and lettering. CR Wren's guide *The Short Cross Coinage 1180–1247* is the best book to identify coins of this series.

RICHARD I 1189–99

	F	VF
Pennies short cross	£90	£250

JOHN 1189–1216

	F	VF
Pennies short cross	£85	£200

ABOVE: John short cross Penny

HENRY III 1216–72

	F	VF
Pennies short cross	£40	£110
Long cross no sceptre	£30	£70
Long cross with sceptre	£30	£70

ABOVE: Henry III, long cross Penny with sceptre

The 'long cross' pennies, first introduced in 1247, are divided into two groups: those with sceptre and those without. They also fall into five basic classes, with many varieties. CR Wren's *The Voided Long Cross Coinage, 1247–79* is the best guide to identification.

ABOVE: Edward I, 1st coinage, long cross Penny

MALCOLM BORD

GOLD COIN EXCHANGE

16 CHARING CROSS ROAD,
LONDON WC2H 0HR
TELEPHONE: 020 7240 0479
FAX: 020 7240 1920

As one of London's leading dealers in most branches of Numismatics we are able to offer you unrivalled advice when it comes to both the buying or selling of coins or whether you wish to buy or sell coins or medals, we will endeavour to offer the most competitive price.

REMEMBER

That any offer we make is not subject to commission and we offer immediate payment.

A comprehensive selection of coins and medals is always available for viewing at our showroom.

HAMMERED SILVER

EDWARD I 1272–1307

1st coinage 1272–78

		F	VF
Long cross pennies	from	£30	£85

Similar in style to those of Henry III but with more realistic beard.

New coinage 1278–1307

		F	VF
Groats		£2700	£7500
Pennies, various classes, mints	from	£20	£55
Halfpennies	from	£35	£90
Farthings	from	£35	£100

ABOVE: Edward I Farthing London

The best guide to this era of coinage is *Edwardian English Silver Coins 1278–1351* (Sylloge of Coins of the British Isles no39).

EDWARD II 1307–27

		F	VF
Pennies, various classes, mints	from	£30	£65
Halfpennies	from	£50	£170
Farthing	from	£35	£120

EDWARD III 1327–77

1st and 2nd coinages 1327–43

	F	VF
Pennies (only 1st coinage) various types and mints	£225	£750
Halfpennies, different types and mints	£25	£75
Farthings	£30	£80

3rd coinage 1344–51, florin coinage

	F	VF
Pennies, various types and mints	£25	£95
Halfpennies	£25	£70
Farthings	£30	£100

ABOVE: Edward III, post-treaty Groat

4th coinage 1351–77

		F	VF
Groats, many types and mints	from	£75	£200
Halfgroats		£40	£130
Pennies		£25	£90
Halfpennies, different types		£30	£125
Farthings, a few types		£110	£350

RICHARD II 1377–99

		F	VF
Groats, four types	from	£500	£1850

ABOVE: Richard II Groat

	F	VF
Halfgroats	£325	£825
Pennies, various types, London	£200	£575
York	£70	£250
Durham	£135	£475
Halfpennies, three main types	£35	£110
Farthings, some varieties	£120	£450

HENRY IV 1399–1413

		F	VF
Groats, varieties	from	£3000	£8750
Halfgroats		£1250	£3250
Pennies	from	£650	£1500
Halfpennies		£225	£725
Farthings		£825	£2150

ABOVE: Henry V Groat

HENRY V 1413–22

	F	VF
Groats, Type A	£1250	£3750
Groats, Type B	£425	£1250
Groats, Type C	£150	£525
Halfgroats, various types, from	£150	£485
Pennies, various types, from	£45	£145
Halfpennies, various types, from	£30	£120
Farthings, various types, from	£500	£1500

HENRY VI 1422–61

Annulet issue 1422–1427

Different mints, from

	F	VF
Groats	£55	£180
Halfgroats	£35	£135
Pennies	£35	£120
Halfpennies	£25	£70
Farthings	£180	£500

Annulet-Trefoil sub issue

	F	VF
Groats	£60	£200

72 BRITISH COINS MARKET VALUES 2022

HAMMERED SILVER

	F	VF
Halfgroats	£45	£150
Penny	£75	£225

Rosette-mascle issue 1427–1430
Groats	£75	£200
Halfgroats	£50	£160
Pennies	£40	£120
Halfpennies	£25	£80
Farthings	£165	£550

Pinecone-mascle issue 1430–1434
Groats	£60	£165
Halfgroats	£45	£135
Pennies	£40	£125
Halfpennies	£25	£75
Farthings	£200	£525

Leaf-mascle issue 1434–1435
Groats	£165	£550
Halfgroats	£175	£475
Pennies	£80	£225
Halfpennies	£35	£100

Leaf-trefoil issue 1435–1438
Groats	£90	£265
Halfgroats	£80	£225
Pennies	£95	£300
Halfpennies	£30	£85
Farthings	£250	£850

Trefoil issue 1438–1443
Groats	£90	£325
Halfgroats	£175	£500
Halfpennies	£30	£100
Farthings	£275	£875

Trefoil-pellet issue 1443–1445
Groats	£175	£525

ABOVE: Henry VI, leaf-mascle issue Groat

Leaf-pellet issue 1445–1454
Groats	£75	£240
Halfgroats	£95	£260
Pennies	£60	£165
Halfpennies	£25	£85
Farthings	£265	£775

	F	VF
Unmarked issue 1445–1454		
Groats	£600	£1850
Halfgroats	£400	£1100

Cross-pellet issue 1454–1460
Groats	£165	£450
Halfgroats	£325	£975
Pennies	£65	£175
Halfpennies	£35	£85
Farthings	£295	£825

Lis-pellet issue 1454–1460
Groats	£295	£875

There are many different varieties, initial marks and mints in this reign. These prices are for commonest prices in each issue.

EDWARD IV 1st Reign 1461–1470
Heavy coinage 1461–4
Groats, many classes, all London	£160	£485
Halfgroats, many classes, all London	£300	£900
Pennies, different classes, London, York and Durham	£135	£385
Halfpennies, different classes, all London	£45	£140
Farthings, London	£400	£1100

ABOVE: Edward IV light coinage Groat

Light coinage 1464–70
Groats, many different issues, varieties, ims and mints from	£60	£175
Halfgroats, ditto	£50	£165
Pennies, ditto	£40	£130
Halfpennies, ditto	£30	£90
Farthings, two issues	£400	£1100

ABOVE: Henry VI restored) Groat London

BRITISH COINS MARKET VALUES 2022

HAMMERED SILVER

HENRY VI restored 1470–71

		F	VF
Groats, different mints, different ims	from	£285	£650
Halfgroats	from	£425	£975
Pennies	from	£275	£800
Halfpennies	from	£200	£675

EDWARD IV 2nd reign 1471–83

	F	VF
Groats, different varieties, mints	£70	£200
Halfgroats	£45	£150
Pennies	£35	£120
Halfpennies	£30	£100

EDWARD IV or V 1483
im halved sun and rose

	F	VF
Groats	£1650	£4750
Pennies	£1100	£4000
Halfpennies	£325	£925

ABOVE: Richard III Groat London

RICHARD III 1483–85

	F	VF
Groats, reading EDWARD, initial mark boar's head on obverse, halved sun and rose on reverse	£2000	£5500
Groats, reading Ricard, London and York mints, various combinations of ims	£1000	£2500
Halfgroats	£1750	£4850
Pennies, York and Durham from	£365	£925
London mint	£2000	£6000
Halfpennies	£285	£825
Farthing	£1650	£4250

PERKIN WARBECK, PRETENDER

	F	VF
Groat, 1494	£2750	£5500

■ THE TUDOR MONARCHS

HENRY VII 1485–1509
Facing bust issues

ABOVE: Henry VII open crown type Groat London

	F	VF
Groats, all London		
Open crown without arches	£120	£385
Crown with two arches unjewelled	£100	£300
Crown with two jewelled arches	£85	£300
Similar but only one arch jewelled	£85	£300
Similar but tall thin lettering	£85	£300
Similar but single arch, tall thin lettering	£90	£300
Halfgroats, London		
Open crown without arches, tressure unbroken	£300	£925
Double arched crown	£50	£175
Unarched crown	£50	£150
Some varieties and different ims.		
Halfgroats, Canterbury		
Open crown, without arches	£50	£175
Double arched crown	£50	£175
Some varieties and different ims.		
Halfgroats, York		
Double arched crown	£55	£185
Unarched crown with tressure broken	£50	£160
Double arched crown with keys at side of bust	£50	£150
Many varieties and different ims.		
Pennies, facing bust type		
London	£175	£675
Canterbury, open crown	£250	£625
Canterbury, arched crown	£65	£200
Durham, Bishop Sherwood, S on breast	£60	£165
York	£50	£150
Many varieties and ims.		
Pennies, 'sovereign enthroned' type		
London, many varieties	£40	£130
Durham, many varieties	£35	£100
York, many varieties	£35	£100
Halfpennies, London		
Open crown	£40	£130
Arched crown	£30	£90
Crown with lower arch	£25	£80
Some varieties and ims.		
Halfpennies, Canterbury		
Open crown	£70	£200
Arched crown	£60	£175
Halfpennies, York		
Arched crown and key below bust	£65	£150
Farthings, all London	£500	£1500

Profile issues

	F	VF
Testoons im lis, three different legends	£22500	£42000
Groats, all London		
Tentative issue, double band to crown	£295	£975

ABOVE: Henry VII regular issue Groat

	F	VF
Regular issue, triple band to crown	£160	£425
Some varieties and ims.		
Halfgroats		
London	£100	£350
London, no numeral after king's name	£500	£1400
Canterbury	£80	£265
York, two keys below shield	£75	£265
York, XB by shield	£250	£700

HENRY VIII 1509–47
First coinage 1509–26 with portrait of Henry VII

	F	VF
Groats, London	£150	£425
Tournai	£1350	£3250
Tournai, without portrait	£8750	*
Halfgroats, London	£130	£425
Canterbury, varieties	£70	£200
York, varieties	£70	£200
Tournai	£950	£2950
Pennies, 'sovereign enthroned' type, London	£50	£165
Canterbury, varieties	£90	£275
Durham, varieties	£50	£125
Halfpennies, facing bust type, London	£30	£110
Canterbury	£60	£175
Farthings, portcullis type, London	£285	£775

ABOVE: Henry VIII second coinage Groat York

Second coinage 1526–44 with young portrait of Henry VIII

	F	VF
Groats, London, varieties, ims	£165	£450
Irish title, HIB REX	£350	£1000
York, varieties, ims	£165	£450
Halfgroats, London, varieties, ims	£70	£200
Irish title, HIB REX	£485	£1525
Canterbury, varieties, ims	£60	£185
York, varieties, ims	£60	£185

	F	VF
Pennies 'sovereign enthroned' type		
London, varieties, ims	£40	£120
Canterbury, varieties, ims	£75	£225
Durham	£35	£120
York	£400	£1150
Halfpennies, facing bust type		
London, varieties, ims	£25	£80
Canterbury	£35	£120
York, varieties, ims	£75	£225
Farthings, portcullis type	£385	£825

Third coinage 1544–47 and posthumous issues 1547–51 with old bearded portrait

	F	VF
Testoons or shillings		
London, Tower mint, varieties, ims	£950	£4750
Southwark, varieties, ims	£950	£4750
Bristol, varieties, ims	£1000	£5000
Groats, six different busts, varieties, ims		
London, Tower mint	£125	£525
Southwark	£125	£525
Bristol	£135	£575
Canterbury	£125	£500
York	£120	£500
London, Durham House	£265	£825

ABOVE: Henry VIII third coinage Groat

Halfgroats, only one style of bust, except York which has two, varieties, ims

	F	VF
London, Tower mint	£85	£350
Southwark	£100	£325
Bristol	£90	£300
Canterbury	£70	£225
York	£80	£240
London, Durham House	£485	£1375

ABOVE: Henry VIII third coinage Halfgroat Bristol

HAMMERED SILVER

ABOVE: Henry VIII posthumous coinage Halfgroat Canterbury

	F	VF
Pennies, facing bust, varieties, ims		
London, Tower mint	£45	£140
Southwark	£50	£150
London, Durham House	£485	£1375
Bristol	£70	£225
Canterbury	£50	£150
York	£50	£150
Halfpennies, facing bust varieties, ims		
London, Tower mint	£45	£125
Bristol	£85	£250
Canterbury	£60	£150
York	£50	£135
Farthing	£950	£2450

EDWARD VI 1547–53
First period 1547–49

Shillings, London, Durham House, im bow, patterns?		ext. rare
Groats, London, Tower, im arrow	£950	£4500
London, Southwark, im E, none	£950	£4500
Halfgroats, London, Tower, im arrow	£750	£2250
London, Southwark, im arrow, E	£650	£1950
Canterbury, im none	£425	£1350
Pennies, London, Tower, im	£400	£1385
London, Southwark, im E	£495	£1500
Bristol, im none	£425	£1385
Halfpennies, London, Tower im uncertain	£600	£1575
Bristol, im none	£600	£1750

ABOVE: Edward VI second period Shilling

Second period 1549–50

Shillings, London, Tower various ims	£295	£1500
Bristol, im TC	£975	£4000
Canterbury, im T or t	£250	£1125
London (Durham House), im bow, varieties	£195	£975

Third period 1550–53

	F	VF
Base silver (similar to issues of second period)		
Shillings, London, Tower, im lis, lion, rose	£175	£825
Pennies, London, Tower, im escallop	£65	£200
York, im mullet	£60	£180
Halfpennies, London, Tower	£175	£650

Fine silver issue
Crown 1551 im Y, 1551–53 im tun	£1150	£3750

ABOVE: Edward VI 1551 Crown

Halfcrown, walking horse, 1551, im Y	£800	£2250
Galloping horse, 1551–52, im tun	£800	£2500

ABOVE: Edward VI, fine silver issue Sixpence

1553, im tun	£1500	£4000
Shillings, im Y, tun	£150	£675
Sixpences, London (Tower), im y, tun	£140	£575
York, im mullet	£265	£1300
Threepences, London (Tower), im tun	£250	£950
York, im mullet	£500	£2000
Pennies, sovereign type	£1250	£4650
Farthings, portcullis type	£1500	*

ABOVE: Mary Groat

MARY 1553–54	F	VF
Groats, im pomegranate	£250	£850
Halfgroats, similar	£850	£2350
Pennies, reverse VERITAS TEMP FILIA	£700	£2500
Reverse CIVITAS LONDON	£700	£2500

PHILIP AND MARY 1554–58	F	VF
Shillings, full titles, without date	£425	£1875
Full titles, without date also without XII	£450	£1875
Full titles, dated 1554	£425	£1850
Dated 1554, English titles only	£450	£1875
Dated 1555, English titles only	£425	£1850
Dated 1554, English titles only, also without XII	£475	£2000
Dated 1555, English titles only, also without XII	£800	*
Dated 1554 but date below bust	£3750	*
1555 but date below bust	£3750	*
1555 similar to previous but without ANG	£4250	*
Sixpences, full titles, 1554	£400	£1500
Full titles, undated		ext. rare
English titles, 1555	£450	£1650
Similar but date below bust, 1554	£1500	*
English titles, 1557	£425	£1750
Similar, but date below bust, 1557	£1850	*
Groats, im lis	£165	£525
Halfgroats, im lis	£750	£2500

ABOVE: Philip and Mary Halfgroat

	F	VF
Pennies, im lis	£525	£1850
Base pennies, without portrait	£75	£225

ELIZABETH I 1558–1603
Hammered coinage, first issue 1558–61

Shillings ELIZABETH	F	VF
Wire-line circles	£600	£2500
Beaded inner circles	£300	£1100
ET for Z	£150	£525
Groats		
Wire-line inner circles	£175	£675
Beaded inner circles	£75	£350
ET for Z	£70	£300
Halfgroats		
Wire-line inner circles	£170	£775
Beaded inner circles	£50	£150
Pennies		
Wire-line inner circles	£395	£1475

Countermarked shillings of Edward VI, 1560–61

	F	VF
with portcullis mark (current for 4½d) F	£6000	*
with greyhound mark (current for 2½d) F	£7000	*

Hammered coinage, second issue 1561–82

	F	VF
Sixpences, dated 1561–82	£65	£275
Threepences, 1561–82	£45	£150
Halfgroats, undated	£50	£170
Threehalfpences, 1561–62, 1564–70, 1572–79, 1581–82	£45	£185
Pennies, undated	£35	£120
Threefarthings, 1561–62, 1568, 1572–78, 1581–82	£75	£225

ABOVE: Elizabeth I 1601 Crown

Hammered coinage, third issue 1583–1603

	F	VF
Crowns, im 1	£1975	£4925

HAMMERED SILVER

	F	VF
im 2	£4000	£11000
Halfcrowns, im 1	£1300	£2950
im 2 F	£3250	£11000
Shillings ELIZAB	£120	£500
Sixpences, 1582–1602	£60	£200
Halfgroats, E D G ROSA etc	£25	£80
Pennies	£30	£120
Halfpennies	£30	£100

There are many different initial marks, such as lis, bell or lion, featured on the hammered coins of Elizabeth I, and these marks enable collectors to date those coins which are not themselves dated. For more details see J J North's *English Hammered Coinage, Volume 2*.

ABOVE: Elizabeth I milled coinage 1561 Sixpence

Milled Coinage

Shillings		
Large size	£595	£2950
Intermediate	£350	£950
Small	£285	£850
Sixpences		
1561	£150	£500
1562	£150	£500
1563–64, 1566	£130	£500
1567–68	£150	£500
1570–71	£400	£1450
Groats, undated	£160	£650
Threepences, 1561, 1562–64	£200	£700
Halfgroats	£250	£800
Threefarthings	£4000	*

■ THE STUART KINGS

JAMES I 1603–25
First coinage 1603–04

Crowns, reverse begins EXURGAT	£1500	£3750
Halfcrowns	£1250	£4250

ABOVE: James I second coinage Shilling

Shillings, varieties	£100	£525
Sixpences, dated 1603–04, varieties	£95	£350
Halfgroats, undated	£45	£135
Pennies	£35	£125

Second coinage 1604–19

Crowns reverse begins QVAE DEVS	£975	£2950
Halfcrowns	£1625	£4850
Shillings, varieties	£80	£325
Sixpences, dated 1604–15, varieties	£60	£235
Halfgroats, varieties	£25	£60
Pennies	£28	£70
Halfpennies	£15	£55

ABOVE: James I third coinage Shilling

Third coinage 1619–25

Crowns	£1100	£2250
Plume over reverse shield	£1100	£3000
Halfcrowns	£225	£750
Plume over reverse shield	£525	£1650
Shillings	£100	£350
Plume over reverse shield	£250	£850
Sixpences dated 1621–24	£75	£285
Halfgroats	£25	£60
Pennies	£20	£50
Halfpennies	£15	£40

CHARLES 1 1625–1649
Tower Mint 1625–1643

Crowns, obverse King on horseback, reverse shield

1st horseman/square shield im lis, cross-calvary	£1000	£2750
Horseman/square shield, plume above shield im lis, cross-calvary, castle	£1450	£4250
2nd horseman/oval shield im plume, rose harp, some varieties from	£800	£1950
2nd horseman/oval shield, plume above shield, im plume, rose, harp	£1000	£2650
3rd horseman/round shield im bell, crown, tun, anchor, triangle, star, portcullis, triangle-in-circle, some varieties, from	£775	£1950
3rd horseman/round shield, plume above shield, im tun	£900	£2500

Halfcrowns, obverse King on horseback, reverse shield

HAMMERED SILVER

ABOVE: Charles I Tower mint Crown, plume on rev

	F	VF
1st horseman/square shield im lis, cross-calvary, negro's head, castle, anchor, many varieties from	£245	£1100
1st horseman/square shield plume above shield im lis, cross-calvary, negro's head castle, anchor,	£525	£2350
2nd horseman/oval shield im plume, rose, harp, portcullis, many varieties from	£125	£385
2nd horseman/oval shield, plume above shield, im plume, rose, harp, portcullis	£300	£900
3rd horseman/round shield im bell, crown, tun, portcullis, anchor, triangle, star many varieties from	£75	£265
3rd horseman/round shield plume above shield, im portcullis, bell, crown, tun,	£150	£500
4th horseman/round shield im star, triangle in circle	£70	£220

ABOVE: Charles I Tower mint Halfcrown, im triangle

Shillings

	F	VF
Group A, 1st bust/square shield im lis, cross-calvary, some varieties	£125	£500
1st bust/square shield, plume above shield, im lis, cross-calvary	£650	£2650
Group B, 2nd bust/square shield im cross-calvary, negro's head, castle, anchor, heart, plume many varieties	£95	£395
Group B, 1st bust/square shield, plume above shield, im cross calvary, negro's head, castle, anchor, heart, plume	£1250	£3750
Group C, 3rd bust/oval shield im plume, rose	£70	£260
Group C, 3rd bust/oval shield, plume above im plume, rose	£150	£600
Group D 4th bust/oval or round shield im harp, portcullis, bell, crown, tun, many varieties from	£50	£200
Group D 4th bust/oval or round shield, plume above, im harp, portcullis, bell, crown, tun,	£650	£2650
Group E, 5th bust/square shield im tun, anchor, triangle, many varieties	£60	£225
Group F, 6th bust/square shield im anchor, triangle, star, triangle-in-circle, many varieties	£45	£165

Sixpences

	F	VF
1st bust/square shield, date above, 1625 im lis, cross-calvary, 1626 im cross-calvary	£110	£450
2nd bust/square shield, date above, 1625, 1626 im cross-calvary, 1626, 1627 im negro's head, 1628, 1629 im castle, 1629 im heart, 1630 im heart, plume	£150	£475
3rd bust/oval shield, im plume, rose,	£80	£275
3rd bust/oval shield, plume above, im plume, rose,	£110	£485
4th bust/oval or round shield, im harp, portcullis, bell, crown, tun	£50	£185

ABOVE: Charles I Tower mint Sixpence im crown

	F	VF
5th bust/square shield im tun, anchor, triangle, many varieties from	£60	£210
6th bust/square shield im triangle, star	£50	£200
Halfgroats, crowned rose both sides im lis, cross-calvary, negro's head	£25	£80
2nd bust/oval shield im plume, rose	£25	£90
2nd bus/oval shield, plume above, im plume, rose	£30	£140
3rd bust/oval shield im rose, plume	£30	£95
3rd bust/oval shield, plume above, im rose, plume	£30	£140

HAMMERED SILVER

	F	VF
4th bust/oval or round shield, im harp, crown, portcullis, bell, tun, anchor, triangle, star, many varieties from	£20	£65
5th bust/round shield, im anchor	£35	£110
Pennies, uncrowned rose both sides im one or two pellets, lis, negro's head	£20	£60
2nd bust/oval shield im plume	£30	£90
3rd bust/oval shield im plume, rose	£20	£75
4th bust/oval shield im harp, one or two pellets, portcullis, bell, triangle	£15	£55
5th bust/oval shield im one or two pellets, none	£15	£55
Halfpennies, uncrowned rose both sides im none	£15	£40

Tower Mint, under Parliament 1643–48
Crowns, obverse King on horseback, reverse shield

	F	VF
4th horseman/round shield im P, R, eye sun	£825	£2450
5th horseman/round shield im sun, sceptre	£900	£3000

ABOVE: Charles I Parliament Shilling

	F	VF
Halfcrowns, obverse King on horseback, reverse shield		
3rd horseman/round shield im P, R, eye sun	£50	£200
im P, foreshortened horse	£150	£500
5th tall horseman/round shield im sun, sceptre	£75	£250
Shillings, reverse all square shield		
6th bust, crude, im P, R, eye, sun	£45	£165
7th bust, tall, slim, im sun, sceptre	£60	£250
8th bust, shorter, older, im sceptre	£70	£285
Sixpences, reverse all square shields		
6th bust im P, R,	£75	£225
7th bust im P, R, eye, sun, sceptre	£65	£200
8th bust (crude style) im eye, sun	£125	£450
Halfgroats, 4th bust/round shield im P, R, eye sceptre	£20	£70
7th bust, old/round shield im eye, sun, sceptre	£20	£70
Pennies, 7th bust/oval shield im one or two pellets	£25	£75

ABOVE: Charles I Briot's issue Crown

	F	VF
Briot's first milled issue 1631–32, im flower and B		
Crowns	£1300	£3750
Halfcrowns	£600	£1625
Shillings	£425	£1100
Sixpences	£175	£475
Halfgroats	£65	£165
Pennies	£70	£195
Briot's second milled issue 1638–39, im anchor and B, anchor and mullet		
Halfcrowns	£450	£1250
Shillings	£175	£525
Sixpences	£90	£265

ABOVE: Briot's first milled issue Sixpence

	F	VF
Briot's hammered issue 1638–39, im anchor, triangle over anchor		
Halfcrowns	£600	£1500
Shillings	£325	£875

ABOVE: Charles I 1645 Exeter Crown

		F	VF
Halfpounds		£1650	£5000
Crowns		£1250	£3450
Halfcrowns		£875	£3250
Shillings		£2000	£6000

Oxford 1642–46 im plume with band
			F	VF
Pounds, varieties	from		£4500	£13000
Halfpounds			£1800	£4000
Crowns			£1750	£4000
Halfcrowns			£325	£925
Shillings			£375	£1200
Sixpences			£325	£950
Groats			£250	£700
Threepences			£150	£450
Halfgroats			£140	£400
Pennies			£225	£675

Bristol 1643–45 im Bristol monogram, acorn, plumelet
			F	VF
Halfcrowns, varieties	from		£450	£1250

Provincial Mints

York 1642–44, im lion
		F	VF
Halfcrowns, varieties	from	£385	£1100
Shillings		£250	£700
Sixpences		£295	£850
Threepences		£70	£200

Aberystwyth 1638–42 im open book
		F	VF
Halfcrowns, varieties	from	£1100	£4850
Shillings		£600	£1600
Sixpences		£400	£1200
Groats		£75	£200

Charles I Aberystwyth Groat

	F	VF
Threepences	£50	£175
Halfgroats	£55	£185
Pennies	£70	£250
Halfpennies	£300	£800

Aberystwyth–Furnace 1647–48, im crown
		F	VF
Halfcrowns	from	£3500	£7500
Shillings		£4250	*
Sixpences		£1950	£4850
Groats		£285	£800
Threepences		£300	£950
Halfgroats		£350	£975
Pennies		£800	£2250

Shrewsbury 1642 im plume without band
		F	VF
Pounds, varieties	from	£3850	£11000

ABOVE: Charles I York Shilling

	F	VF
Shillings	£485	£1475
Sixpences	£400	£1350
Groats	£265	£800
Threepences	£375	£875
Halfgroats	£300	£900
Pennies	£475	£1100

ABOVE: Charles I 1644 Bristol Halfcrown

BRITISH COINS MARKET VALUES 2022 **81**

HAMMERED SILVER

HAMMERED SILVER

Late 'Declaration' issues 1645–6
These bear the marks A, B and plume.

Ashby de la Zouch mint, 1645

		F	VF
Halfcrowns, varieties	from	£4000	*
Shillings, varieties		£1500	4500
Sixpences, varieties		£1375	*
Groats, varieties		£975	£3000
Threepences, varieties		£685	£2000

Bridgnorth-on-Severn, 1646

		F	VF
Halfcrowns, varieties	from	£1750	£6000
Shillings, varieties		£750	£2500
Sixpences, varieties		£300	£875
Groats, varieties		£265	£700
Threepence, varieties		£250	£625
Halfgroats, varieties		£500	£1375

Truro 1642–43 im rose, bugle

		F	VF
Crowns, varieties	from	£600	£1300
Halfcrowns		£1250	£3750
Shillings		£5000	*

ABOVE: Charles I 1646 Bridgnorth-on-Severn Halfcrown

Exeter 1643–46 im Ex, rose, castle

		F	VF
Halfpounds			ext. rare
Crowns, varieties	from	£500	£1425
Halfcrowns		£450	£950
Shillings		£575	£1750
Sixpences		£375	£1000
Groats		£150	£475
Threepences		£165	£425
Halfgroats		£300	£800
Pennies		£400	£1000

Worcester 1644–5 im castle, helmet, leopard's head, lion, two lions, lis, rose, star

		F	VF
Halfcrowns, many varieties	from	£950	£4750

Salopia (Shrewsbury) 1644 im helmet, lis, rose in legend

		F	VF
Halfcrowns, many varieties	from	£1400	£5500

Worcester or Salopia (Shrewsbury) 1643–4 im bird, boar's head, lis, castle, cross and annulets, helmet, lion, lis, pear, rose, scroll

	F	VF
Shillings, varieties	£2200	£6000
Sixpences	£1850	£5000
Groats	£675	£2000
Threepences	£425	£975
Halfgroats	£475	£1200

'HC' mint (probably Hartlebury Castle, Worcester, 1646) im pear, three pears

	F	VF
Halfcrowns	£1650	£6000

Chester 1644 im cinquefoil, plume, prostrate gerb, three gerbs

		F	VF
Halfcrowns, varieties	from	£1250	£3850
Shillings		£3250	£9750
Threepences		£950	£2950

Welsh Marches mint? 1644

	F	VF
Halfcrowns	£1000	£3250

Carlisle besieged 1644–45

	F	VF
Three shillings	£13500	£30000
Shillings F	£9750	£21500

Newark besieged 1645–6, surrendered May 1646

	F	VF
Halfcrowns, F	£850	£2000

ABOVE: Charles I 1645 Newark Halfcrown

	F	VF
Shillings, 1645–46, varieties F	£900	£1950
Ninepences, 1645–46	£800	£1625
Sixpences	£900	£1850

Pontefract besieged 1648–49

	F	VF
Two shillings, 1648	£8000	£25000
Shillings, 1648, varieties	£2750	£6000

ABOVE: Charles I 1648 Pontefract Shilling

Scarborough besieged 1644–45

Many odd values issued were issued in Scarborough, all of which are extremely rare. The coin's value was decided by the intrinsic value of the piece of metal from which it was made.

Examples: 5s 8d, 2s 4d, 1s 9d, 1s 3d, 7d F

Collectors can expect to pay at least £25000 or more in F and £40000 in VF for any of these.

COMMONWEALTH 1649–60

	F	VF
Crowns, im sun 1649, 51–54, 56	£1500	£3750
Halfcrowns, im sun 1649, 1651–6	£400	£900
im anchor 1658–60	£1500	£3850
Shillings, im sun 1649, 1661–87	£300	£700
im anchor 1658–60	£1200	£2750
Sixpences, im sun 1649, 1651–7	£250	£600
im anchor 1658–6	£800	£1850
Halfgroats undated	£35	£110
Pennies undated	£30	£85
Halfpennies	£30	£85

CHARLES II 1660–85

Hammered coinage 1660–62

First issue

		F	VF
Halfcrown	from	£1600	£4750
Shilling		£525	£1650
Sixpence		£300	£1150
Twopence		£50	£125
Penny		£30	£110

ABOVE: Charles II hammered first issue Shilling

Second issue

		F	VF
Halfcrown		£1200	£4500
Shilling		£700	£2250
Sixpence		£1375	£4000
Twopence	from	£25	£90
Penny		£30	£80

Third issue

	F	VF
Halfcrown	£200	£650
Shilling	£165	£550
Sixpence	£125	£450
Fourpence	£35	£120
Threepence	£20	£80
Twopence	£20	£65
Penny	£20	£70

HALLS HAMMERED COINS
British Hammered Coin Specialist - From early Saxon to late Stuart

BNTA

Halls Hammered Coins

Contact - Simon Hall

Email - Simon@HallsHammeredCoins.com

Phone - 07830019584

Website - www.HallsHammeredCoins.com

BRITISH COINS MARKET VALUES 2019

'ROYAL' AND 'ROSE' BASE METAL FARTHINGS

Until 1613 English coins were struck only in gold or silver, because the monarchy thought base metal would diminish the royal prerogative of coining.

However silver coins became far too small and farthings so tiny that they had to be discontinued.

So to meet demands for small change, James I authorised Lord Harington to issue copper farthing tokens.

Subsequently this authority passed in turn to the Duke of Lennox, the Duchess of Richmond and Lord Maltravers.

It ceased by order of Parliament in 1644.

ROYAL FARTHING TOKENS

	Fair	F	VF	EF
JAMES I				
Type 1 Harington, c1613. Larger flan with tin-washed surface, mint-mark between sceptres below crown	£15	£30	£90	£370
Type 2 Harington, c1613. Larger flan, no tin wash	£15	£20	£50	£175
Type 3 Lennox, 1614–25. IACO starts at 1 o'clock position	£10	£15	£40	£140
Type 4 Lennox, 1622–25. Oval flan, IACO starts at 7 o'clock	£15	£30	£90	£300

	Fair	F	VF	EF
CHARLES I				
Type 1 Richmond, 1625–34 single arched crown	£10	£18	£40	£100
Type 2 Transitional, c1634 double arched crown	£10	£25	£70	£260
Type 3 Maltravers, 1634–36 inner circles	£10	£20	£40	£120
Type 4 Richmond, 1625–34 as Type 1 but oval	£12	£30	£75	£295
Type 5 Maltravers, 1634–36 double arched crown	£15	£35	£80	£220

ROSE FARTHING TOKENS

These have a rose on the reverse.

	Fair	F	VF	EF
Type 1 Small thick flan	£10	£18	£35	£140
Type 2 Small thick flan, but single arched crown	£8	£15	£30	£100
Type 3 Small thick flan, but sceptres below crown	£15	£35	£70	£160

ABOVE: From left to right: James I Harington farthings, types 1, 2 and 3

ABOVE: From left to right: Charles I Richmond, Maltravers and rose farthings

GUERNSEY STAMPS AND COLLECTABLES | GUERNSEY POST

Banknotes

Guernsey issues its own sterling currency in the form or notes and coins, which are legal tender in the Bailiwick but not outside, where their acceptability is limited.
In collaboration with the States of Guernsey Treasury, a set of circulating Guernsey coins, produced by The Royal Mint and £1, £5, £10, £20 & £50 bank notes are available in mint uncirculated condition. The bank notes are designed and printed by De La Rue Currency which was set up by Guernsey-man Thomas De La Rue in the 19th Century.
Every coin and note gives you a piece of Guernsey's rich history, something for collectors to treasure.

NEW £1 B.Haines signatory Guernsey Bank Note (AA Prefix)

Coins

Guernsey Mint Coin Pack £15

Mint, uncirculated Banknote: £1

A new 'AA' String Guernsey Bank Note featuring Daniel De Lisle Brock, Bailiff of Guernsey between 1762 - 1842 and The Royal Court, St Peter Port 1840. They have been designed and printed by De La Rue Currency, a company started by Guernseyman Thomas De La Rue in the 19th Century.

Uncirculated banknotes can be purchased from Guernsey Stamps.

Limited Edition British Isles Coastal Wildlife 10p collectors set £60

Uncirculated coins & banknotes available on our website

Guernsey Uncirculated Coins

A set of seven Guernsey coins are supplied in a Presentation Pack containing design information and specifications.
Coins included are:-
£2, 50p, 20p, 10p, 5p, 2p, 1p.

Limited Edition British Isles Woodland Wildlife 10p colour set £60

rder Guernsey banknotes and stamps
line or by tel: +44 (0) 1481 716486
ail philatelic@guernseypost.com

Guernsey Stamps   @guernseystamps

www.guernseystamps.com/bank-notes

MILLED COINAGE FROM 1656

This listing gives a general indication of value throughout the entire milled series. It is a guide for collectors only, not dealers' buying prices. The prices are a reasonable assessment of the market at the time of compilation, and for strictly graded coins, pieces of exceptional quality can sell for considerably more. Standards of grading also vary, so always seek advice if you are unsure, contact the British Numismatic Trade Association.

Prices are drawn from auction results and dealers' lists, with the aim of determining firm valuations, but prices still vary enormously from sale to sale and from one dealer's list to another. For practical reasons, only some of the varieties, dates and errors are mentioned.

The silver and base metal coinage up to the beginning of the reign of George III is graded to extremely fine, afterwards they are graded up to uncirculated. The condition, or grade, of a coin is of great importance in determining its value.

For further assistance see the sections on grading (pp44–45), abbreviations and terms (pp46–47).

For practical reasons we have ceased cataloguing coins produced beyond 2010, so please refer to the Royal Mint website.

■ CROMWELL GOLD PATTERNS

These were struck by order of Cromwell, with the consent of the Council of State.

Thomas Simon made the dies, and the coins were struck on Peter Blondeau's machine.

The fifty shillings and the broad were struck from the same dies, but the fifty shillings has the edge inscription PROTECTOR LITERIS LITERAE NUMMIS CORONA ER SALUS, while the broad is not as thick and has a grained edge.

No original strikings of the half-broad are known, but some were struck from dies made by Joh(n) Tanner in 1738.

All three denominations are dated 1656.

	F	VF	EF	Unc
Fifty shillings	*	£75000	£230000	*
Broad	*	£12000	£29000	£45000
Half-broad	*	*	£25000	*

ABOVE: Oliver Cromwell gold Broad 1656

■ FIVE GUINEAS

CHARLES II	F	VF	EF	Unc
1668–78 pointed end of trnctn of bust	£5750	£12250	£45000	*
1668, 69, 75 as above, eleph below bust	£5750	£12250	£45000	*
1675–8 as above, eleph & castle below bust	£5750	£12250	£45000	*
1678–84 rounded end to trnctn	£5750	£12250	£45000	*
1680–4 as above, eleph & castle	£5750	£12250	£45000	*

ABOVE: Charles II 1670 proof Five Guineas

JAMES II				
1686 sceptres in wrong order on rev	£5850	£11000	£45000	*
1687–8 sceptres correct	£5850	£11000	£45000	*
1687–8 eleph & castle	£5850	£11000	£45000	*

WILLIAM AND MARY				
1691–4 no prov mark	£5000	£11000	£40000	*
1691–4 eleph & castle	£5000	£11250	£40000	*

ABOVE: William and Mary 1692 elephant & castle Five Guineas

MILLED COINAGE

WILLIAM III	F	VF	EF	Unc
1699–1700 no prov mark	£4500	£10000	£37000	*
1699 eleph & castle	£4500	£9500	£32500	*
1701 new bust 'fine work'	£4500	£10000	£37000	*

ANNE				
Pre-Union with Scotland				
1703 VIGO below bust	*	£200000	£500000	*
1705–6 plain below	£7000	£15000	£50000	*
Post-Union with Scotland				
1706	£7000	£12500	£40000	*
1709 larger lettering wider shield and crowns	£5500	£12500	£40000	*
1711, 1713–4 broader bust	£5500	£10000	£35000	*

The pre-Union reverse has separate shields, top and right, for England and Scotland, while post-Union reverses have the English and Scottish arms side by side on the top and bottom shields.

GEORGE I				
1716, 17, 20, 26	£6000	£12500	£60000	*

ABOVE: George I 1716 Five Guineas

GEORGE II				
1729, 31, 35, 38, 41 YH	£4000	£6500	£27500	*
1729 YH, E.I.C. below head	£4000	£6500	£27500	*
1746 OH, LIMA below	£4000	£6500	£26000	*
1748, 53 OH plain below	£4000	£6500	£27000	*

GEORGE III				
1770, 73, 77 patterns only	*	*	£150000	£325000

■ TWO GUINEAS

CHARLES II	F	VF	EF	Unc
1664, 65, 69, 71 pointed end to trnctn	£2250	£4750	£20000	*
1664 elephant below	£2250	£4250	£20000	*
1675–84 rounded end to trnctn	£2250	£4000	£17500	*
1676, 78, 82–84 eleph & castle below bust	£2250	£4250	£17500	*
1678 eleph below				ext. rare

JAMES II				
1687	£2500	£5750	£23000	*
1688/7	£2500	£5750	£23000	*

WILLIAM AND MARY				
1691, 93, 94 eleph & castle	£2650	£5500	£17500	*
1693, 94 no prov mark	£2650	£5750	£17500	*

WILLIAM III				
1701	£2750	£4850	£17000	*

ANNE				
1709, 11, 13, 14	£2250	£3750	£12000	*

GEORGE I				
1717, 20, 26	£2000	£4000	£13000	£30000

GEORGE II				
1734, 35, 38, 39, YH F	£1300	£1700	£4500	£9000
1739–40 IH	£1350	£1750	£4700	*
1748, 53, OH	£1450	£1950	£5000	*

GEORGE III				
1768, 73, 77 patterns only	*	*	£50000	£95000

■ BROAD

CHARLES II				
1662	£2250	£3250	£9250	*

■ GUINEAS

	F	VF	EF	Unc
1663 pointed trnctn	£3250	*	*	*
1663 eleph	£2500	£7000	*	*
1664 trnctn indented	£2500	£7750	*	*
1664 eleph	£2500	£8000	*	*
1664–73 sloping pointed trnctn	£900	£2950	£11000	*
1664, 65, 68 eleph	£1200	£4000	£16000	*
1672–84 rounded trnctn	£800	£2450	£8250	*
1674–84 eleph & castle	£1100	£2750	£9250	*
1677–8 eleph				ext. rare

BRITISH COINS MARKET VALUES 2022

MILLED COINAGE

ABOVE: Charles II 1663 Guinea, elephant below bust

JAMES II	F	VF	EF	Unc
1685–6 1st bust	£775	£2500	£8500	*
1685 1st bust eleph & castle	£800	£3000	£10500	*
1686–8 2nd bust	£750	£2000	£7250	*
1686–8 2nd bust eleph & castle	£850	£2850	£9000	*
WILLIAM AND MARY				
1689–94 no prov mark	£850	£2500	£8500	*
1689–94 eleph & castle	£950	£2850	£9000	*
1692 eleph	£1350	£3000	£10500	*
WILLIAM III				
1695–6 1st bust	£600	£1650	£5250	*
1695, 6 eleph & castle	£600	£1650	£5250	*
1697–1701 2nd bust	£625	£1500	£4750	*
1697–1701 eleph & castle	£1250	£5000	*	*
1701 3rd bust 'fine work'	£900	£2350	£8500	*
ANNE				
Pre-Union				
1702, 1705–07 plain below bust	£975	£3000	£11000	*
1703 VIGO below	£10000	£28000	£75000	*
Post-Union				
1707–8 1st bust	£750	£1850	£5750	*
1707 eleph & castle	£950	£2500	£7000	*
1707–9 2nd bust	£650	£1500	£4250	£7250
1708–9 eleph & castle	£950	£3250	*	*
1710–1714 3rd bust	£575	£1000	£3850	£6500

Pre-Union reverse has separate shields, top and right, for England and Scotland. Post-Union reverses have the English and Scottish arms side by side on both the top and bottom shields.

GEORGE I	F	VF	EF	Unc
1714 1st hd PR. EL. (Prince Elector) in rev legend	£1250	£3500	£11000	£25000
1715 2nd hd, tie with two ends	£650	£1600	£4500	£7000
1715–16 3rd hd, hair not curling round trnctn	£650	£1600	£4000	£6500
1716–23 4th hd, tie with loop	£650	£1350	£3850	£6000
1721–2 eleph & castle	*			ext. rare
1723–7 5th hd, smaller, older bust	£550	£1200	£3850	£5500
1726 eleph & castle	£1650	£6250	*	*
GEORGE II				
1727 1st YH, small lettering	£950	£2850	£9500	*
1727–28 1st YH larger lettering	£1000	£3250	£9500	*
1729–32 2nd YH	£800	£2650	£7000	*
1729, 31–32 E.I.C. below	£825	£2850	£8250	*
1732–38 larger lettering	£600	£1450	£4000	£6250
1732 E.I.C. below	£850	£2750	£7500	*
1739–40, 43 intermediate hd	£625	£1200	£3850	£6500
1739 E.I.C. below	£850	£2750	£8250	*
1745–6 larger lettering	£550	£1350	£3750	£6500
1746 LIMA below	£3000	£6000	£17500	*
1746–53, 55–56, 58–59, 60, OH	£475	£1000	£3850	£5850
GEORGE III				
1761 1st hd	£1350	£3250	£8500	£13750
1763–64 2nd hd	£1250	£3250	£7000	*
1765–73 3rd hd	£450	£725	£1950	£4250
1774–79, 81–86 4th hd	£400	£550	£1425	£2650
1789–99 5th hd, 'spade' rev F	£400	£600	£850	£1500
1813 6th hd, rev shield in Garter ('Military guinea')	£725	£1500	£4000	£7000

ABOVE: George II 1760 Guinea

ABOVE: George III 1813 Guinea

88 BRITISH COINS MARKET VALUES 2022

■ HALF-GUINEAS

	F	VF	EF	Unc
CHARLES II				
1669–72 bust with pointed trnctn	£650	£1650	£5750	*
1672–84 rounded truncation	£650	£1500	£5000	*
1676–78, 80, 82, 84 eleph & castle	£750	£1800	£7000	*
JAMES II				
1686–88 no prov mark	£500	£1650	£5000	£9000
1686 eleph & castle	£2000	*	*	*
WILLIAM AND MARY				
1689 1st busts	£650	£1850	£5500	*
1690–4 2nd busts	£700	£1750	£5000	*
1691–2 eleph & castle	£750	£1950	£5500	*
1692 eleph	£1500	*	*	*

ABOVE: William and Mary 1689 Half-guinea

WILLIAM III				
1695 no prov mark	£475	£950	£3750	£6000
1695–6 eleph & castle	£650	£1500	£5250	*
1697–1701 larger harp on rev	£475	£900	£3750	£6000
1698 eleph & castle	£600	£1650	£5750	*

ANNE				
Pre-Union				
1702, 05 plain below bust	£750	£2750	£7750	£12750
1703 VIGO below	£5250	£14500	£37500	*

Post-Union
| 1707–1714 plain | £450 | £700 | £2250 | £6000 |

Pre-Union reverse has separate shields, top and right, for England and Scotland. Post-Union reverses have the English and Scottish arms side by side on the top and bottom shields.

GEORGE I				
1715, 17–24 1st hd	£375	£700	£2650	£4250
1721 eleph & castle	*	*	*	ext. rare
1725–27 smaller older hd	£295	£600	£2500	£3650

GEORGE II				
1728–39 YH	£425	£975	£3500	*

	F	VF	EF	Unc
1729–32, 39 E.I.C. below	£550	£1350	£4750	*
1740, 43, 45–46 intermediate hd	£395	£750	£2850	*
1745 LIMA below	£1500	£3000	£9750	*
1747–53, 55–56, 58–60 OH	£325	£550	£1650	£3250

ABOVE: George II 1756 Half-guinea

GEORGE III				
1762–63 1st hd	£575	£1725	£4250	*
1764–66, 68–69, 72–75 2nd hd	£250	£525	£1650	*
1774–75 3rd hd	£850	£1950	£6000	*
1775–79, 81, 83–86 4th hd	£295	£400	£975	£2000
1787–91, 93–98, 1800 5th hd	£225	£300	£925	£1700
1801–03 6th hd	£225	£3005	£750	£1100
1804, 06, 08–11, 13 7th hd	£225	£300	£350	£1400

■ THIRD-GUINEAS

GEORGE III				
1797–1800 1st hd	£100	£150	£500	£800
1801–03 date close to crown on rev	£100	£150	£500	£850
1804–05, 08–11 2nd hd	£90	£150	£425	£800

■ QUARTER-GUINEAS

GEORGE I				
1718	£110	£250	£525	£1000

GEORGE III				
1762	£165	£300	£575	£975

ABOVE: George III 1762 Quarter-guinea

■ FIVE POUNDS

GEORGE III				
1820 pattern F	*	*	*	£375000

MILLED COINAGE

BRITISH COINS MARKET VALUES 2022 **89**

MILLED COINAGE

	F	VF	EF	Unc
GEORGE IV				
1826 proof	*	*	£2200	£60000
VICTORIA				
1839 proof, 'Una and the Lion' rev F	*	*	£95000	£230000

ABOVE: Victoria 1839 proof Five Pound with 'Una and the Lion'

	F	VF	EF	Unc
1887 JH F	£1500	£1750	£2500	£3750
1887 proof	*	*	£4850	£14000
1887 proof no B.P.	*	*	£5850	£12500
1893 OH F	£1700	£2100	£3700	£5950
1893 proof	*	*	£7000	£20000
EDWARD VII				
1902 F	£1350	£1600	£2450	£3750
1902 proof	*	*	£2650	£3875
GEORGE V				
1911 proof F	*	*	*	£12000
GEORGE VI				
1937 proof	*	*	*	£7000

In 1984 the Royal Mint issued the first of an annual issue of Brilliant Uncirculated £5 coins.

These bear the symbol 'U' in a circle to the left of the date on the reverse to indicate the standard of striking.

BV indicates bullion value. At the time of going to press gold is approximately £1050 per troy oz.

ELIZABETH II Sovereign Issues	Unc
1953 proof	ext. rare
1980 proof, originally issued in Royal Mint set	BV
1981 proof	BV
1982 proof, originally issued in Royal Mint set	BV
1984 proof	BV
	Unc
1984 BU	BV
1985 proof	BV
1985 BU	BV

	F	VF	EF	Unc
1986 BU				BV
1987 new effigy, BU				BV
1988 BU				BV
1989 proof, 500th anniversary of the sovereign, originally issued in Royal Mint set				£2250
1989 BU, 500th anniversary of the sovereign				BV
1990 proof, originally issued in Royal Mint set				BV
1990 BU				BV
1991 proof, originally issued in Royal Mint set				BV
1991 BU				BV
1992 proof, originally issued in Royal Mint set				BV
1992 BU				BV
1993 proof, originally issued in Royal Mint set				BV
1993 BU				BV
1994 proof, originally issued in Royal Mint set				BV
1994 BU				BV
1995 proof, originally issued in Royal Mint set				BV
1995 BU				BV
1996 proof, originally issued in Royal Mint set				BV
1996 BU				BV
1997 proof, originally issued in Royal Mint set				BV
1997 BU				BV
1998 proof, originally issued in Royal Mint set				BV
1998 BU				BV
1999 proof, originally issued in Royal Mint set				BV
1999 BU				BV
2000 proof, originally issued in Royal Mint set				BV
2000 BU				BV
2001 proof, originally issued in Royal Mint set				BV
2001 BU				BV
2002 shield reverse, proof, originally issued in Royal Mint set				BV
2002 BU				BV
2003 proof, originally issued in Royal Mint set				BV
2003 BU				BV
2004 proof, originally issued in Royal Mint set				BV
2004 BU				BV
2005 proof, originally issued in Royal Mint set				BV
2005 BU				BV
2006 proof, originally issued in Royal Mint set				BV
2006 BU				BV
2007 proof, originally issued in Royal Mint set				BV
2008 proof, originally issued in Royal Mint four coin set				BV
2009 proof, Countdown to London 2012				BV
2009 proof, Henry VIII				BV
2009 BU				BV
2010 proof				BV
2011 proof				BV
2011 BU				BV
2012 proof				BV
2012 BU				BV
2013 proof				BV
2013 BU				BV
2014 proof				BV
2014 BU				BV
2015 proof				BV
2015 proof, new portrait				BV
2015 BU				BV

2016 proof, Butler portrait	BV
2016 BU	BV

ABOVE: George IV 1823 Two pounds

■ TWO POUNDS

	F	VF	EF	Unc
GEORGE III				
1820 pattern F	*	*	£25000	£65000
GEORGE IV				
1823 St George on rev F	*	£800	£2000	£5000
1826 proof, shield rev	*	*	£6000	£13000
WILLIAM IV				
1831 proof	*	*	£7250	£20000
VICTORIA				
1887 JH F	£550	£650	£1000	£1650
1887 proof	*	*	£1750	£3000
1893 OH F	£650	£850	£1750	£3000
1893 proof	*	*	£2500	£6000
EDWARD VII				
1902 F	£525	£600	£1100	£2200
1902 proof	*	*	£1100	£2200
GEORGE V				
1911 proof F	*	*	*	£3500
GEORGE VI				
1937 proof	*	*	*	£2500

ELIZABETH II		Unc
1953 proof		ext. rare
1980 proof, originally issued in Royal Mint set		BV
1982 proof, originally issued in Royal Mint set		BV
1983 proof		BV
1985 proof, originally issued in Royal Mint set		BV
1987 proof		BV
1988 proof		BV
1989 500th anniversary of the sovereign, proof		£1100
1990 proof		BV
1991 proof		BV
1992 proof		BV
1993 proof		BV
1996 proof		BV
1998 proof, originally issued in Royal Mint set		BV
2000 proof, originally issued in Royal Mint set		BV
2002 shield rev, proof, originally issued in Royal Mint set		BV
2003 proof, originally issued in Royal Mint set		BV
2004 proof, originally issued in Royal Mint set		BV
2005 proof, originally issued in Royal Mint set		BV
2006 proof, originally issued in Royal Mint set		BV
2007 proof, originally issued in Royal Mint set		BV
2008 proof, originally issued in Royal Mint set		BV
2009 proof, originally issued in Royal Mint set		BV
2010 proof		BV
2011 proof		BV
2012 proof		BV
2012 BU		BV
2013 proof		BV
2013 BU		BV
2014 proof		BV
2014 BU		BV
2015 proof		BV
2015 proof, new portait		BV
2016 proof, Butler portait		BV

■ SOVEREIGNS

ABOVE: George III 1817 Sovereign

Early sovereigns can attain considerably higher prices if flawless

	F	VF	EF	Unc
GEORGE III				
1817 F	£500	£750	£1950	£4200
1818	£800	£1500	£4500	£9000
1819	£35000	£55000	*	*
1820	£500	£650	£1700	£3200
GEORGE IV				
Type Laureate head/St George				
1821 F	£450	£550	£1300	£3200
1821 proof	*	*	£3500	£10000
1822 F	£450	£650	£1300	£3500
1823	£875	£2000	£6250	£10500
1824	£450	£650	£1750	£5000
1825	£600	£1575	£4650	£9000
Type bare head/shield				
1825 F	£450	£650	£1450	£2950
1826	£450	£650	£1450	£3500
1826 proof	*	*	£3500	£11000
1827 F	£450	£650	£1500	£3250
1828 F	£4000	£10000	£25000	*
1829	£450	£650	£1500	£3700
1830	£450	£675	£1600	£3700
WILLIAM IV				
1831	£495	£875	£2250	£4500

BRITISH COINS MARKET VALUES 2022

MILLED COINAGE

	F	VF	EF	Unc
1831 proof	*	*	£3950	£11000
1832 F	£450	£750	£1675	£3250
1833	£450	£650	£1750	£4000
1835	£450	£750	£2000	£4250
1836	£450	£725	£2000	£3750
1837	£450	£775	£2250	£4250

ABOVE: William IV 1833 Sovereign

VICTORIA
Type 1, YH/shield

	F	VF	EF	Unc
1838	£700	£1275	£2950	£6000
1838 wreath leaves different	£2000	£5000	£20000	*
1839	£1000	£1750	£4250	£9500
1839 proof	*	*	£5000	£12500
1841	£4500	£8250	£13500	£25000
1842	*	*	£585	£1850
1843	*	*	£585	£1850
1843 narrow shield	£3000	£6500	£16500	*
1844	*	*	£585	£1850
1845	*	*	£700	£2000
1846	*	*	£700	£2000
1847	*	*	£475	£1250
1848	*	*	£475	£1250
1849	*	*	£700	£3000
1850	*	*	£425	£1450
1851	*	*	£400	£1350
1852	*	*	£395	£1250
1853	*	*	£395	£1350
1853 proof	*	*	£9000	£23000
1854	*	*	£395	£1500
1855	*	*	£395	£1500
1856	*	*	£395	£1500
1857	*	*	£395	£1500
1858	*	*	£395	£1500
1859	*	*	£395	£1500
1859 'Ansell'	£675	£2500	£6750	*
1860	*	*	£400	£1850
1861	*	*	£365	£975
1862	*	*	£365	£975

ABOVE: Victoria 1859 'Ansell' Sovereign

	F	VF	EF	Unc
1863	*	*	£325	£650
1863 '827' on trnctn	£5250	£8500	*	*
1863 die number below wreath on rev	*	*	£300	£650
1863 '827' on trnctn	£4500	£7500	£14000	*
1864 die no	*	*	£385	£900
1865 die no	*	*	£400	£925
1866 die no	*	*	£385	£900
1868 die no	*	*	£385	£900
1869 die no	*	*	£385	£900
1870 die no	*	*	£385	£900
1871 die no	*	*	£325	£500
1871 S (Sydney mint) below wreath	*	*	£350	£700
1872	*	*	£300	£425
1872 die no	*	*	£315	£450
1872 M (Melbourne mint) below wreath	*	*	£350	£825
1872 S	*	*	£350	£1000
1873 die no	*	*	£350	£450
1873 S	*	*	£350	£1000
1874 die no	£1750	£3750	£8500	*
1874 M	*	*	£325	£725
1875 S	*	*	£350	£1000
1877 S	*	*	£350	£1000
1878 S	*	*	£325	£875
1879 S	*	*	£325	£725
1880 M	£600	£1100	£4000	*
1880 S	*	*	£350	£1000
1881 M	*	*	£500	£6500
1881 S	*	*	£445	£1250
1882 M	*	*	£425	£900
1882 S	*	*	£500	£1450
1883 M	*	£425	£1250	£2250
1883 S	*	*	£315	£800
1884 M	*	*	£315	£725
1884 S	*	*	£300	£925
1885 M	*	*	£315	£650
1885 S	*	*	£315	£650
1886 M	£1400	£3000	£6000	£11000
1886 S	*	*	£375	£1500
1887 M	£875	£1850	£5250	£9000
1887 S	*	*	£475	£1450

ABOVE: Victoria 1871 St George Sovereign

Type II, YH/St George and dragon

	F	VF	EF	Unc
1871	*	*	£325	£575
1871 S below hd	*	*	£500	£1750
1872	*	*	£325	£575

92 BRITISH COINS MARKET VALUES 2022

MILLED COINAGE

	F	VF	EF	Unc
1872 M below hd	*	*	£750	£3250
1872 S	*	*	£350	£950
1873	*	*	£325	£575
1873 M	*	*	£395	*
1873 S	*	*	£475	£2225
1874	*	*	£325	£575
1874 M	*	*	£375	£1250
1874 S	*	*	£350	£1200
1875 M	*	*	£375	£900
1875 S	*	*	£400	£875
1876	*	*	£285	£600
1876 M	*	*	£375	£900
1876 S	*	*	£375	£900
1877 M	*	*	£375	£900
1878	*	*	£300	£600
1878 M	*	*	£375	£900
1879	£475	£1000	£4000	*
1879 M	*	*	£400	£900
1879 S	*	*	£900	£2750
1880	*	*	£375	£550
1880 M	*	*	£400	£775
1880 S	*	*	£400	£775
1881 M	*	*	£550	£1100
1881 S	*	*	£400	£775
1882 M	*	*	£400	£775
1882 S	*	*	£400	£585
1883 M	*	*	£400	£600
1883 S	*	*	£400	£585
1884	*	*	£375	£525
1884 M	*	*	£400	£585
1884 S	*	*	£400	£585
1885	*	*	£375	£525
1885 M	*	*	£400	£700
1885 S	*	*	£375	£600
1886 M	*	*	£375	£975
1886 S	*	*	£375	£600
1887 M	*	*	£375	£700
1887 S	*	*	£375	£800

ABOVE: Victoria 1887 Jubilee Head Sovereign

Jubilee head coinage

	F	VF	EF	Unc
1887 F	*	*	£350	£450
1887 proof	*	*	£850	£2850
1887 M (Melbourne mint)	*	*	£375	£675
1887 S (Sydney mint)	*	*	£600	£2250
1888	*	*	£300	£400
1888 M	*	*	£250	£600
1888 S	*	*	£300	£825
1889	*	*	£350	£450
1889 M	*	*	£350	£450
1889 S	*	*	£350	£475
1890	*	*	£350	£400
1890 M	*	*	£350	£600
1890 S	*	*	£350	£900
1891	*	*	£350	£450
1891 M	*	*	£350	£500
1891 S	*	*	£350	£450
1892	*	*	£350	£450
1892 M	*	*	£350	£450
1892 S	*	*	£350	£495
1893 M	*	*	£350	£450
1893 S	*	*	£350	£485

Old head coinage

	F	VF	EF	Unc
1893	*	*	£325	£450
1893 proof	*	*	£1250	£3250
1893 M	*	*	£350	£575
1893 S	*	*	£350	£450
1894	*	*	£350	£450
1894 M	*	*	£350	£450
1894 S	*	*	£350	£450
1895	*	*	£350	£450
1895 M	*	*	£350	£450
1895 S	*	*	£350	£450
1896	*	*	£350	£450
1896 M	*	*	£350	£450
1896 S	*	*	£350	£475
1897 M	*	*	£350	£450
1897 S	*	*	£350	£450
1898	*	*	£350	£450
1898 M	*	*	£350	£450
1898 S	*	*	£350	£450
1899	*	*	£350	£450
1899 M	*	*	£350	£450
1899 P (Perth mint)	*	*	£485	£1350
1899 S	*	*	£350	£450
1900	*	*	£350	£400
1900 M	*	*	£350	£450
1900 P	*	*	£350	£450
1900 S	*	*	£350	£450
1901	*	*	£350	£400
1901 M	*	*	£350	£450
1901 P	*	*	£350	£450
1901 S	*	*	£350	£450

EDWARD VII

	F	VF	EF	Unc
1902	*	*	*	£350
1902 proof	*	*	£375	£650
1902 M	*	*	*	£350
1902 P	*	*	*	£350
1902 S	*	*	*	£350
1903	*	*	*	£325
1903 M	*	*	*	£350
1903 P	*	*	*	£350
1903 S	*	*	*	£350
1904	*	*	*	£325
1904 M	*	*	*	£350
1904 P	*	*	*	£350
1904 S	*	*	*	£350

MILLED COINAGE

	F	VF	EF	Unc
1905	*	*	*	£325
1905 M	*	*	*	£350
1905 P	*	*	*	£350
1905 S	*	*	*	£350
1906	*	*	*	£395
1906 M	*	*	*	£350
1906 P	*	*	*	£350
1906 S	*	*	*	£350
1907	*	*	*	£395
1907 M	*	*	*	£350
1907 P	*	*	*	£350
1907 S	*	*	*	£350
1908	*	*	*	£325
1908 C on ground below dragon F	*	*	£5850	£10500
1908 M	*	*	*	£350
1908 P	*	*	*	£350
1908 S	*	*	*	£350
1909	*	*	*	£325
1909 C	*	£350	£500	£1500
1909 M	*	*	*	£350
1909 P	*	*	*	£350
1909 S	*	*	*	£350
1910	*	*	*	£325
1910 C	*	£295	£400	£1150
1910 M	*	*	*	£350
1910 P	*	*	*	£350
1910 S	*	*	*	£350

GEORGE V

	F	VF	EF	Unc
1911	*	*	*	£325
1911 proof	*	*	*	£1375
1911 C	*	*	£2300	£325
1911 M	*	*	*	£325
1911 P	*	*	*	£325
1911 S	*	*	*	£325
1912	*	*	*	£325
1912 M	*	*	*	£325
1912 P	*	*	*	£325
1912 S	*	*	*	£325
1913	*	*	*	£325
1913 C F	£300	£465	£1550	*
1913 M	*	*	*	£325
1913 P	*	*	*	£325
1913 S	*	*	*	£325
1914	*	*	*	£325
1914 C	*	£300	£395	£800
1914 M	*	*	*	£325
1914 P	*	*	*	£325
1914 S	*	*	*	£325
1915	*	*	*	£325
1915 M	*	*	*	£325
1915 P	*	*	*	£425
1915 S	*	*	*	£325
1916	*	*	*	£425
1916 C F	*	£8000	£13500	£18500
1916 M	*	*	*	£325
1916 P	*	*	*	£325

	F	VF	EF	Unc
1916 S	*	*	*	£300
1917 F	*	£4000	£10000	£15000
1917 C	*	*	£295	£385
1917 M	*	*	*	£325
1917 P	*	*	*	£325
1917 S	*	*	*	£325
1918 C	*	*	£295	£365
1918 I	*	*	£295	£400
1918 M	*	*	*	£400
1918 P	*	*	*	£325
1918 S	*	*	*	£325
1919 C	*	*	£295	£385
1919 M	*	*	*	£495
1919 P	*	*	*	£325
1919 S	*	*	*	£325
1920 M	£900	£2000	£3750	£5750
1920 P	*	*	*	£285
1920 S	*	*	highest	rarity
1921 M	£3000	£5250	£9000	£16000
1921 P	*	*	*	£325
1921 S	*	£650	£1100	£2250
1922 M	£3000	£5000	£7750	£11000
1922 P	*	*	*	£300
1922 S	£5000	£8500	£12500	£17500
1923 M	*	*	*	£350
1923 S	£2500	£4000	£7250	£13500
1923 SA (Pretoria Mint)	£3000	£4000	£8000	*
1923 SA proof	*	*	*	£3000
1924 M	*	*	*	£325
1924 P	*	*	*	£325
1924 S	*	£600	£1375	£2250
1924 SA	*	*	£7500	*
1925	*	*	*	£325
1925 M	*	*	*	£325
1925 P	*	*	*	£350
1925 S	*	*	*	£300
1925 SA	*	*	*	£325
1926 M	*	*	*	£365
1926 P	*	£400	£750	£1000
1926 S	£4750	£8250	£13500	*
1926 SA	*	*	*	£325
1927 P	*	*	£285	£495
1927 SA	*	*	*	£325
1928 M	£550	£825	£1750	£3000
1928 P	*	*	*	£325
1928 SA	*	*	*	£300
1929 M	*	£700	£1875	£3750
1929 P	*	*	*	£325
1929 SA	*	*	*	£325
1930 M	*	*	£295	£350
1930 P	*	*	£295	£325
1930 SA	*	*	*	£300
1931 M	*	*	£325	£825
1931 P	*	*	*	£325
1931 SA	*	*	*	£325
1932	*	*	*	£325

GEORGE VI

	F	VF	EF	Unc
1937 proof only	*	*	*	£2600

ABOVE: George VI 1937 proof Sovereign

ELIZABETH II	F	VF	EF	Unc
1953 proof	*	*	*	£375000

One sold at Baldwins in 2014 for £396,000 including premium

	F	VF	EF	Unc
1957	*	*	*	£325
1958	*	*	*	£325
1959	*	*	*	£325
1962	*	*	*	£325
1963	*	*	*	£325
1964	*	*	*	£325
1965	*	*	*	£325
1966	*	*	*	£325
1967	*	*	*	£325
1968	*	*	*	£325
1974	*	*	*	£325
1976	*	*	*	£325
1976 proof	*	*	*	ext. rare
1977	*	*	*	£325
1978	*	*	*	£325
1979	*	*	*	£325
1979 proof				£375
1980	*	*	*	£325
1980 proof				£375
1981	*	*	*	£325
1981 proof				£375
1982	*	*	*	£325
1982 proof				£375
1983 proof				£375
1984 proof				£375
1985 proof				£375
1986 proof				£375
1987 proof				£375
1988 proof				£375
1989 500th anniversary of sovereign, proof				£1100
1990 proof				£375
1991 proof				£375
1992 proof				£375
1993 proof				£375
1994 proof				£375
1995 proof				£375
1996 proof				£375
1997 proof				£375
1998 proof				£375
1999 proof				£375
2000 proof				£375
2000 BU				£250
2001 proof				£375
2001 BU				BV
2002 shield, proof				£375
2002 BU				BV
2003 proof				£375

	F	VF	EF	Unc
2003 BU				BV
2004 Proof				£375
2004 BU				BV
2005 proof				£375
2005 BU				BV
2006 proof				£375
2006 BU				BV
2007 proof				£375
2007 BU				BV
2008 BU				BV
2008 proof				£375
2009 BU				BV
2009 proof				£375
2010 proof				£375
2010 BU				BV
2011 proof				£375
2011 BU				BV
2012 proof				£375
2012 BU				BV
2013 proof				£375
2013 BU				BV
2013 BU "I" mint mark				BV
2014 proof				£375
2014 BU				BV
2015 proof				£375
2015 BU				BV
2015 proof, new portrait				£375
2016 proof				£375
2016 BU				BV
2017 proof				£400
2017 BU				BV
2018 proof				£400
2018 BU				BV
2019 proof				£400
2019 BU				BV

■ HALF-SOVEREIGNS

GEORGE III	F	VF	EF	Unc
1817	£185	£300	£600	£1625
1818	£200	£325	£700	£1825
1820	£165	£250	£650	£1750

GEORGE IV
Laureate hd/ornate shield date

	F	VF	EF	Unc
1821	£625	£1000	£2750	£5500
1821 proof	*	*	£3750	£8000
1823 plain shield	£200	£350	£875	£1875
1824	£200	£325	£750	£1750
1825	£200	£325	£750	£1650

Bare hd, date/shield and full legend

	F	VF	EF	Unc
1826	£200	£275	£700	£1600
1826 proof	*	*	£1650	£4250
1827	£200	£275	£800	£1825
1828	£200	£275	£800	£1825

WILLIAM IV

	F	VF	EF	Unc
1831 proof	*	*	£2500	£5250

MILLED COINAGE

BRITISH COINS MARKET VALUES 2022

MILLED COINAGE

	F	VF	EF	Unc
1834 reduced size	£265	£485	£1250	£2650
1835 normal size	£225	£400	£925	£1750
1836 sixpence obv die	£1350	£3000	£7250	*
1836	£225	£400	£1000	£2250
1837	£225	£400	£1100	£2250

VICTORIA

	F	VF	EF	Unc
1838	*	£175	£675	£1350
1839 proof only	*	*	£1450	£2850
1841	*	£175	£725	£1500
1842	*	£175	£525	£1100
1843	*	£175	£625	£1275
1844	*	£175	£525	£1100
1845	£250	£550	£2500	*
1846	*	£175	£525	£1100
1847	*	£175	£525	£1100
1848	*	£175	£575	£1100
1849	*	£175	£575	£1100
1850	£200	£400	£1525	*
1851	*	£175	£500	£975
1852	*	£175	£575	£1100
1853	*	£175	£495	£950
1853 proof	*	*	£4000	£10000
1855	*	£175	£525	£925
1856	*	£175	£575	£1100
1857	*	£175	£575	£1100
1858	*	£175	£525	£1100
1859	*	£175	£395	£900
1860	*	£175	£425	£725
1861	*	£175	£425	£725
1862	£1100	£3000	£7000	*
1863	*	£175	£395	£825
1863 die no	*	£175	£525	£875
1864 die no	*	£175	£400	£800
1865 die no	*	£175	£400	£800
1866 die no	*	£175	£400	£800
1867 die no	*	£175	£400	£800
1869 die no	*	£175	£400	£800
1870 die no	*	£175	£375	£700
1871 die no	*	£175	£400	£800
1871 S below shield	£150	£385	£1500	£4000
1872 die no	*	£175	£385	£675
1872 S	£150	£200	£1000	£3500
1873 die no	*	£175	£385	£675
1873 M below shield	£150	£195	£1000	£3500
1874 die no	*	£175	£385	£675
1875 die no	*	£175	£385	£675
1875 S	£165	£250	£1500	*
1876 die no	*	£175	£350	£595
1877 die no	*	£175	£350	£595
1877 M	£165	£285	£2000	£8000
1878 die no	*	£175	£385	£500
1879 die no	*	£175	£325	£500
1879 S	£165	£250	£1500	*
1880	*	£175	£375	£700
1880 die no	*	£195	£495	*
1880 S	£165	£225	£1375	*
1881 S	£200	£500	*	*
1881 M	£300	£525	*	*
1882 S	£250	£625	£3500	*
1882 M	£150	£285	£1100	*
1883	*	£175	£325	£500
1883 S	£150	£285	£1100	*
1884	*	£175	£325	£575
1884 M	£165	£325	£1500	*
1885	*	£175	£325	£575
1885 M	£165	£265	£1200	£4250
1886 S	£175	£300	£1300	£4500
1886 M	£195	£350	£1500	*
1887 S	£150	£245	£875	£3000
1887 M	£175	£475	£1650	*

JH/shield

	F	VF	EF	Unc
1887	*	*	£150	£225
1887 proof	*	*	£650	£1650
1887 M	*	£165	£475	£2500
1887 S	*	£165	£475	£2500
1889 S	*	£185	£685	*
1890	*	*	£195	£295
1891	*	*	£225	£325
1891 S	£165	£300	£850	£3000
1892	*	*	£195	£295
1893	*	*	£195	£295
1893 M	*	£195	£600	£1450

OH/St George and dragon

	F	VF	EF	Unc
1893	*	*	£145	£275
1893 proof	*	*	£725	£1900
1893 M				ext. rare
1893 S	*	£175	£575	£1850
1894	*	*	£145	£275
1895	*	*	£145	£275
1896	*	*	£145	£275
1896 M	*	£175	£575	*
1897	*	*	£145	£275
1897 S	*	£175	£575	£1850
1898	*	*	£145	£225
1899	*	*	£145	£225
1899 M	£150	£195	£575	£1850
1899 P proof only	*	*	*	ext. rare
1900	*	*	£145	£275
1900 M	*	£175	£600	*
1900 P	£150	£250	£875	£2750
1900 S	*	£150	£350	£1375
1901	*	*	£150	£275
1901 P proof only	*	*	*	ext. rare

EDWARD VII

	F	VF	EF	Unc
1902	*	*	£150	£200
1902 proof	*	*	£195	£450
1902 S	*	*	£250	£750
1903	*	*	£150	£200
1903 S	*	*	£295	£1100
1904	*	*	£150	£200
1904 P	*	*	*	ext.rare
1905	*	*	£150	£200
1906	*	*	£150	£200
1906 M	£150	£325	£1375	*

MILLED COINAGE

	F	VF	EF	Unc
1906 S	*	*	£185	£650
1907	*	*	£150	£200
1907 M	*	*	£300	£925
1908	*	*	£150	£200
1908 M	*	*	£275	£725
1908 P	*	£475	£1300	*
1908 S	*	*	£165	£650
1909	*	*	£150	£200
1909 M	*	*	£295	£875
1909 P	*	£325	£800	*
1910	*	*	£150	£200
1910 S	*	*	£150	£575

GEORGE V

	F	VF	EF	Unc
1911	*	*	*	£185
1911 proof	*	*	£375	£875
1911 P	*	*	£150	£265
1911 S	*	*	£150	£185
1912	*	*	*	£185
1912 S	*	*	£150	£185
1913	*	*	*	£185
1914	*	*	*	£185
1914 S	*	*	£150	£185
1915	*	*	*	£185
1915 M	*	*	£150	£185
1915 P	*	*	£150	£265
1915 S	*	*	£150	£185
1916 S	*	*	£150	£185
1918 P	*	£1250	£2850	£5000
1923 SA proof	*	*	*	£1500
1925 SA	*	*	*	£160
1926 SA	*	*	*	£160

GEORGE VI

	F	VF	EF	Unc
1937 proof	*	*	*	£775

ELIZABETH II

	Unc
1953 proof	ext. rare
1980 proof	£175
1982 proof	£190
1982 BU	BV
1983 proof	£230
1984 proof	£260
1985 proof	£220
1986 proof	£220
1987 proof	£220
1988 proof	£285
1989 500th anniversary of the sovereign, proof	£400
1990 proof	£230
1991 proof	£230
1992 proof	£230
1993 proof	£230
1994 proof	£230
1995 proof	£230
1996 proof	£230
1997 proof	£230
1998 proof	£230
1999 proof	£230
2000 proof	£285
2000 BU	BV
2001 proof	£225
2001 BU	£BV
2002 shield, proof	£260
2002 BU	BV
2003 proof	£230
2003 BU	BV
2004 proof	£245
2004 BU	BV
2005 proof	£230
2005 BU	BV
2006 proof	£230
2006 BU	BV
2007 proof	£230
2007 BU	BV
2008 BU	BV
2008 proof	£230
2009 BU	BV
2009 proof	£230
2010 BU	BV
2010 proof	£225
2011 BU	BV
2011 proof	£225
2012 BU	BV
2012 proof	£320
2013 BU	BV
2013 proof	£225
2014 BU	BV
2014 proof	£200
2014 BU "I" mint mark	BV
2015 proof	£225
2015 BU	BV
2015 proof, new portrait	£225
2016 BU	BV
2016 proof	£265
2017 BU	BV
2017 proof	£365
2018 BU	BV
2018 proof	£250
2019 proof	£365
2019 BU	BV

■ CROWNS

Exceptionally well struck coins of the early milled series can command considerably higher prices.

CROMWELL	F	VF	EF
1658	£2500	£4500	£9500
1658 Dutch copy	£4000	£4750	£14500
1658 Tanner's copy	*	£4500	£12000

CHARLES II			
1662 1st bust	£225	£850	£9000
1663	£225	£850	£9000
1664 2nd bust	£225	£850	£9500
1665	£825	£2250	*
1666	£250	£1250	£11000
1666 eleph	£800	£2850	£13500

BRITISH COINS MARKET VALUES 2022 **97**

MILLED COINAGE

	F	VF	EF
1667	£195	£600	£7000
1668	£195	£600	£7000
1668/7	£195	£600	£6000
1668/5			ext. rare
1669	£325	£1200	*
1669/8	£375	£1350	
1670	£195	£600	£6250
1670/69	£400	£700	*
1671	£195	£600	£6250
1671 3rd bust	£195	£600	£6250
1672	£195	£600	£6250
1673	£195	£600	£6250
1673/2	£195	£600	£6250
1674	*	*	ext. rare
1675	£700	£2250	*
1675/3	£600	£1875	*
1676	£195	£600	£5000
1677	£195	£600	£5000
1677/6	£195	£600	£5000
1678/7	£275	£800	*
1679	£195	£600	£5000
1679 4th bust	£195	£600	£5000
1680 3rd bust	£265	£695	£6500
1680/79 3rd bust	£265	£695	£6500
1680 4th bust	£265	£695	£6500
1680/79	£325	£750	*
1681 eleph & castle	£4000	£8750	*
1681	£265	£695	£6500
1682	£265	£695	£6500
1682/1	£265	£695	£6500
1683	£325	£875	*
1684	£295	£775	*

JAMES II
1686 1st bust	£400	£1500	*
1687 2nd bust	£200	£600	£2250
1688	£200	£600	£2450
1688/7	£200	£600	£2450

WILLIAM & MARY
1691	£625	£1650	£5500
1692	£625	£1650	£5500
1692/2 inv QVINTO	£625	£1650	£5500
1692/2 inv QVARTO	£625	£1650	£5500

WILLIAM III
1695 1st bust	£120	£325	£2000
1696	£110	£325	£2000
1696 GEI error	£625	£1250	*
1696/5	£225	£500	*
1696 2nd bust			unique
1696 3rd bust	£120	£325	£2000
1697	£1500	£3750	£17500
1700 3rd bust var	£120	£425	£2500

ANNE
1703 1st bust VIGO	£400	£1100	£4750
1705	£600	£1850	£5000
1706	£275	£725	£2500

	F	VF	EF
1707	£275	£725	£3000
1707 2nd bust	£175	£475	£1950
1707 E	£175	£475	£2500
1708	£175	£475	£1950
1708 E	£175	£495	*
1708/7	£175	£500	*
1708 plumes	£275	£750	£3000
1713 3rd bust	£275	£725	£2500

GEORGE I
1716 rev r & p	£375	£925	£4250

ABOVE: George I 1716 Crown

1718	£400	£1200	£4750
1718/6	£425	£1250	£5000
1720	£425	£1250	£5000
1720/18	£400	£1200	£5000
1723 SS C	£400	£1200	£4750
1726 small r & p	£750	£1650	£7000

GEORGE II
1732 YH	£400	£875	£3500
1732 proof	*	*	£16500
1734	£400	£875	£3850
1735	£400	£875	£3850
1736	£375	£850	£3000
1739	£295	£725	£2350
1741	£375	£675	£2500
1743 OH	£295	£700	£2650
1746 OH LIMA	£400	£800	£2850
1746 OH proof	*	£4250	£1000
1750	£400	£800	£2850
1751	£425	£825	£3000

ABOVE: William & Mary 1691 Crown

MILLED COINAGE

GEORGE III

	F	VF	EF
Oval counterstamp	£250	£375	£850
Octagonal counterstamp	£550	£900	£1750
1804 Bank of England Dollar	£150	£300	£675

Collectors should beware of contemporary forgeries on these three coins. The counterstamps are usually on Spanish–American dollars.

	F	VF	EF	Unc
1818 LVIII	£30	£65	£450	£1000
1818 LVIII error edge	£250	*	*	*
1818 LIX	£30	£65	£450	£1000
1819 LIX	£30	£65	£450	£1000
1819 LIX no edge stops	£60	£150	£600	*
1819/8 LIX	£45	£165	£550	*
1819 LIX no stop after TUTAMEN	£45	£165	£525	*
1820 LX	*	*	£450	£1000
1820/19 LX	£50	£200	£575	*

GEORGE IV

	F	VF	EF	Unc
1821 1st hd SECUNDO	£35	£150	£875	£2000
1821 SECUNDO proof	*	*	*	£4500
1821 TERTIO proof error edge	*	*	*	£6250
1822 SECUNDO	£60	£175	£875	£2250
1822 SECUNDO proof	*	*	*	*
1822 TERTIO	£50	£175	£875	£2250
1822 TERTIO proof	*	*	*	£6000
1823 proof only	*	*	*	ext. rare
1826 2nd head proof	*	*	£6500	£17500

WILLIAM IV proof only

			EF	Unc
1831 W.W.	*	*	£10250	£27500
1831 W.WYON	*	*	£12000	£35000
1834 W.W.	*	*	£2000	£55000

ABOVE: George IV 1821 Crown

VICTORIA

	F	VF	EF	Unc
1839 proof	*	*	£8500	£27500
1844 star stops	£35	£100	£950	£4000
1844 star stops proof	*	*	ext. rare	*
1844 cinquefoil stops	£35	£100	£950	£4000
1845	£35	£100	£950	£4000
1845 proof	*	*	*	£25000
1847	£35	£100	£975	£4500

ABOVE: Victoria 1847 Gothic Crown

	F	VF	EF	Unc
1847 Gothic	£550	£950	£2700	£7500
1847 Gothic plain edge	*	£1100	£2950	£9500
1853 SEPTIMO	*	*	£9500	£25000
1853 plain	*	*	£10500	£27500
1887 JH	£18	£30	£85	£175
1887 JH proof	*	*	£750	£2500
1888 close date	£25	£35	£125	£285
1888 wide date	£65	£195	£450	*
1889	£25	£35	£95	£275
1890	£25	£35	£125	£300
1891	£25	£45	£150	£350
1892	£25	£50	£175	£400
1893 LVI	£25	£35	£165	£350
1893 LVI proof	*	*	£900	£3000
1893 LVII	£25	£65	£250	£575
1894 LVII	£25	£45	£225	£450
1894 LVIII	£25	£45	£225	£450
1895 LVIII	£25	£45	£195	£400
1895 LIX	£25	£45	£185	£385
1896 LIX	£35	£45	£295	£595
1896 LX	£25	£45	£225	£450
1897 LX	£25	£45	£185	£425
1897 LXI	£25	£45	£185	£385
1898 LXI	£25	£75	£325	£600
1898 LXII	£25	£45	£225	£450
1899 LXII	£25	£45	£225	£450
1899 LXIII	£25	£45	£225	£500
1900 LXIII	£25	£45	£200	£425
1900 LXIV	£25	£45	£185	£395

EDWARD VII

	F	VF	EF	Unc
1902	£35	£90	£200	£350

	F	VF	EF	Unc
1902 matt proof	*	*	£225	£375

GEORGE V

	F	VF	EF	Unc
1927 proof	*	*	£165	£325
1928	£85	£150	£275	£385
1929	£85	£165	£285	£450
1930	£85	£150	£275	£400
1931	£85	£150	£275	£400
1932	£140	£250	£475	£700
1933	£85	£140	£275	£385
1934	£975	£1975	£3250	£4650
1935	£13	£20	£20	£25
1935 raised edge proof	*	*	*	£525
1935 gold proof	*	*	*	£50000
1935 proof in good silver (.925)	*	*	*	£2650
1935 specimen	*	*	*	£65
1936	£125	£250	£400	£750

ABOVE: George V 1935 raised edge proof Crown

GEORGE VI

	F	VF	EF	Unc
1937	*	*	£20	£30
1937 proof	*	*	*	£75
1937 'VIP' proof	*	*	*	ext. rare
1951	*	*	*	£10
1951 'VIP' proof	*	*	*	£875

ELIZABETH II

	F	VF	EF	Unc
1953	*	*	*	£8
1953 proof	*	*	*	£35
1953 'VIP' proof	*	*	*	£650
1960	*	*	*	£10
1960 'VIP' proof	*	*	*	£750
1960 polished dies	*	*	*	£25
1965 Churchill	*	*	*	£100
1965 Churchill 'satin' finish	*	*	*	£1500

For issues from 1972 onwards see under 25 pence in Decimal Coinage section.

■ DOUBLE–FLORINS

VICTORIA	F	VF	EF	Unc
1887 Roman 'I'	£13	£25	£65	£135
1887 Roman 'I' proof	*	*	£300	£1250
1887 Arabic '1'	£13	£25	£60	£125
1887 Arabic '1' proof	*	*	£300	£1250
1888	£13	£25	£80	£175
1888 inv '1'	£28	£45	£185	£450
1889	£13	£25	£80	£175
1889 inv '1'	£28	£45	£185	£450
1890	£13	£25	£80	£175

■ THREE SHILLING BANK TOKENS

Contemporary forgeries of these pieces, as well as of other George III coins, were produced in quite large numbers. Several varieties exist for the pieces dated 1811 and 1812. Prices given here are for the commonest types of these years.

GEORGE III

	F	VF	EF	Unc
1811	£17	£55	£165	£300
1812 draped bust	£17	£55	£165	£300
1812 laureate hd	£17	£55	£165	£300
1813	£17	£55	£165	£300
1814	£17	£55	£165	£300
1815	£17	£55	£165	£300
1816	*	£300	£975	£1650

■ HALFCROWNS

CROMWELL	F	VF	EF
1656	£2850	£7000	£15000
1658	£1275	£2650	£5500

ABOVE: Cromwell 1658 Halfcrown

CHARLES II

	F	VF	EF
1663 1st bust	£275	£875	£7500
1664 2nd bust	£275	£1250	£7250
1666/3 3rd bust	£850	*	*
1666/3 eleph	£1000	£2750	*

MILLED COINAGE

	F	VF	EF
1667/4			ext. rare
1668/4	£275	£950	*
1669	£350	£1100	*
1669/4	£250	£750	*
1670	£150	£575	£3750
1671 3rd bust var	£150	£575	£3750
1671/0	£150	£575	£3750
1672	£150	£575	£3750
1672 4th bust	£150	£575	£3750
1673	£150	£575	£3750
1673 plume below	£8750	*	*
1673 plume both sides	£8000	*	*
1674	£150	£575	£3750
1674/3	£265	£750	*
1675	£135	£450	£2950
1676	£135	£450	£2950
1677	£135	£450	£2950
1678	£175	£685	*
1679	£135	£400	£2750
1680	£165	£550	£3750
1681	£150	£525	£3750
1681/0	£275	£750	*
1681 eleph & castle	£2950	£7500	£25000
1682	£150	£525	£3750
1682/79	£300	£875	*
1683	£150	£595	£3750
1683 plume below	ext. rare	*	*
1684/3	£300	£875	

JAMES II

	F	VF	EF
1685 1st bust	£195	£800	£3750
1686	£195	£800	£3750
1686/5	£250	£850	*
1687	£195	£800	£3750
1687/6	£525	£725	£3250
1687 2nd bust	£175	£725	£3250
1688	£225	£725	£3250

WILLIAM AND MARY

	F	VF	EF
1689 1st busts 1st shield	£95	£400	£1950
1689 1st busts 2nd shield	£95	£400	£1950

ABOVE: William and Mary 1690 Halfcrown

	F	VF	EF
1690	£140	£575	£2950
1691 2nd busts 3rd shield	£110	£400	£2750
1692	£110	£400	£2750
1693	£110	£400	£2750
1693 2nd busts 3rd shield 3 inv	£125	£475	£3000
1693 3 over 3 inv	£110	£425	£3000

WILLIAM III

	F	VF	EF
1696 1st bust large shield early hp	£60	£250	£975
1696 B	£95	£300	£2500
1696 C	£150	£450	£3000
1696 E	£150	£425	£2500
1696 N	£200	£700	*
1696 Y	£110	£375	£2500
1696 y/E			ext. rare
1696 large shield ord hp	£150	£475	£1350
1696 C	£150	£425	£2500
1696 E	£150	£425	£2500
1696 N	£250	£675	*
1696 small shield	£65	£275	£1100
1696 B	£95	£350	£2250
1696 C	£175	£500	£2250
1696 E	£175	£500	£2250
1696 N	£150	£425	£2250
1696 y	£150	£400	£2250
1696 2nd bust			unique
1697 1st bust large shield	£65	£225	£900
1697 B	£110	£300	£2250
1697 C	£110	£300	£2250
1697 E	£110	£295	£2250
1697 E/C	£150	£525	*
1697 N	£110	£300	£2250
1697 y	£110	£295	£2250
1698	£65	£200	£800
1699	£140	£350	£2250
1700	£60	£165	£800
1701	£85	£350	£1350
1701 eleph & castle	£2850	*	*
1701 plumes	£265	£800	£5000

ANNE

	F	VF	EF
1703 plain	£700	£1850	£9000
1703 VIGO	£175	£425	£1750
1704 plumes	£250	£775	£3250
1705	£185	£575	£2250
1706 r & p	£120	£300	£1450
1707	£120	£275	£1375
1707 plain	£75	£200	£975
1707 E	£75	£225	£1425
1708 plain	£75	£200	£850
1708 E	£75	£300	£2250
1708 plumes	£150	£395	£1650
1709 plain	£70	£250	£900
1709 E	£400	*	*
1710 r & p	£120	£300	£1375
1712	£85	£200	£975
1713 plain	£95	£300	£1450
1713 r & p	£85	£275	£1250
1714	£75	£275	£1250

BRITISH COINS MARKET VALUES 2022 **101**

MILLED COINAGE

	F	VF	EF
1714/3	£125	£400	£1475

GEORGE I
	F	VF	EF
1715 proof	*	*	£6500
1715 r & p	£225	£575	£2875
1717	£225	£575	£2875
1720	£275	£650	£3250
1720/17	£225	£575	£2875
1723 SS C	£200	£500	£2500
1726 small r & p	£2500	£4500	£13500

GEORGE II
	F	VF	EF
1731 YH proof	*	£2500	£7250
1731	£150	£450	£1750
1732	£150	£450	£1750
1734	£165	£495	£1975
1735	£150	£450	£1750
1736	£165	£495	£1975
1739	£125	£285	£1500
1741	£125	£285	£1500
1741/39	£100	£300	£1500
1743 OH	£95	£225	£975
1745	£95	£225	£975
1745 LIMA	£70	£175	£725
1746 LIMA	£65	£175	£700
1746 plain, proof	*	*	£4750
1750	£165	£400	£1975
1751	£165	£475	£2000

GEORGE III
	F	VF	EF	Unc
Oval counterstamp, usually on Spanish Half-Dollar	£250	£395	£750	*
1816 large hd	£10	£50	£275	£625
1817	£10	£50	£275	£625
1817 small hd	£10	£50	£245	£625

ABOVE: George III oval countermarked Spanish 4 Reales (Half-Dollar)

1818	£10	£50	£300	£675
1819	£10	£50	£275	£625
1819/8				ext. rare
1820	£10	£60	£300	£625

GEORGE IV
1st hd
	F	VF	EF	Unc
1820 1st rev	£25	£70	£325	£700

	F	VF	EF	Unc
1821	£30	£70	£350	£750
1821 proof	*	*	£1100	£2750
1823	£1000	£2650	£9250	*
1823 2nd rev	£30	£70	£395	£875
1824	£35	£85	£400	£975

ABOVE: George IV 1820 Halfcrown

2nd hd
1824 3rd rev				ext. rare
1825	£30	£70	£375	£725
1826	£30	£70	£375	£800
1826 proof	*	*	£1000	£3200
1828	£50	£150	£725	£2250
1829	£40	£90	£385	£950

WILLIAM IV
1831				ext. rare
1831 proof	*	*	£975	£3500
1834 ww	£35	£125	£495	£1250
1834 ww in script	£25	£75	£375	£900
1835	£35	£100	£465	£1200
1836	£25	£75	£365	£825
1836/5	£45	£150	£625	*
1837	£40	£140	£595	£1350

ABOVE: William IV 1831 proof Halfcrown

VICTORIA

From time to time Halfcrowns bearing dates ranging from 1861 to 1871 are found (usually worn), but except for rare proofs in 1853, 1862 and 1864, no Halfcrowns were struck between 1850 and 1874, so pieces dated from this period are now considered to be contemporary or later forgeries.

ABOVE: Victoria 1839 proof Halfcrown

Young Head	F	VF	EF	Unc
1839 ww in relief	£825	£1650	£6250	*
1839 plain and ornate fillets, plain edge proof	*	*	£1800	£5000
1839 ww incuse	£925	£2500	£7500	*
1840	£45	£110	£625	£1650
1841	£550	£1375	£4850	*
1842	£45	£110	£685	£1500
1843	£90	£250	£2000	£3850
1844	£40	£90	£625	£1525
1845	£40	£110	£625	£1525
1846	£40	£110	£625	£1525
1848	£175	£525	£1675	£3850
1848/6	£150	£485	£1575	£3250
1849 large date	£65	£195	£825	£1850
1849 small date	£90	£300	£975	£2250
1850	£50	£200	£775	£2000
1853 proof	*	*	*	£7500
1862 proof	*	*	*	£9000
1864 proof	*	*	*	£9000
1874	£18	£48	£225	£675
1875	£18	£48	£235	£675
1876	£18	£48	£235	£675
1876/5	£20	£60	£375	£800
1877	£18	£48	£250	£600
1878	£18	£48	£675	£675
1879	£18	£50	£295	£800
1880	£18	£48	£225	£550
1881	£18	£48	£225	£550
1882	£18	£48	£295	£750
1883	£18	£48	£225	£550
1884	£18	£48	£225	£550

	F	VF	EF	Unc
1885	£18	£48	£225	£550
1886	£18	£48	£225	£550
1887	£18	£48	£225	£550

Jubilee Head

1887	£8	£15	£35	£80
1887 proof	*	*	£250	£675
1888	£9	£20	£65	£175
1889	£9	£20	£65	£175
1890	£9	£25	£75	£200
1891	£9	£25	£75	£275
1892	£9	£25	£75	£235

Old Head

1893	£9	£22	£55	£135
1893 proof	*	*	£285	£850
1894	£9	£27	£110	£245

ABOVE: Edward VII 1909 Halfcrown

	F	VF	EF	Unc
1895	£9	£25	£85	£195
1896	£9	£25	£85	£195
1897	£9	£22	£55	£170
1898	£9	£22	£80	£190
1899	£9	£22	£66	£185
1900	£9	£22	£55	£150
1901	£9	£22	£55	£140

EDWARD VII

1902	£12	£30	£75	£150
1902 matt proof	*	*	*	£225
1903	£125	£400	£2000	£4950
1904	£50	£225	£800	£1950
1905 F	£600	£1350	£5850	£12000
1906	£15	£45	£225	£650
1907	£15	£45	£225	£650
1908	£20	£60	£425	£1100
1909	£15	£50	£350	£875
1910	£15	£40	£175	£425

GEORGE V

1911	*	£10	£60	£200

MILLED COINAGE

BRITISH COINS MARKET VALUES 2022

MILLED COINAGE

	F	VF	EF	Unc
1911 proof	*	*	*	£300
1912	*	£15	£60	£300
1913	*	£15	£70	£300
1914	*	*	£25	£95
1915	*	*	£20	£65
1916	*	*	£20	£65
1917	*	*	£30	£75
1918	*	*	£20	£60
1919	*	*	£25	£90
1920	*	*	£30	£150
1921	*	*	£40	£130
1922	*	*	£30	£100
1923	*	*	£12	£45
1924	*	*	£30	£100
1925	*	£45	£350	£800
1926	*	*	£45	£150
1926 mod eff	*	*	£60	£185
1927	*	*	£25	£60
1927 new rev, proof only	*	*	*	£70
1928	*	*	£10	£27
1929	*	*	£10	£28
1930	£7	£35	£285	£875
1931	*	*	£12	£45
1932	*	*	£15	£50
1933	*	*	£10	£35
1934	*	*	£35	£125
1935	*	*	£8	£20
1936	*	*	£8	£17

GEORGE VI

	F	VF	EF	Unc
1937	*	*	*	£14
1937 proof	*	*	*	£30
1938	*	*	£4	£35
1939	*	*	*	£17
1940	*	*	*	£14
1941	*	*	*	£14
1942	*	*	*	£12
1943	*	*	*	£14
1944	*	*	*	£12
1945	*	*	*	£12
1946	*	*	*	£10
1947	*	*	*	£10
1948	*	*	*	£10
1949	*	*	*	£17
1950	*	*	*	£24
1950 proof	*	*	*	£25
1951	*	*	*	£24
1951 proof	*	*	*	£25
1952				2 known

ELIZABETH II

	F	VF	EF	Unc
1953	*	*	*	£12
1953 proof	*	*	*	£15
1954	*	*	£4	£45
1955	*	*	*	£10
1956	*	*	*	£10
1957	*	*	*	£8
1958	*	*	*	£28
1959	*	*	*	£45

	F	VF	EF	Unc
1960	*	*	*	£4
1961	*	*	*	£4
1962	*	*	*	£4
1963	*	*	*	£2
1964	*	*	*	£2
1965	*	*	*	£2
1966	*	*	*	£1
1967	*	*	*	£1

■ FLORINS

The first Florins produced in the reign of Victoria bore the legend VICTORIA REGINA and the date, omitting DEI GRATIA or 'By the Grace of God'. They are therefore known as 'godless' Florins.

The date of a Victorian Gothic Florin is shown in Roman numerals in Gothic lettering on the obverse, for example mdccclvii (1857). Gothic Florins were issued between 1851–1887.

VICTORIA

	F	VF	EF	Unc
1848 'Godless' proof with milled edge	*	*	*	£3700
1848 'Godless' proof with plain edge	*	*	*	£2500
1849 'Godless' ww obliterated by circle	£25	£60	£225	£475
1849 'Godless' ww inside circle	£18	£45	£150	£395
1851 proof only	*	*	*	£15000
1852	£20	£45	£150	£485
1853	£20	£45	£150	£485
1853 no stop after date	£20	£50	£200	£500
1853 proof	*	*	*	£4850
1854	£650	£1650	£5750	*
1855	£20	£55	£250	£685
1856	£20	£55	£250	£685
1857	£20	£45	£250	£685
1858	£20	£45	£250	£685
1859	£20	£45	£250	£685
1859 no stops after date	£20	£50	£225	£685
1860	£20	£50	£250	£750
1862	£185	£425	£1650	£4250
1863	£650	£1500	£5000	*
1864	£20	£50	£235	£685
1865	£35	£95	£395	£800

ABOVE: Victoria 1871 Gothic Florin

	F	VF	EF	Unc
1865 colon after date	*	*	£900	*
1866	£30	£75	£250	£625
1866 colon after date				ext. rare
1867	£30	£75	£225	£685
1868	£30	£85	£295	£725
1869	£30	£85	£275	£700
1870	£20	£50	£235	£685
1871	£20	£50	£235	£685
1872	£20	£35	£200	£600
1873	£20	£35	£200	£600
1874	£20	£50	£235	£650
1874 xxiv/iii die	£75	£200	£500	*
1875	£20	£45	£225	£625
1876	£20	£45	£200	£600
1877	£20	£45	£200	£625
1877 no ww	*	*	*	ext. rare
1877 42 arcs	£30	£85	£325	£675
1878	£20	£50	£200	£550
1879 die no	*	*	*	ext.rare
1879 ww 42 arcs	£85	£195	£575	*
1879 ww 48 arcs	£20	£40	£200	£625
1879 no ww, 38 arcs	£20	£45	£200	£525
1880	£20	£40	£200	£475
1881	£20	£40	£200	£475
1881 xxri error	£25	£80	£295	£525
1883	£20	£40	£200	£450
1884	£20	£40	£200	£450
1885	£20	£40	£200	£450
1886	£20	£40	£185	£400
1887 46 arcs	£30	£75	£250	£625
1887 JH	*	£10	£25	£65
1887 JH proof	*	*	*	£400
1888	*	£15	£55	£135
1889	*	£20	£80	£175
1890	*	£25	£165	£425
1891	£20	£60	£265	£525
1892	£20	£70	£295	£600
1893 OH	*	£15	£50	£125
1893 proof	*	*	*	£550
1894	*	£20	£90	£250
1895	*	£18	£70	£200
1896	*	£18	£70	£200
1897	*	£15	£60	£145
1898	*	£18	£70	£200
1899	*	£18	£70	£200
1900	*	£15	£55	£120
1901	*	£15	£55	£125

EDWARD VII

	F	VF	EF	Unc
1902	*	£12	£55	£110
1902 matt proof	*	*	*	£100
1903	*	£28	£140	£400
1904	*	£40	£185	£500
1905	£60	£175	£750	£1750
1906	*	£28	£125	£400
1907	*	£30	£135	£425
1908	*	£45	£295	£550
1909	*	£40	£245	£575
1910	*	£20	£100	£285

ABOVE: George V 1932 Florin

GEORGE V

	F	VF	EF	Unc
1911	*	*	*	£125
1911 proof	*	*	*	£195
1912	*	*	£50	£165
1913	*	*	£70	£225
1914	*	*	£25	£75
1915	*	*	£45	£100
1916	*	*	£28	£70
1917	*	*	£35	£80
1918	*	*	£20	£55
1919	*	*	£30	£75
1920	*	*	£35	£135
1921	*	*	£30	£100
1922	*	*	£20	£85
1923	*	*	£18	£50
1924	*	*	£27	£55
1925	*	£35	£165	£500
1926	*	*	£45	£95
1927 proof	*	*	*	£120
1928	*	*	£7	£25
1929	*	*	£7	£30
1930	*	*	£25	£70
1931	*	*	£12	£50
1932	£15	£60	£300	£900
1933	*	*	£12	£45
1935	*	*	£8	£25
1936	*	*	£5	£20

GEORGE VI

	F	VF	EF	Unc
1937	*	*	*	£12
1937 proof	*	*	*	£20
1938	*	*	*	£35
1939	*	*	*	£12
1940	*	*	*	£15
1941	*	*	*	£10
1942	*	*	*	£8
1943	*	*	*	£10
1944	*	*	*	£10
1945	*	*	*	£8
1946	*	*	*	£8
1947	*	*	*	£8
1948	*	*	*	£8
1949	*	*	*	£20
1950	*	*	*	£20
1950 proof	*	*	*	£20
1951	*	*	*	£25
1951 proof	*	*	*	£25

MILLED COINAGE

ELIZABETH II

	F	VF	EF	Unc
1953	*	*	*	£9
1953 proof	*	*	*	£12
1954	*	*	*	£45
1955	*	*	*	£7
1956	*	*	*	£7
1957	*	*	*	£45
1958	*	*	*	£30
1959	*	*	*	£35
1960	*	*	*	£4
1961	*	*	*	£4
1962	*	*	*	£2
1963	*	*	*	£2
1964	*	*	*	£2
1965	*	*	*	£2
1966	*	*	*	£1
1967	*	*	*	£1

■ EIGHTEENPENCE BANK TOKENS

GEORGE III

	F	VF	EF	Unc
1811	£12	£25	£100	£225
1812	£12	£25	£100	£225
1812 laureate hd	£12	£25	£110	£225
1813	£12	£25	£110	£225
1814	£12	£25	£110	£225
1815	£12	£25	£110	£225
1816	£12	£25	£125	£225

■ SHILLINGS

ABOVE: Cromwell 1658 Shilling

CROMWELL

	F	VF	EF
1658	£850	£1750	£3500
1658 Dutch copy	*	*	£11500

ABOVE: Charles II 1671 Shilling, plumes both sides

SOVEREIGN RARITIES

For the rarest historic coins, and the most exciting modern issues.

17-19 MADDOX STREET, LONDON, W1S 2QH
INFO@SOVR.COM   TEL: +44 (0)20 3019 1185
WWW.SOVR.CO.UK

TOM HART COINS

The largest specialist buyer of coins in the Southwest
Covering Devon Cornwall West Somerset and Dorset
Whole collections sought from Ancient to Modern
Anything Considered

Phone **07745 985510**
email **woosworlduk@aol.com**
Website **woosworld.co.uk**

LONDON COINS
REGULAR PAPER MONEY SALES

Sign up to receive our catalogues and updates

Web: www.londoncoins.co.uk
Email: info@londoncoins.co.uk
Phone: +44 (0) 1474 871 464

www.londoncoins.co.uk

Regular High Volume Auctions of Quality Paper Money

MILLED COINAGE

CHARLES II	F	VF	EF
1663 1st bust	£135	£525	£2850
1663 1st bust var	£135	£375	£2700
1666 1st bust	*	*	*
1666 eleph	£650	£2750	£9000
1666 guinea head, eleph	£2750	*	*
1666 2nd bust	£1700	*	*
1668 1st bust var	£400	£1650	*
1668 2nd bust	£135	£525	£2500
1668/7	£150	£600	£2500
1669/6 1st bust var	ext. rare	*	*
1669 2nd bust	ext. rare	*	*
1670	£150	£600	£2250
1671	£150	£600	£2500
1671 plumes both sides	£750	£1950	£5500
1672	£150	£600	£2500
1673	£150	£600	£2500
1673/2	£150	£600	£2500
1673 plumes both sides	£750	£1950	£5500
1674	£150	£525	£2500
1674/3	£150	£600	£2500
1674 plumes both sides	£750	£2250	£5000
1674 plumes rev only	£1200	£3500	*
1674 3rd bust	£525	£1500	*
1675	£525	£1500	*
1675/3	£525	£1500	£3950
1675/4 2nd bust	£325	£1100	*
1675 plumes both sides	£900	£2500	*
1676	£160	£675	£2250
1676/5	£160	£675	£2250
1676 plumes both sides	£900	£2500	£5500
1677	£150	£525	£2500
1677 plumes obv only	£900	£2250	£5250
1678	£160	£675	*
1678/7	£160	£675	*
1679	£150	£600	£2500
1679/7	£150	£600	£2500
1679 plumes	£900	£2500	£5500
1679 plumes obv only	£1500	£3250	*
1680/79 plumes	£1500	*	*
1681	£625	£1500	*
1681/0	£675	£1650	*
1681/0 eleph & castle	£3000	£8750	*
1682/1	£975	*	*
1683	£975	*	*
1683 4th bust	£275	£750	£2850
1684	£275	£750	£2850
1685	£225	£575	£2350

JAMES II	F	VF	EF
1685 no stops on rev	£225	£575	£2500
1685 plume on rev			ext. rare
1686	£225	£575	£2350
1686/5	£225	£575	£2350
1686 V/S	£225	£575	£2500
1687	£225	£575	£2350
1687/6	£225	£575	£2350
1688	£225	£575	£2350
1688/7	£225	£575	£2500

WILLIAM AND MARY	F	VF	EF
1692	£265	£650	£2500
1693	£265	£650	£2500

WILLIAM III	F	VF	EF
1695 1st bust	£35	£125	£525
1696	£30	£100	£450
1696 no stops on rev	£150	£350	£750
1669 in error	£875	*	*
1696 B	£45	£165	£850
1696 C	£65	£200	£975
1696 E	£60	£190	£850
1696 N	£85	£265	*
1696 y	£60	£190	£750
1696 Y	£90	£300	*
1696 2nd bust		unique	
1696 3rd bust C	£165	£575	*
1696 E		ext. rare	
1696 y		ext. rare	
1697 1st bust	£35	£100	£475
1697 no stops on rev	£85	£295	£725
1697 B	£90	£285	£725
1697 C	£100	£350	£725

ABOVE: William III 1699 roses Shilling

1697 E	£90	£285	£725
1697 N	£125	£325	*
1697 y	£90	£275	£725
1697 Y	£75	£285	£875
1697 3rd bust	£30	£100	£450
1697 B	£125	£350	£1250
1697 C	£75	£250	£800
1697 E	£90	£300	£1000
1697 N	£95	£300	£1375
1697 y	£90	£325	£1100
1697 3rd bust var	£35	£110	£495
1697 B	£110	£385	£1375
1697 C	£165	£400	£1600

ABOVE: James II 1687 Shilling

MILLED COINAGE

	F	VF	EF
1698 plain	£75	£250	£925
1698 plumes	£250	£750	£2850
1698 4th bust	£300	£750	£2750
1699 4th bust	£300	£750	£2750
1699 5th bust	£175	£450	£1950
1699 plumes	£250	£550	£2250
1699 roses	£325	£750	*
1700	£30	£100	£475
1700 no stops on rev	£80	£250	£800
1700 plume below bust	£3000	*	*
1701	£85	£295	£1100
1701 plumes	£250	£585	£2850

ABOVE: Anne 1702 Shilling

ANNE

	F	VF	EF
1702 1st bust	£90	£265	£1100
1702 plumes	£90	£300	£900
1702 VIGO	£90	£275	£900
1703 2nd bust VIGO	£90	£275	£900
1704	£500	£1500	£3750
1704 plumes	£200	£475	£1850
1705	£150	£450	£1850
1705 plumes	£135	£400	£1750
1705 r&p	£110	£325	£1100
1707 r&p	£125	£375	£1350
1707 E	£75	£265	£900
1707 E*	£100	£300	£1350
1707 E* local dies	£225	£700	*
1707 3rd bust	£25	£145	£465
1707 plumes	£85	£295	£1100
1707 E	£65	£225	£825
1707 Edin bust E*	£500	*	*
1708 2nd bust E	£165	£525	*
1708 E*	£250	£700	*
1708/7 E*			ext. rare
1708 r&p	£150	£450	£1275
1708 3rd bust	£30	£100	£450
1708 plumes	£100	£300	£1100
1708 r&p	£120	£350	£1200
1708 E	£75	£225	£875
1708/7 E	£150	£300	£1100
1708 Edin bust E*	£250	£700	*
1709	£60	£100	£475
1709 Edin bust E	£375	£1100	*
1709 Edin bust E*	£100	£350	£1100
1710 3rd bust r&p	£85	£300	£900
1710 4th bust proof			ext. rare
1710 r&p	£65	£200	£775

	F	VF	EF
1711 3rd bust	£175	£475	£1200
1711 4th bust	£35	£90	£375
1712 r&p	£50	£165	£575
1713/2	£65	£195	£675
1714	£55	£165	£575
1714/3	£60	£250	£675

ABOVE: George I 1721/0 roses & plumes Shilling

GEORGE I

	F	VF	EF
1715 1st bust r&p	£60	£195	£750
1716 r&p	£150	£375	£1200
1717 r&p	£85	£265	£775
1718 r&p	£60	£185	£750
1719 r&p	£150	£375	£1250
1720 r&p	£85	£285	£875
1720/18	£150	£475	£1450
1720 plain	£60	£175	£550
1720 large 0	£60	£175	£575
1721 plain	£175	£625	£1350
1721 r&p	£85	£285	£900
1721/0 r&p	£80	£250	£800
1721/19 r&p	£85	£265	£875
1721/18 r&p	ext. rare	*	*
1722 r&p	£85	£300	£875
1723 r&p	£85	£300	£875
1723 SSC	£30	£80	£300
1723 SSC C/SS	£35	£110	£395
1723 SSC French arms at date	£175	£500	£1500
1723 2nd bust SS C	£50	£120	£350
1723 r&p	£95	£285	£900
1723 WCC	£600	£1850	£6500
1724 r&p	£95	£300	£975
1724 WCC	£600	£1850	£6500
1725 r&p	£110	£325	£950
1725 no obv stops	£110	£325	£1100
1725 WCC	£600	£1850	£6500
1726 r&p	£600	£1750	*
1726 WCC	£700	£1850	£6500
1727 r&p	£500	£1250	£2850
1727 r&p no stops on obv	£500	£1250	£3000

GEORGE II

	F	VF	EF
1727 YH plumes	£165	£425	£1500
1727 r&p	£110	£300	£1350
1728	£150	£425	£1825
1728 r&p	£100	£295	£1350
1729 r&p	£100	£295	£1350
1731 r&p	£85	£295	£1500

BRITISH COINS MARKET VALUES 2022 **109**

MILLED COINAGE

	F	VF	EF
1731 plumes	£120	£400	£1500
1732 r&p	£85	£250	£975
1734 r&p	£85	£275	£975
1735 r&p	£85	£250	£975
1736 r&p	£70	£185	£825
1736/5 r&p	£85	£250	£925
1737 r&p	£85	£250	£925
1739 r&p roses	£45	£165	£625
1741 roses	£45	£165	£600
1741/39 roses	£100	£300	£1100

ABOVE: George II 1729 young head Shilling

	F	VF	EF
1743 OH roses	£55	£145	£575
1743/1 roses	£65	£175	£675
1745	£40	£110	£485
1745/3 roses	£65	£175	£650
1745 LIMA	£25	£90	£425
1746 LIMA	£80	£200	£675
1746/5 LIMA	£80	£200	£750
1746 proof	*	£800	£2500
1747 roses	£55	£120	£550
1750	£55	£165	£600
1750/6	£70	£185	£675
1751	£80	£225	£850
1758	£17	£45	£150

ABOVE: George III 1763 'Northumberland' Shilling

GEORGE III

	F	VF	EF	Unc
1763 'Northumberland' F	*	£450	£900	£1900
1764 pattern	*	*	*	£7000
1778 pattern	*	*	*	£8000
1786 proof or pattern	*	*	*	£8500
1787 no hearts	£15	£30	£70	£165
1787 no hearts no stop over head	£20	£45	£100	£225
1787 no hearts no stops at date	£20	£65	£150	£285

	F	VF	EF	Unc
1787 no stops on obv	£250	£600	*	*
1787 hearts	£15	£25	£70	£165
1798 'Dorrien and Magens'	£5000	£12500	£23000	*
1816	*	£10	£85	£165
1817	*	£10	£85	£165
1817 GEOE error	£75	£150	£525	*
1818	£10	£25	£145	£250
1819	*	£10	£90	£185
1819/8	*	*	£150	£325
1820	*	£10	£90	£185

GEORGE IV

	F	VF	EF	Unc
1820 1st head 1st rev pattern or proof	*	*	*	£5250
1821 1st rev	£12	£45	£185	£450
1821 proof	*	*	£775	£1850
1823 1st head 2nd rev	£30	£85	£325	£650
1824 2nd rev	£10	£40	£185	£450
1825 2nd rev	£15	£50	£200	£475
1825 2nd head	£10	£25	£150	£325
1826	*	£25	£120	£265

ABOVE: George IV 1824 Shilling

	F	VF	EF	Unc
1826 proof	*	*	£325	£800
1827	£25	£80	£350	£685
1829	*	£40	£200	£525

WILLIAM IV

	F	VF	EF	Unc
1831 proof	*	*	£650	£1500
1834	£12	£35	£195	£485
1835	£12	£40	£200	£585
1836	£12	£35	£195	£485
1837	£25	£75	£250	£650

ABOVE: William IV 1836 Shilling

VICTORIA

	F	VF	EF	Unc
1838 YH	£20	£25	£175	£450
1839	£25	£50	£250	£575

MILLED COINAGE

	F	VF	EF	Unc
1839 2nd YH	£15	£30	£165	£450
1839 proof	*	*	*	£1250
1840	£20	£45	£200	£485
1841	£20	£50	£285	£525
1842	£15	£30	£150	£450
1843	£25	£45	£210	£550
1844	£20	£30	£150	£450
1845	£20	£30	£135	£465
1846	£10	£30	£150	£450
1848/6	£75	£250	£700	*
1849	£15	£35	£175	£550
1850	£500	£1750	£4650	*
1850/49	£625	£1850	£4850	*
1851	£40	£150	£475	£975
1852	£12	£20	£120	£450
1853	£12	£20	£120	£450
1853 proof	*	*	*	£2500
1854	£175	£425	£1750	£4500
1855	£12	£20	£145	£375
1856	£12	£20	£120	£325
1857	£12	£20	£120	£325
1857 F:G:	£250	£575	£2000	*
1858	£12	£20	£120	£325
1859	£12	£20	£120	£325
1860	£12	£25	£150	£550
1861	£12	£25	£150	£325
1862	£22	£50	£225	£525

ABOVE: Victoria 1860 Shilling

1863	£40	£100	£500	£1175
1863/1	£60	£200	£675	*
1864	£12	£25	£120	£325
1865	£12	£25	£120	£325
1866	£12	£25	£120	£325
1866 BBRITANNIAR error	£90	£325	£875	£1750
1867	£12	£25	£120	£350
1867 3rd YH, die no	£175	£350	£1900	£2850
1868	£10	£25	£120	£325
1869	£15	£40	£150	£350
1870	£10	£25	£135	£325
1871	£10	£20	£150	£350
1872	£10	£20	£120	£325
1873	£10	£20	£120	£325
1874	£10	£20	£120	£325
1875	£10	£20	£120	£325
1876	£10	£25	£120	£350
1877	£10	£20	£120	£325

	F	VF	EF	Unc
1878	£12	£28	£150	£365
1879 no die		ext. rare		
1879 4th YH	£10	£20	£120	£265
1880	£10	£15	£100	£225
1880 longer line below SHILLING	*	*	*	*
1881	£10	£20	£95	£195
1881 longer line below SHILLING	£10	£20	£95	£195
1881 longer line below SHILLING, large rev lettering	£10	£20	£95	£195
1882	£15	£20	£120	£285
1883	£10	£20	£90	£225
1884	£10	£20	£90	£225
1885	£10	£20	£90	£225
1886	£10	£20	£90	£225
1887	£10	£25	£110	£265
1887 JH	*	£5	£12	£35
1887 proof	*	*	*	£350
1888/7	*	£8	£45	£90
1889	£40	£100	£425	£650
1889 large JH	*	£8	£50	£135
1890	*	£8	£50	£150
1891	*	£8	£50	£165
1892	*	£8	£50	£165
1893 OH	£4	£12	£35	£95
1893 proof	*	*	*	£350
1893 small obv letters	*	*	£40	£80
1894	*	£8	£45	£110
1895	*	*	£40	£120
1896	*	*	£40	£100

ABOVE: Victoria 1896 Shilling

1897	*	£8	£48	£125
1898	*	£8	£48	£125
1899	*	£8	£48	£135
1900	*	£8	£48	£125
1901	*	£8	£48	£125

EDWARD VII

1902	*	*	£45	£75
1902 matt proof	*	*	£50	£110
1903	*	£20	£165	£425
1904	*	£15	£135	£385
1905	£90	£250	£1350	£3000
1906	*	*	£65	£185
1907	*	*	£70	£200

BRITISH COINS MARKET VALUES 2022 111

MILLED COINAGE

	F	VF	EF	Unc
1908	£8	£20	£175	£525
1909	£8	£20	£175	£525
1910	*	*	£45	£125

GEORGE V

	F	VF	EF	Unc
1911	*	*	£28	£75
1911 proof	*	*	*	£150
1912	*	*	£35	£135
1913	*	*	£75	£200
1914	*	*	£30	£65
1915	*	*	£30	£65
1916	*	*	£30	£65
1917	*	*	£38	£85
1918	*	*	£30	£65
1919	*	*	£40	£90
1920	*	*	£35	£80
1921	*	*	£45	£120
1922	*	*	£30	£80
1923	*	*	£25	£65
1923 nickel	*	*	*	£1500
1924	*	*	£30	£80
1924 nickel	*	*	*	£1500
1925	*	*	£50	£135
1926	*	*	£30	£70
1926 mod eff	*	*	£20	£50
1927	*	*	£25	£55
1927 new type	*	*	£12	£40
1927 new type proof	*	*	*	£60
1928	*	*	*	£25
1929	*	*	£8	£25
1930	*	*	£37	£110
1931	*	*	£8	£30
1932	*	*	£8	£30
1933	*	*	£8	£30
1934	*	*	£15	£50
1935	*	*	£4	£20
1936	*	*	£4	£20

GEORGE VI

	F	VF	EF	Unc
1937 Eng	*	*	*	£10
1937 Eng proof	*	*	*	£20
1937 Scot	*	*	*	£10
1937 Scot proof	*	*	*	£20
1938 Eng	*	*	£5	£35
1938 Scot	*	*	£5	£30
1939 Eng	*	*	*	£15
1939 Scot	*	*	*	£18
1940 Eng	*	*	*	£15
1940 Scot	*	*	*	£18
1941 Eng	*	*	£2	£15
1941 Scot	*	*	£2	£18
1942 Eng	*	*	*	£15
1942 Scot	*	*	*	£18
1943 Eng	*	*	*	£15
1943 Scot	*	*	*	£15
1944 Eng	*	*	*	£15
1944 Scot	*	*	*	15
1945 Eng	*	*	*	£10
1945 Scot	*	*	*	£10

	F	VF	EF	Unc
1946 Eng	*	*	*	£10
1946 Scot	*	*	*	£10
1947 Eng	*	*	*	£8
1947 Scot	*	*	*	£8
1948 Eng	*	*	*	£8
1948 Scot	*	*	*	£8
1949 Eng	*	*	*	£25
1949 Scot	*	*	*	£25
1950 Eng	*	*	*	£25
1950 Eng proof	*	*	*	£25
1950 Scot	*	*	*	£25
1950 Scot proof	*	*	*	£25
1951 Eng	*	*	*	£25
1951 Eng proof	*	*	*	£25
1951 Scot	*	*	*	£25
1951 Scot proof	*	*	*	£25

ELIZABETH II

	F	VF	EF	Unc
1953 Eng	*	*	*	£5
1953 Eng proof	*	*	*	£10
1953 Scot	*	*	*	£5
1953 Scot proof	*	*	*	£10
1954 Eng	*	*	*	£5
1954 Scot	*	*	*	£5
1955 Eng	*	*	*	£5
1955 Scot	*	*	*	£5
1956 Eng	*	*	*	£10
1956 Scot	*	*	*	£9
1957 Eng	*	*	*	£4
1957 Scot	*	*	*	£20
1958 Eng	*	*	*	£50
1958 Scot	*	*	*	£4
1959 Eng	*	*	*	£4
1959 Scot	*	*	*	£75
1960 Eng	*	*	*	£2
1960 Scot	*	*	*	£3
1961 Eng	*	*	*	£2
1961 Scot	*	*	*	£10
1962 Eng	*	*	*	£1
1962 Scot	*	*	*	£1
1963 Eng	*	*	*	£1
1963 Scot	*	*	*	£1
1964 Eng	*	*	*	£1
1964 Scot	*	*	*	£1
1965 Eng	*	*	*	£1
1965 Scot	*	*	*	£1
1966 Eng	*	*	*	£1
1966 Scot	*	*	*	£1

■ SIXPENCES

CROMWELL

	F	VF	EF
1658		highest rarity	
1658 Dutch copy	*	£4000	£7500

CHARLES II

	F	VF	EF
1674	£50	£250	£750
1675	£50	£245	£785

	F	VF	EF
1675/4	£50	£245	£785
1676	£50	£250	£825
1676/5	£50	£250	£825
1677	£50	£225	£750
1678/7	£50	£245	£785
1679	£50	£250	£825
1680	£70	£250	£825
1681	£50	£245	£785
1682	£65	£285	£875
1682/1	£50	£245	£785
1683	£50	£225	£750
1684	£65	£245	£750

ABOVE: James II 1686 Sixpence

JAMES II
	F	VF	EF
1686 early shields	£100	£350	£1500
1687 early shields	£100	£350	£1500
1687/6	£100	£350	£1500
1687 later shields	£100	£350	£1500
1687/6	£100	£375	£1750
1688	£100	£375	£1500

WILLIAM AND MARY
	F	VF	EF
1693	£110	£375	£1200

ABOVE: William and Mary 1693 Sixpence

	F	VF	EF
1693 3 upside down	£125	£425	£1250
1694	£140	£400	£1400

WILLIAM III
	F	VF	EF
1695 1st bust early hp	£30	£95	£375
1696	£25	£70	£200
1696 no obv stops	£40	£125	£450
1696/5	£30	£100	£450
1696 B	£30	£80	£350
1696 C	£35	£100	£450
1696 E	£35	£100	£450
1696 N	£35	£100	£450
1696 y	£30	£95	£425
1696 Y	£40	£100	£425
1696 1st bust later hp	£50	£135	£400
1696 B	£75	£200	*
1696 C	£60	£225	£500
1696 N	£70	£225	£525
1696 2nd bust	£185	£500	£1750
1696 3rd bust, early hp, E			ext. rare
1696 3rd bust, early hp, y			ext. rare
1697 1st bust early hp	£25	£60	£275
1697 B	£40	£100	£425
1697 C	£60	£150	£500
1697 E	£40	£110	£425
1697 N	£40	£110	£425
1697 y	£40	£110	£425
1697 2nd bust	£145	£475	£1250
1697 3rd bust later hp	£25	£75	£250
1697 B	£40	£100	£425
1697 C	£60	£185	£650
1697 E	£65	£120	£485
1697 Y	£60	£150	£500
1698	£45	£95	£300
1698 plumes	£80	£200	£700
1699	£85	£200	£685
1699 plumes	£70	£185	£625
1699 roses	£85	£225	£700

ABOVE: William III 1699 plumes Sixpence

	F	VF	EF
1700	£25	£60	£300
1700 plume below bust	£3250	*	*
1701	£40	£100	£450

ANNE
	F	VF	EF
1703 VIGO	£40	£110	£395
1705	£60	£185	£575
1705 plumes	£55	£165	£500
1705 r&p	£60	£175	£500
1707	£40	£140	£425
1707 plain	£25	£75	£275
1707 E	£25	£100	£385
1707 plumes	£35	£100	£395

ABOVE: Anne 1707 plumes Sixpence

BRITISH COINS MARKET VALUES 2022 **113**

MILLED COINAGE

MILLED COINAGE

	F	VF	EF
1708 plain	£30	£95	£285
1708 E	£35	£110	£450
1708/7 E	£60	£165	£525
1708 E*	£40	£150	£500
1708/7 E*	£60	£185	£550
1708 Edin bust E*	£60	£195	£700
1708 plumes	£45	£125	£485
1710 r&p	£45	£135	£450
1711	£20	£75	£200

ABOVE: George I 1726 roses and plumes Sixpence

GEORGE I

1717 r&p	£50	£195	£600
1720/17 r&p	£50	£175	£575
1723 SS C, small letters on obv	£25	£85	£250
1723 SS C, large letters on both sides	£25	£85	£250
1726 small r&p	£35	£200	£725

ABOVE: George II 1728 roses and plumes Sixpence

GEORGE II

1728 YH	£65	£225	£600
1728 plumes	£45	£175	£500
1728 YH r&p	£45	£165	£495
1731	£25	£110	£400
1732	£25	£110	£400
1734	£35	£125	£465
1735	£35	£125	£425
1735/4	£35	£125	£485
1736	£30	£125	£400
1739 roses	£25	£100	£325
1739 O/R	£60	£185	£475
1741	£25	£110	£325
1743 OH roses	£25	£110	£325
1745	£25	£110	£325
1745/3	£30	£125	£350
1745 LIMA	£20	£85	£225
1746	£20	£85	£225
1746 plain proof	*	*	£1650

		F	VF	EF
1750		£35	£135	£325
1751		£35	£175	£400
1757		£10	£20	£60
1757		£10	£20	£60
1758/7		£15	£35	£70

GEORGE III

	F	VF	EF	Unc
1787 hearts	£10	£20	£50	£125
1787 no hearts	£10	£20	£50	£130
1816	£8	£12	£60	£130
1817	£8	£12	£60	£130
1818	£8	£18	£75	£165
1819	£8	£15	£70	£165
1819/8	£8	£15	£80	£185
1819 small 8	£10	£20	£75	£165
1820	£8	£15	£65	£140
1820 1 inv	£50	£200	£525	*

GEORGE IV

1820 1st head 1st rev pattern or proof	*	*	*	£5500
1821 proof	*	*	*	£1000
1821 BBITANNIAR error	£100	£285	£800	*
1824 1st head 2nd rev	£8	£25	£165	£395
1825	£8	£20	£150	£395
1826	£20	£90	£295	£600
1826 2nd head 3rd rev	£5	£20	£120	£300
1826 proof	*	*	*	£500
1827	£15	£45	£325	£675
1828	£8	£20	£225	£525
1829	£6	£20	£150	£425

ABOVE: William IV 1831 proof Sixpence

WILLIAM IV

1831	£10	£20	£110	£250
1831 proof	*	*	*	£450
1834	£10	£30	£120	£285
1835	£10	£20	£120	£285
1836	£15	£35	£175	£325
1837	£12	£30	£175	£325

VICTORIA

1838 1st YH	£7	£17	£110	£300
1839	£8	£17	£110	£300
1839 proof	*	*	*	£750
1840	£8	£18	£125	£300
1841	£8	£20	£150	£325
1842	£8	£18	£125	£300
1843	£8	£18	£125	£300

MILLED COINAGE

	F	VF	EF	Unc		F	VF	EF	Unc
1844	£8	£18	£125	£300	1883	£5	£10	£70	£125
1845	£8	£18	£110	£300	1884	£5	£10	£65	£135
1846	£8	£18	£125	£300	1885	£5	£10	£65	£135
1848	£30	£110	£465	£875	1886	£5	£10	£65	£135
1848/6	£25	£100	£425	£800	1887	£5	£10	£65	£135
1850	£12	£18	£125	£300	1887 JH shield rev	£2	£5	£10	£28
1850 5/3	£17	£45	£200	£400	1887 proof	*	*	*	£275
1851	£8	£18	£125	£300	1887 new rev	£2	£5	£10	£30
1852	£8	£18	£125	£300	1888	£3	£5	£30	£90
1853	£6	£17	£95	£225	1889	£3	£7	£30	£90
1853 proof	*	*	*	£1200	1890	*	£8	£30	£90
1854	£135	£395	£975	*	1891	*	£8	£40	£110
1855	£8	£15	£120	£280	1892	*	£10	£45	£120
1855/3	£10	£17	£120	£285	1893	£250	£725	£2450	£4250
1856	£8	£15	£120	£280	1893 OH	*	£5	£20	£85
1857	£8	£15	£120	£280	1893 proof	*	*	*	£300
1858	£8	£15	£120	£280	1894	*	£7	£35	£110
1859	£8	£15	£120	£280	1895	*	£7	£32	£120
1859/8	£8	£20	£120	£280	1896	*	£7	£30	£100
1860	£8	£17	£120	£280	1897	*	£7	£30	£100
1862	£50	£110	£475	£975	1898	*	£7	£35	£120
1863	£40	£85	£365	£775	1899	*	£7	£35	£120
1864	£8	£15	£120	£280	1900	*	£7	£35	£100
1865	£8	£15	£120	£280	1901	*	£7	£30	£100
1866	£7	£15	£120	£280	**EDWARD VII**				
1866 no die no				ext. rare	1902	*	£8	£40	£80
1867	£10	£20	£125	£295	1902 matt proof	*	*	*	£95
1868	£10	£20	£125	£295	1903	*	£10	£55	£120
1869	£12	£18	£135	£325	1904	*	£20	£100	£265
1870	£12	£25	£150	£325	1905	*	£20	£90	£225
					1906	*	£10	£50	£110
					1907	*	£10	£55	£120
					1908	*	£15	£60	£130
					1909	*	£10	£55	£120
					1910	*	£7	£40	£80

ABOVE: Victoria 1871 proof Sixpence

	F	VF	EF	Unc
1871	£7	£12	£100	£285
1871 no die no	£7	£15	£100	£295
1872	£7	£15	£100	£295
1873	£7	£12	£95	£275
1874	£7	£12	£95	£240
1875	£7	£12	£95	£275
1876	£9	£20	£125	£325
1877	£7	£12	£95	£275
1877 no die no	£5	£12	£95	£275
1878	£7	£10	£95	£275
1878/7	£40	£115	£600	£1000
1878 DRITANNIAR error	£65	£185	£850	*
1879 die no	£10	£20	£120	£300
1879 no die no	£7	£15	£100	£275
1880 2nd YH	£7	£15	£80	£235
1880 3rd YH	£5	£8	£70	£125
1881	£5	£10	£60	£110
1882	£8	£25	£100	£285

GEORGE V

	F	VF	EF	Unc
1911	*	*	£22	£50
1911 proof	*	*	*	£120
1912	*	*	£30	£70
1913	*	*	£35	£75
1914	*	*	£18	£45
1915	*	*	£22	£55
1916	*	*	£18	£45
1917	*	*	£40	£120
1918	*	*	£18	£45
1919	*	*	£22	£55
1920	*	*	£27	£65
1920 debased	*	*	£27	£65
1921	*	*	£20	£70
1922	*	*	£20	£70
1923	*	*	£27	£65
1924	*	*	£18	£50
1925	*	*	£18	£45
1925 new rim	*	*	£15	£40
1926	*	*	£15	£35
1926 mod eff	*	*	£12	£30
1927	*	*	£15	£35

BRITISH COINS MARKET VALUES 2022

MILLED COINAGE

	F	VF	EF	Unc
1927 new rev proof	*	*	*	£50
1928	*	*	£7	£25
1929	*	*	£7	£25
1930	*	*	£8	£28
1931	*	*	£8	£28
1932	*	*	£12	£45
1933	*	*	£8	£28
1934	*	*	£10	£40
1935	*	*	£5	£18
1936	*	*	£5	£18

GEORGE VI

	F	VF	EF	Unc
1937	*	*	£2	£10
1937 proof	*	*	*	£15
1938	*	*	£4	£20
1939	*	*	£2	£15
1940	*	*	£2	£20
1941	*	*	£4	£10
1942	*	*	£2	£10
1943	*	*	£2	£10
1944	*	*	£2	£10
1945	*	*	£2	£10
1946	*	*	£2	£10
1947	*	*	£1	£7
1948	*	*	£1	£7
1949	*	*	£1	£10
1950	*	*	£1	£12
1950 proof	*	*	*	£18
1951	*	*	£1	£15
1951 proof	*	*	*	£18
1952	*	£5	£20	£110

ELIZABETH II

	F	VF	EF	Unc
1953	*	*	*	£5
1953 proof	*	*	*	£7
1954	*	*	*	£5
1955	*	*	*	£3
1956	*	*	*	£4
1957	*	*	*	£3
1958	*	*	*	£6
1959	*	*	*	£2
1960	*	*	*	£4
1961	*	*	*	£4
1962	*	*	*	£1
1963	*	*	*	£1
1964	*	*	*	£1
1965	*	*	*	£1
1966	*	*	*	£1
1967	*	*	*	£1

■ GROATS 'BRITANNIA' TYPE

Earlier dates are included in Maundy sets (see p134).

WILLIAM IV

	F	VF	EF	Unc
1836	*	*	£45	£100
1836 proof	*	*	*	£850
1837	*	*	£60	£120

VICTORIA

	F	VF	EF	Unc
1837 proof	*	*	*	£1200
1838	*	£5	£40	£110
1838 8/8 on side	*	£15	£60	£165
1839	*	£8	£40	£110
1839 proof	*	*	*	£550
1840	*	£10	£40	£110
1840 narrow 0	*	£12	£40	*
1841	*	£10	£50	£125
1841 I for last 1	*	*	*	*
1842	*	£8	£50	£125
1842/1	*	£15	£70	£180
1843	*	£5	£50	£125
1843 4/5	*	£15	£65	£185
1844	*	£8	£50	£125
1845	*	£8	£50	£125
1846	*	£8	£50	£125
1847/6	£25	£70	£325	*
1848	*	£8	£45	£120
1848/6	£10	£25	£75	*
1848/7	*	£20	£90	£265
1849	*	£10	£45	£120
1849/8	*	£10	£50	£125
1851	£20	£95	£350	*
1852	£45	£185	£500	*

ABOVE: Victoria 1852 Groat

	F	VF	EF	Unc
1853	£45	£195	£475	*
1853 proof	*	*	*	£1200
1854	*	£8	£45	£120
1854 5/3	*	£20	£85	*
1855	*	£8	£45	£120
1857 proof	*	*	*	£1875
1862 proof	*	*	*	£2250
1888 JH	*	£20	£40	£90

■ SILVER THREEPENCES

Earlier dates are included in Maundy sets.

WILLIAM IV

	F	VF	EF	Unc
1834	*	£12	£70	£195
1835	*	£12	£65	£175
1836	*	£12	£70	£195
1837	*	£20	£85	£200

ABOVE: Victoria 1866 Threepence

MILLED COINAGE

VICTORIA	F	VF	EF	Unc
1838	*	£15	£60	£175
1839	*	£20	£95	£225
1840	*	£15	£85	£225
1841	*	£15	£95	£195
1842	*	£15	£100	£200
1843	*	£15	£68	£165
1844	*	£15	£85	£200
1845	*	£12	£60	£135
1846	*	£60	£200	£425
1847	£45	£125	£400	£800
1848	£35	£100	£400	£750
1849	*	£15	£95	£195
1850	*	£10	£50	£120
1851	*	£12	£68	£165
1852	£45	£175	£450	*
1853	*	£50	£195	£385
1854	*	£10	£60	£150
1855	*	£15	£85	£180
1856	*	£10	£60	£150
1857	*	£15	£70	£180
1858	*	£12	£50	£165
1858 BRITANNIAB error		ext. rare		
1858/6	£10	£25	£150	£275
1859	*	£8	£50	£125
1860	*	£15	£95	£195
1861	*	£8	£68	£165
1862	*	£8	£50	£125
1863	*	£10	£85	£175
1864	*	£10	£50	£125
1865	*	£10	£70	£150
1866	*	£8	£50	£125
1867	*	£8	£50	£125
1868	*	£8	£50	£125
1868 RRITANNIAR error		ext. rare		
1869	£10	£30	£100	£250
1870	*	£6	£50	£125
1871	*	£7	£60	£125
1872	*	£5	£55	£125
1873	*	£5	£38	£95
1874	*	£5	£38	£90
1875	*	£5	£38	£90
1876	*	£5	£38	£90
1877	*	£5	£38	£100
1878	*	£5	£40	£100
1879	*	£5	£40	£100
1880	*	£6	£38	£90
1881	*	£6	£40	£80
1882	*	£8	£60	£125
1883	*	£5	£40	£80
1884	*	£5	£40	£80
1885	*	£5	£40	£80
1886	*	£5	£40	£80
1887 YH	*	£6	£38	£90
1887 JH	*	£2	£5	£15
1887 proof	*	*	*	£95
1888	*	£2	£12	£40
1889	*	£2	£10	£35
1890	*	£2	£10	£35
1891	*	£2	£10	£35

	F	VF	EF	Unc
1892	*	£3	£12	£40
1893	£20	£60	£145	£400
1893 OH	*	*	£12	£40
1893 proof	*	*	*	£110
1894	*	£2	£20	£50
1895	*	£2	£18	£45
1896	*	£2	£18	£45
1897	*	*	£12	£35
1898	*	*	£12	£35
1899	*	*	£12	£35
1900	*	*	£10	£30
1901	*	*	£10	£30

EDWARD VII				
1902	*	*	£10	£25
1902 matt proof	*	*	*	£30
1903	*	£2	£25	£50
1904	*	£6	£35	£100
1905	*	£6	£25	£75
1906	*	£3	£35	£95
1907	*	£2	£25	£50
1908	*	£2	£12	£45
1909	*	£2	£25	£60
1910	*	£2	£12	£35

GEORGE V				
1911	*	*	£6	£20
1911 proof	*	*	*	£30
1912	*	*	£6	£20
1913	*	*	£6	£20
1914	*	*	£4	£20
1915	*	*	£4	£25
1916	*	*	£3	£15
1917	*	*	£3	£15
1918	*	*	£3	£15
1919	*	*	£3	£15
1920	*	*	£3	£20
1920 debased	*	*	£3	£20
1921	*	*	£3	£20
1922	*	*	£14	£60
1925	*	£1	£12	£50
1926	*	£5	£35	£100
1926 mod eff	*	£1	£10	£40
1927 new rev proof	*	*	*	£95
1928	*	£2	£15	£45
1930	*	£1	£8	£30
1931	*	*	£2	£12
1932	*	*	£1	£9
1933	*	*	£1	£9
1934	*	*	£2	£12
1935	*	*	£2	£15
1936	*	*	£2	£12

GEORGE VI				
1937	*	*	£2	£5
1937 proof	*	*	*	£10
1938	*	*	£2	£6
1939	*	£1	£5	£20
1940	*	*	£2	£8

BRITISH COINS MARKET VALUES 2022 117

MILLED COINAGE

	F	VF	EF	Unc
1941	*	*	£2	£12
1942	*	£2	£6	£35
1943	*	£3	£17	£55
1944	*	£6	£28	£80
1945	*	*	*	*

Some of the Threepences were issued for use in the Colonies. Note: all specimens of 1945 were probably melted down but it appears that one or two still exist.

■ SMALL SILVER FOR COLONIES

These tiny coins were struck for issue in some of the Colonies but they were never issued for circulation in Britain. However, they are often included in collections of British coins, so we have given the prices.

Twopences

Other dates are included in Maundy sets.

VICTORIA	F	VF	EF	Unc
1838	*	£5	£20	£45
1838 2nd 8 like S	*	£8	£30	£75
1848	*	£5	£20	£50

Threehalfpences

WILLIAM IV				
1834	*	£5	£40	£90
1835	*	£5	£65	£165
1835/4	*	£10	£40	£110
1836	*	£5	£35	£100
1837	£10	£25	£100	£300

VICTORIA				
1838	*	£8	£25	£85
1839	*	£8	£25	£70
1840	*	£15	£65	£150
1841	*	£8	£30	£90
1842	*	£8	£30	£90
1843	*	£8	£20	£75
1843/34	£5	£20	£65	£150
1860	£4	£15	£45	£140
1862	£4	£15	£45	£140
1870 proof				£900

■ NICKEL–BRASS THREEPENCES

ABOVE: Edward VIII 1937 Threepence, extremely rare

The 1937 Edward VIII threepences, struck in 1936 ready for issue, were melted after Edward's abdication.

A few, however, escaped into circulation to become highly prized collectors' pieces.

George VI 1937 threepences were struck in large numbers, and are consequently worth much less.

EDWARD VIII	F	VF	EF	BU
1937	*	*	£35000	*

GEORGE VI				
1937	*	*	£1	£6
1938	*	*	£3	£28
1939	*	*	£6	£50
1940	*	*	£2	£20
1941	*	*	£1	£8
1942	*	*	£1	£8
1943	*	*	£1	£8
1944	*	*	£1	£8
1945	*	*	£1	£12
1946	*	£15	£185	£800
1948	*	*	£5	£45
1949	*	£15	£145	£700
1950	*	*	£15	£85
1951	*	*	£25	£110
1952	*	*	*	£12

ELIZABETH II				
1953	*	*	*	£5
1953 proof	*	*	*	£8
1954	*	*	*	£5
1955	*	*	*	£7
1956	*	*	*	£7
1957	*	*	*	£4
1958	*	*	*	£13
1959	*	*	*	£3
1960	*	*	*	£3
1961	*	*	*	£1
1962	*	*	*	£1
1963	*	*	*	£1
1964	*	*	*	£1
1965	*	*	*	£1
1966	*	*	*	£1
1967	*	*	*	*

■ COPPER TWOPENCE

GEORGE III				
1797	£20	£75	£375	£1200

■ COPPER PENNIES

GEORGE III				
1797 10 leaves	£5	£35	£250	£575
1797 11 leaves	£5	£45	£250	£575
1806	£3	£8	£90	£350
1806 no incuse curl	£3	£8	£90	£375
1807	£3	£8	£90	£385
1808 unique	*	*	*	£130000

BRITISH COINS MARKET VALUES 2022

ABOVE: George III 1806 Penny

GEORGE IV

	F	VF	EF	BU
1825	£5	£25	£175	£650
1826	£3	£12	£150	£600
1826 proof	*	*	£300	£850
1826 thin line down St Andrew's cross	£5	£25	£175	£600
1826 thick line	£5	£40	£225	*
1827	£350	£775	£4250	*

ABOVE: William IV 1831

WILLIAM IV

	F	VF	EF	BU
1831	£10	£50	£285	£1000
1831 proof	*	*	*	£950
1831 .ww inc				ext. rare
1831 w.w inc	£15	£75	£375	*
1834	£15	£75	£365	£1375
1837	£20	£90	£600	£2000

ABOVE: Victoria 1841 Penny

MILLED COINAGE

VICTORIA	F	VF	EF	BU
1839 proof	*	*	*	£2000
1841	£20	£60	£300	£800
1841 no colon after REG	£3	£15	£65	£385
1843	£90	£300	£1650	£3950
1843 no colon after REG	£65	£200	£1350	£3500
1844	£3	£20	£100	£485
1845	£8	£20	£145	£725
1846 DEF far colon	£3	£15	£110	£485
1846 DEF close colon	£3	£15	£135	£465
1847 DEF close colon	£3	£15	£95	£375
1847 DEF far colon	£3	£15	£85	£350
1848	£3	£15	£95	£400
1848/6	£15	£75	£475	*
1848/7	£3	£15	£95	£400
1849	£100	£425	£1500	£3500
1851 DEF far colon	£3	£18	£125	£475
1851 DEF close colon	£4	£15	£110	£450
1853 OT	£2	£10	£80	£285
1853 proof	*	*	*	£2500
1853 PT	£2	£10	£85	£375
1854 PT	£2	£10	£80	£265
1854/3	£15	£40	£165	£475
1854 OT	£2	£10	£80	£285
1855 OT	£2	£10	£80	£285
1855 PT	£2	£10	£80	£285
1856 PT	£50	£165	£725	£2000
1856 OT	£60	£200	£875	£2500
1857 OT	£2	£10	£80	£325
1857 PT	£2	£10	£80	£300
1857 small date	£2	£10	£85	£325
1858	£2	£10	£65	£250
1858 small date	£3	£10	£85	£325
1858/3	£3	£10	£85	£325
1858/7	£2	£5	£85	£365
1858 no ww	£2	£5	£65	£285
1858 no ww (large 1 and 5, small 8s)	£3	£8	£65	£285
1859	£3	£10	£95	£400
1859 small date	£4	£15	£100	£400
1860/59	£325	£875	£3250	*

■ BRONZE PENNIES

For fuller details of varieties in bronze pennies see *English Copper, Tin and Bronze Coins in the British Museum 1558–1958* by C W Peck, *The Bronze Coinage of Great Britain* by M J Freeman and *The British Bronze Penny 1860–1970* by Michael Gouby.

The die pairings below are from Gouby, a must for the penny collector. There are many varieties and die combinations, and only the more significant are listed below.

VICTORIA	F	VF	EF	BU
1860 BB, dies C/a	£100	£300	£700	*
1860 BB dies C/b	£40	£100	£245	£500
1860 BB rev rock to left of lighthouse, dies C/c	£80	£200	£750	*
1860 obv BB/rev TB, dies C/d	£400	£750	£1500	£3000

BRITISH COINS MARKET VALUES 2022 119

MILLED COINAGE

ABOVE: Victoria 1860 bronze Penny

	F	VF	EF	BU
1860 obv TB/rev BB, dies D/b	£300	£625	£2250	£6000
1860 TB, signature on cape, dies D/d	*	£15	£60	£235
1860 TB, rev L.C.W. inc below foot, dies E/e	£300	£575	£1000	£2850
1860 TB, rev L.C.W inc below shield, dies F/d	*	£15	£90	£225
1860 TB obv, no signature on cape, dies H/d	*	£150	£400	£800

ABOVE: 1861 bronze Penny

	F	VF	EF	BU
1861 signature on cape, rev LCW below shield, dies D/d	£80	£225	£450	£1500
1861 signature on cape, rev no signature, dies D/g	£80	£225	£450	£1500
1861 signature below cape, L.C.W. below shield, dies F/d	*	£10	£90	£300
1861 signature below cape, rev no signature, dies F/g	£80	£350	£850	*
1861 obv no signature, L.C.W. below shield, dies H/d	*	£20	£100	£300
1861 date: 6 over 8	£400	£1250	£2850	*
1861 no signature either side, dies J/g	*	£12	£75	£275
1862 obv signature, rev no LCW, dies D/g	£450	£875	£2000	*
1862 obv no signature dies J/g	*	£10	£75	£275
1862 date: small figures (½d size)	£475	£1500	£4000	*
1863 dies J/g	*	£10	£60	£200

	F	VF	EF	BU
1863 die no 2 below date	£2000	*	*	*
1863 die no 3 below date	£1850	£3250	*	*
1863 die no 4 below date	£2500	*	*	*
1863 die no 5 below date	£20,000	*	*	*
1864 upper serif to 4 in date	£20	£165	£1650	£4000
1864 crosslet serif to 4 in date	£25	£195	£1950	£4750
1865	*	£25	£150	£525
1865/3	£40	£125	£525	£1675
1866	*	£15	£90	£425
1867	£10	£35	£250	£750
1868	£10	£40	£285	£925
1869	£150	£450	£2950	£6500
1870	£10	£40	£250	£600
1871	£30	£85	£825	£1850
1872	*	£12	£85	£300
1873	*	£12	£85	£350
1874	*	£20	£125	£400
1874 H dies J/g	*	£12	£80	£325
1874 rev lighthouse tall and thin, dies J/j	£20	£95	£300	£600
1874 H dies J/j	£25	£95	£250	£675
1874 obv, aged portrait, dies K/g	*	£20	£85	£325
1874 H	*	£20	£85	£325
1875 dies L/k	*	£15	£80	£285
1875 H	£30	£200	£925	£2500
1876 H	*	£15	£85	£275
1877	*	£8	£75	£225
1878	*	£35	£175	£500
1879	*	*	£75	£200
1880 no rock to left of lighthouse, dies M/k	£12	£35	£125	£375
1880 rocks to left of lighthouse, dies M/n	£12	£45	£150	£495
1881	*	*	£200	£575
1881 new obv, dies P/k	£45	£145	£350	*
1881 H	*	*	£65	£285
1882 H	*	*	£65	£235
1882 no H	£875	£2500	*	*
1883	*	*	£60	£225
1884	*	*	£50	£165
1885	*	*	£50	£165
1886	*	*	£50	£165
1887	*	*	£45	£140
1888	*	*	£50	£165
1889 14 leaves	*	*	£45	£140
1889 15 leaves	*	*	£50	£165
1890	*	*	£40	£125
1891	*	*	£40	£125
1892	*	*	£40	£145
1893	*	*	£40	£125
1894	*	*	£60	£225
1895 2mm	*	£50	£365	£1500

MILLED COINAGE

	F	VF	EF	BU
1895	*	*	£15	£75
1896	*	*	£12	£70
1897	*	*	£12	£70
1897 higher horizon	£40	£120	£600	*
1898	*	*	£15	£75
1899	*	*	£15	£70
1900	*	*	£12	£55
1901	*	*	£10	£40

EDWARD VII

	F	VF	EF	BU
1902 low horizon	*	£15	£100	£295
1902	*	*	£10	£45
1903	*	*	£20	£85
1904	*	*	£35	£150
1905	*	*	£35	£110
1906	*	*	£25	£100
1907	*	*	£25	£100
1908	*	*	£17	£90
1909	*	*	£25	£100
1910	*	*	£20	£90

ABOVE: George V 1933 Penny

GEORGE V

	F	VF	EF	BU
1911	*	*	£12	£48
1912	*	*	£12	£60
1912 H	*	*	£55	£185
1913	*	*	£20	£75
1914	*	*	£18	£58
1915	*	*	£18	£58
1916	*	*	£18	£58
1917	*	*	£18	£58
1918	*	*	£18	£58
1918 H	*	£35	£265	£700
1918 KN	*	£45	£395	£1000
1919	*	*	£18	£58
1919 H	*	£35	£325	£925
1919 KN	*	£75	£725	£2250
1920	*	*	£15	£48
1921	*	*	£15	£48
1922	*	*	£15	£48
1922 rev as 1927		ext. rare		
1926	*	*	£30	£100
1926 mod eff	£25	£225	£1200	£3750
1927	*	*	£12	£338
1928	*	*	£12	£35

	F	VF	EF	BU
1929	*	*	£12	£35
1930	*	*	£22	£55
1931	*	*	£15	£70
1932	*	*	£30	£125
1933			highest rarity	
1934	*	*	£15	£40
1935	*	*	£4	£15
1936	*	*	£4	£15

ABOVE: Edward VIII proof Penny

EDWARD VIII
Proof penny   highest rarity

GEORGE VI

	F	VF	EF	BU
1937	*	*	*	£5
1938	*	*	*	£5
1939	*	*	£1	£6
1940	*	*	£7	£45
1944	*	*	£5	£27
1945	*	*	£4	£20
1946	*	*	*	£10
1947	*	*	*	£7
1948	*	*	*	£7
1949	*	*	*	£7
1950	*	£7	£20	£60
1951	*	£7	£28	£45
1952 proof				unique

ABOVE: George VI 1952 Penny, unique

BRITISH COINS MARKET VALUES 2022   121

MILLED COINAGE

	F	VF	EF	BU
ELIZABETH II				
1953	*	£1	£4	£20
1953 proof	*	*	*	£20
1954		unique		
1961	*	*	*	£2
1962	*	*	*	£1
1963	*	*	*	£1
1964	*	*	*	£0.50
1965	*	*	*	£0.50
1966	*	*	*	£0.50
1967	*	*	*	£0.25

■ COPPER OR TIN HALFPENNIES

ABOVE: Charles II 1675 Halfpenny

	Fair	F	VF	EF
CHARLES II				
1672	£8	£45	£225	£1350
1672 CRAOLVS error		ext. rare		*
1673	£8	£45	£200	£1350
1673 CRAOLVS error		ext. rare		*
1673 no stops on rev	£10	£65	£325	*
1673 no stops on obv	£12	£60	£300	*
1675	£10	£50	£200	£1475
1675 no stops on obv	£10	£60	£300	*
1675 5/3	£35	£120	£400	*
JAMES II				
1685 tin	£65	£250	£650	£4500
1686 tin	£70	£250	£650	*
1687 tin	£65	£250	£600	*
1687 D/D	*	*	*	*
WILLIAM AND MARY				
1689 tin, ET on right	£650	£1250	£2500	*
1689 tin, ET on left	*	*	*	*
1690 tin, date on edge	£65	£200	£650	£3500
1691 tin, date in exergue and on edge	£65	£200	£650	£3500
1691/2 tin, 1691 in exergue 1692 on edge		ext. rare		*

	Fair	F	VF	EF
1692 tin, date in exergue and on edge	£65	£75	£450	*
1694 copper	£12	£50	£250	£1350
1694 GVLIEMVS error	£150	*	*	*
1694 no stop after MARIA	£25	£65	£300	£1400
1694 BRITANNIA with last I/A	£30	£125	£350	*
1694 no stop on rev	£20	£60	£300	£1350

ABOVE: William III 1696 Halfpenny

WILLIAM III	Fair	F	VF	EF
Type 1, date in exergue				
1695	£10	£35	£175	£1350
1695 BRITANNIA, As unbarred	£50	£175	*	*
1695 no stop on rev	£10	£50	£225	*
1696	£10	£35	£175	£1350
1696 GVLIEMVS, no stop on rev		ext. rare		*
1696 TERTVS error	£85	£200	*	*
1697	£10	£45	£175	£1350
1697 no stops	£35	£150	*	*
1697 I/E on TERTIVS	£35	£150	*	*
1697 GVLILMVS no stop on rev		ext. rare		*
1697 no stop after TERTIVS	£15	£40	£150	£1350
1698	£15	£45	£200	*
Type 2, date in legend				
1698	£10	£45	£225	£1350
1699	£10	£30	£225	£1250
1699 BRITANNIA, As unbarred	£35	£150	*	*
1699 GVLIEMVS error	£35	£150	*	*
Type 3, Britannia's hand on knee, date in exergue				
1699	£10	£30	£200	£1250
1699 stop after date	£35	£150	*	*
1699 BRITANNIA, As unbarred	£20	£70	£250	*
1699 GVILELMVS	£50	£225	*	*
1699 TERTVS	£50	£225	*	*
1699 no stop on rev	£35	£150	*	*
1699 no stops on obv	£15	£60	£250	*
1699 no stops after				

MILLED COINAGE

	Fair	F	VF	EF
GVLIELMVS	£15	£60	£250	*
1700	£8	£20	£200	£1250
1700 no stops on obv	£20	£70	£250	*
1700 no stops after GVLIELMVS	£20	£70	£250	*
1700 BRITANNIA, As unbarred	£8	£20	£200	£1250
1700 no stop on reverse	£8	£25	£200	£1250
1700 GVLIELMS error	£20	£70	£250	*
1700 GVLIEEMVS error	£12	£45	£185	*
1700 TER TIVS error	£8	£20	£200	£1250
1700 I/V on TERTIVS	£50	£225	*	*
1701 BRITANNIA, As unbarred	£8	£20	£200	£1250
1701 no stops on obv	£50	£225	*	*
1701 GVLIELMVS TERTIVS, Vs inverted As	£12	£45	£225	*

GEORGE I
Type 1

	Fair	F	VF	EF
1717	£10	£35	£250	£875
1717 no stops on obv	£15	£65	£475	*

ABOVE: George I 1717 Halfpenny

	Fair	F	VF	EF
1718	£10	£30	£225	£800
1718 no stop on obv	£15	£65	£475	*
1719 on large flan of type 2	£250	*	*	*
1719 on large flan of type 2, edge grained			ext. rare	*

Type 2

	Fair	F	VF	EF
1719 both shoulder straps ornate	£5	£25	£150	£825
1719 both shoulder straps ornate, edge grained			ext. rare	*
1719 bust with left strap plain	£5	£25	£150	£800
1720	£5	£25	£150	£750
1721	£5	£25	£150	£725
1721/0	£5	£25	£150	£725
1721 stop after date	£5	£25	£150	£725
1722	£5	£25	£150	£725
1722 GEORGIVS, V inverted A	£15	£90	£300	*
1723	£5	£25	£150	£725
1723 no stop on reverse	£15	£90	£300	*
1724	£5	£25	£150	£650

ABOVE: George II 1733 Halfpenny

GEORGE II
Young Head

	Fair	F	VF	EF
1729	*	£20	£85	£400
1729 no stop on rev	*	£25	£90	£425
1730	*	£20	£85	£375
1730 GEOGIVS, no stop on reverse	*	£25	£110	£450
1730 stop after date	£5	£20	£85	£375
1730 no stop after REX or on rev	*	£25	£110	£450
1731	*	£20	£85	£365
1731 rev no stop	*	£25	£100	£400
1732	*	£20	£75	£350
1732 rev no stop	*	£25	£100	£400
1733	*	£18	£70	£350
1734	*	£18	£70	£350
1734/3	*	£25	£150	*
1734 no stops on obv	*	£25	£150	*
1735	*	£18	£70	£350
1736	*	£18	£75	£350
1737	*	£18	£75	£350
1738	*	£18	£70	£325
1739	*	£18	£70	£325

Old Head

	Fair	F	VF	EF
1740	*	£7	£55	£285
1742	*	£7	£55	£285
1742/0	*	£10	£80	£325
1743	*	£7	£55	£285
1744	*	£7	£55	£285
1745	*	£7	£55	£285
1746	*	£7	£55	£285
1747	*	£7	£55	£285
1748	*	£7	£55	£285
1749	*	£7	£55	£285
1750	*	£7	£55	£295
1751	*	£7	£55	£275
	Fair	F	VF	EF
1752	*	£7	£55	£275
1753	*	£7	£55	£275
1754	*	£7	£55	£275

www.stampmagazine.co.uk

MILLED COINAGE

ABOVE: George II 1777 Halfpenny

	F	VF	EF	BU
GEORGE III				
1770	£5	£45	£200	£775
1770 Proof	*	*	*	£1750
1771	£5	£45	£200	£775
1771 no stop on rev	£7	£45	£200	£775
1771 ball below spear head	£5	£45	£200	£775
1772	£5	£45	£200	£775
1772 GEORIVS error	£10	£80	£275	*
1772 ball below spear head	£5	£45	£200	£775
1772 no stop on rev	£5	£45	£200	£775
1773	£5	£45	£200	£775
1773 no stop after REX	£5	£45	£200	£775
1773 no stop on reverse	£5	£45	£200	*
1774	£5	£45	£200	£775
1775	£5	£45	£200	£850
1799 five inc gunports	*	£8	£60	£175
1799 six relief gunports	*	£8	£60	£175
1799 nine relief gunports	*	£8	£60	£200
1799 no gunports	*	£8	£60	£185
1799 no gunports and raised line along hull	*	£8	£60	£185
1806 no berries on olive branch	*	£8	£55	£175
1806 line under SOHO three berries	*	£8	£55	£175
1807	*	£8	£45	£175
GEORGE IV				
1825	*	£30	£135	£350
1826 Proof	*	*	*	£385
1826 two inc lines down cross	*	£15	£85	£250
1826 raised line down centre of cross	*	£20	£100	£275
1826 proof	*	*	*	£475
1827	*	£15	£85	£250
WILLIAM IV				
1831	*	£20	£110	£325
1831 Proof	*	*	*	£525
1834	*	£20	£110	£325
1837	*	£15	£100	£350
VICTORIA				
1838	£3	£8	£50	£265
1839 proof	*	*	*	£500
1839 proof, rev inv	*	*	*	£525

	F	VF	EF	BU
1841	£3	£8	£50	£250
1843	£15	£45	£195	£700
1844	£7	£20	£110	£295
1845	£125	£350	£1450	*
1846	£8	£20	£90	£295
1847	£8	£20	£90	£295
1848	£20	£55	£175	£475
1848/7	£5	£20	£95	£300
1851	£3	£8	£50	£265
1851 seven inc dots on and above shield	£2	£5	£35	£245
1852	£3	£8	£50	£245
1852 seven inc dots on and above shield	£2	£8	£50	£225
1853 proof	*	*	*	£800
1853/2	£4	£25	£110	£300
1854	£3	£5	£45	£130

ABOVE: Victoria 1853 proof Halfpenny

	F	VF	EF	BU
1855	£2	£5	£45	£150
1856	£3	£8	£50	£250
1857	£2	£5	£45	£150
1857 seven inc dots on and above shield	£1	£5	£35	£135
1858	£2	£5	£45	£135
1858/6	£3	£10	£45	£150
1858/7	£2	£5	£45	£150
1858 small date	£1	£5	£35	£150
1859	£2	£5	£50	£185
1859/8	£6	£12	£95	£285
1860 proof only	*	*	*	£10500

■ BRONZE HALFPENNIES

For fuller details of varieties in bronze Halfpennies and Farthings see *English Copper, Tin and Bronze Coins in the British Museum 1558–1958* by C W Peck and *The Bronze Coinage of Great Britain* by M J Freeman. There are a large number of varieties and die combinations for this series, only the more significant are listed below.

	F	VF	EF	BU
VICTORIA				
1860 BB	*	£5	£40	£145
1860 rev TB/obv BB		ext. rare		*
1860 TB, 4 berries	*	£6	£58	£200
1860 TB, double				

124   BRITISH COINS MARKET VALUES 2022

ABOVE: Victoria 1860 bronze Halfpenny

	F	VF	EF	BU
inc leaf veins	*	£15	£90	£325
1861 obv 5 berries	*	£30	£110	£350
1861 obv 4 berries, rev L.C.W. on rock	*	£25	£110	£350
1861 rev no signature	£12	£50	£165	*
1861 rev no signature, breastplate has inc lines	*	£30	£100	£325
1861 obv 4 double incuse leaf veins, rev no signature, breastplate has inc lines	*	£20	£95	£265
1861 same obv, rev L.C.W. on rock	*	£6	£58	£200
1861 obv 7 double incuse leaf veins, rev L.C.W. on rock	*	£6	£58	£200
1861 rev no signature	*	£5	£40	£150
1861 obv 16 leaves, rev rounded to top lighthouse	*	£20	£95	£265
1861 rev pointed top to lighthouse	*	£6	£58	£200
1861 no signature	*	£8	£50	£165
1861 HALP error	£225	£585	*	*
1861 6/8	£200	£585	*	*
1862	*	£5	£35	£165
1862 letter A left of lighthouse base	£495	£750	£2000	*
1862 letter B left of lighthouse base	£850	£1500	£4500	*
1862 letter C left of lighthouse base	£800	*	*	*
1863	*	£5	£75	£245
1864	*	£6	£70	£300
1865	*	£10	£100	£450
1865/3	£30	£90	£350	£825
1866	*	£8	£70	£300
1867	*	£8	£85	£385
1868	*	£8	£80	£300
1869	£20	£65	£350	£1200
1870	*	£5	£75	£245
1871	£20	£65	£350	£975
1872	*	£5	£55	£175
1873	*	£8	£75	£245
1874	*	£20	£125	£450
1874 H	*	£5	£50	£180
1875	*	£5	£50	£180
1875 H	*	£6	£75	£245
1876 H	*	£5	£50	£180
1877	*	£5	£50	£180

	F	VF	EF	BU
1878	*	£18	£110	£425
1879	*	£5	£45	£165
1880	*	£4	£45	£180
1881	*	£4	£45	£180
1881 H	*	£4	£45	£180
1882 H	*	£4	£45	£180
1883	*	£4	£45	£180
1884	*	£2	£45	£165
1885	*	*	£45	£165
1886	*	*	£45	£165
1887	*	*	£45	£165
1888	*	*	£45	£165
1889	*	*	£45	£165
1889/8	*	£20	£110	£325
1890	*	*	£40	£140
1891	*	*	£40	£140
1892	*	*	£40	£140
1893	*	*	£40	£140
1894	*	£5	£60	£200
1895 OH	*	*	£12	£70
1896	*	*	£10	£65
1897 normal horizon	*	*	£10	£65
1897 higher horizon	*	*	£10	£65
1898	*	*	£10	£65
1899	*	*	£10	£65
1900	*	*	£5	£40
1901	*	*	£4	£35

EDWARD VII

	F	VF	EF	BU
1902 low horizon	*	£35	£135	£375
1902	*	*	£10	£35
1903	*	*	£15	£95
1904	*	*	£20	£130
1905	*	*	£17	£100
1906	*	*	£17	£100
1907	*	*	£13	£85
1908	*	*	£13	£85
1909	*	*	£17	£95
1910	*	*	£12	£75

GEORGE V

	F	VF	EF	BU
1911	*	*	£8	£38
1912	*	*	£9	£45
1913	*	*	£9	£45
1914	*	*	£10	£50
1915	*	*	£10	£50
1916	*	*	£10	£50
1917	*	*	£6	£38
1918	*	*	£6	£38
1919	*	*	£5	£38
1920	*	*	£7	£45
1921	*	*	£7	£40
1922	*	*	£15	£60
1923	*	*	£7	£45
1924	*	*	£7	£45
1925	*	*	£7	£45
1925 mod eff	*	*	£15	£55
1926	*	*	£7	£45
1927	*	*	£5	£35

MILLED COINAGE

MILLED COINAGE

	F	VF	EF	BU
1928	*	*	£5	£28
1929	*	*	£5	£30
1930	*	*	£5	£35
1931	*	*	£5	£30
1932	*	*	£15	£135
1933	*	*	£5	£30
1934	*	*	£15	£110
1935	*	*	£5	£30
1936	*	*	£4	£22

GEORGE VI

	F	VF	EF	BU
1937	*	*	*	£5
1937 proof	*	*	*	£12
1938	*	*	*	£9
1939	*	*	*	£22
1940	*	*	*	£22
1941	*	*	*	£9
1942	*	*	*	£6
1943	*	*	*	£6
1944	*	*	*	£6
1945	*	*	*	£8
1946	*	*	*	£18
1947	*	*	*	£6
1948	*	*	*	£6
1949	*	*	*	£15
1950	*	*	*	£12
1950 proof	*	*	*	£15
1951	*	*	*	£25
1951 proof	*	*	*	£15
1952	*	*	*	£8

ELIZABETH II

	F	VF	EF	BU
1953	*	*	*	£2
1953 proof	*	*	*	£8
1954	*	*	*	£5
1955	*	*	*	£4
1956	*	*	*	£5
1957	*	*	*	£2
1958	*	*	*	£2
1959	*	*	*	£1
1960	*	*	*	£1
1962	*	*	*	*
1963	*	*	*	*
1964	*	*	*	*
1965	*	*	*	*
1966	*	*	*	*
1967	*	*	*	*

■ COPPER FARTHINGS

OLIVER CROMWELL

	Fair	F	VF	EF
Patterns only	*	£2850	£5750	£9000

CHARLES II

	Fair	F	VF	EF
1671 patterns only	*	*	£350	£750
1672	£2	£35	£175	£685
1672 no stop on obv	£5	£45	£250	£750
1672 loose drapery				

	Fair	F	VF	EF
at Britannia's elbow	£4	£35	£200	£775
1673	£1	£35	£175	£650
1673 CAROLA error	£30	£125	£465	*
1673 BRITINNIA error			ext. rare	
1673 no stops on obv	£30	£125	*	*
1673 rev no stop	£25	£125	*	*
1674	*	£35	£175	£725
1675	*	£35	£175	£685
1675 no stop after CAROLVS	£45	£165	*	*
1679	*	£25	£175	£775
1679 no stop on rev	£7	£75	£300	*
1694 tin, various edge readings	£35	£175	£550	£3000
1685 tin		ext. rare	*	*

ABOVE: James II 1685 tin Farthing

JAMES II

	Fair	F	VF	EF
1684 tin		ext. rare		*
1685 tin, various edge readings	£60	£165	£600	£2650
1686 tin, various edge readings	£70	£185	£600	£3000
1687 tin, draped bust, various readings		ext. rare	*	*

WILLIAM AND MARY

	Fair	F	VF	EF
1689 tin, date in exergue and on edge, many varieties	£250	£500	*	*
1689/90 tin, 1689 in exergue, 1690 on edge	*	*	*	*
1689/90 tin, 1690 in exergue, 1689 on edge	*	*	*	*
1690 tin, various types	£40	£150	£475	£2650
1691 tin, small and large figures	£40	£150	£475	£2650
1692 tin	£40	£150	£475	£2650
1694 copper, many varieties	£10	£50	£165	£800

ABOVE: William and Mary 1694 Farthing

MILLED COINAGE

WILLIAM III	Fair	F	VF	EF
Type 1, date in exergue				
1695	£2	£40	£160	£725
1695 GVLIELMV error	£60	£185	*	*
1696	*	£40	£145	£700
1697	*	£40	£145	£700
1698	£50	£175	£450	*
1699	£2	£40	£150	£700
1700	£2	£40	£145	£700
Type 2, date in legend				
1698	£5	£45	£175	£750
1699	£5	£45	£185	£775

ANNE
1714 patterns F   *   *   £475   £875

ABOVE: George I 1717 'dump' Farthing

GEORGE I
Smaller flan, 'dump type'
1717	*	£150	£375	£875
1718		unique		
1718 silver proof	*	*	*	£3000

Larger flan
1719 large lettering on obv	£3	£35	£200	£600
1719 small lettering on obv	£3	£35	£200	£625
1719 last A over I in BRITANNIA	£10	£60	£295	*

ABOVE: George I 1721 Farthing

1719 legend continuous over bust	£20	£60	*	*
1720 large lettering on obv	£20	£60	£275	*
1720 small lettering on obv	£2	£20	£110	£525
1721	£2	£20	£110	£500
1721/0	£5	£40	£125	£525
1722 large lettering on obv	*	£25	£125	£550
1722 small lettering on obv	*	£20	£110	£500

	Fair	F	VF	EF
1723	*	£20	£125	£525
1723 R/R REX	£12	£75	£150	£650
1724	£5	£25	£125	£550

GEORGE II
1730	*	£10	£55	£300
1731	*	£10	£55	£300
1732	*	£12	£60	£350
1733	*	£10	£50	£300
1734	*	£10	£55	£350
1734 no stops on obv	*	£12	£70	£400
1735	*	£10	£40	£300
1735 3/3	*	£12	£70	£400
1736	*	£10	£50	£300
1736 triple tie-riband	*	£15	£70	£400
1737 small date	*	£10	£45	£300
1737 large date	*	£10	£45	£300
1739	*	£10	£45	£300
1739/5	*	£10	£55	£375
1741 OH	*	£10	£45	£225
1744	*	£10	£55	£265
1746	*	£10	£45	£225
1746 V/U	ext. rare	*	*	*
1749	*	£10	£45	£200
1750	*	£10	£55	£250
1754/0	*	£20	£80	£275
1754	*	£8	£40	£165

GEORGE III
	F	VF	EF	BU
1771	£5	£45	£200	£550
1773	£5	£30	£175	£400
1774	£5	£30	£175	£400
1775	£5	£30	£175	£400
1799	*	*	£50	£120
1806	*	£3	£50	£120
1807	*	£4	£50	£130

GEORGE IV
1821	*	£8	£45	£130
1822	*	£8	£45	£130
1823	*	£8	£45	£130
1825	*	£8	£45	£130
1825 D/U in DEI	*	£50	£175	*
1826 date on rev	*	£10	£60	£150
1826 date on obv	*	£9	£50	£135
1826 I for 1 in date	£15	£65	£300	£575
1826 proof	*	*	*	£300
1827	*	£9	£50	£140
1828	*	£9	£55	£135
1829	*	£10	£60	£180
1830	*	£9	£50	£135

WILLIAM IV
1831	*	£7	£55	£150
1831 proof	*	*	*	£395
1834	*	£7	£55	£150
1835	*	£7	£50	£165
1836	*	£7	£50	£165
1837	*	£7	£55	£165

BRITISH COINS MARKET VALUES 2022   **127**

MILLED COINAGE

	F	VF	EF	BU
VICTORIA				
1838	*	£5	£35	£160
1839	*	£5	£35	£150
1839 proof	*	*	*	£485
1840	*	£5	£35	£150
1841	*	£5	£35	£150
1842	*	£35	£100	£350
1843	*	£5	£40	£150
1843 I for 1	£40	£200	£575	*
1844	£35	£200	£600	£2000
1845	*	£6	£30	£145
1846	*	£6	£60	£165
1847	*	£5	£40	£140
1848	*	£6	£40	£140
1849	*	£50	£325	*
1850	*	£5	£35	£140
1851	*	£15	£50	£165
1851 D/D sideways	£10	£75	£300	£850
1852	*	£12	£55	£165
1853 proof	*	*	*	£750
1853 w.w. raised	*	£5	£35	£125
1853 w.w. inc	*	£20	£85	£275
1854	*	£5	£35	£100
1855	*	£6	£45	£140
1855 w.w. raised	*	£6	£40	£140
1856 w.w. inc	*	£7	£55	£165
1856 R/E in VICTORIA		£10	£50	£275
1857	*	£5	£40	£125
1858	*	£5	£40	£125
1859	*	£15	£50	£195
1860 proof	*	*	*	£8500

ABOVE: Victoria 1859 copper Farthing

■ BRONZE FARTHINGS

VICTORIA				
1860 BB	*	£2	£20	£85
1860 TB/BB (mule)	£100	£200	£485	*
1860 TB	*	£1	£15	£75
1861	*	£1	£12	£75
1862 small 8	*	£1	£12	£65
1862 large 8	£40	£100	£225	*
1863	£20	£40	£150	£395
1864	*	£3	£30	£110
1865	*	£3	£25	£85
1865–5/2	*	£5	£35	£135
1866	*	£2	£20	£80
1867	*	£3	£30	£100
1868	*	£3	£30	£100

	F	VF	EF	BU
1869	*	£8	£40	£125
1872	*	£2	£20	£80
1873	*	£3	£20	£80
1874 H	*	£5	£30	£90
1874 H G sideways/Gs	£65	£175	£475	*
1875 large date	*	£10	£35	£125
1875 small date	£8	£20	£90	£300
1875 older features	*	£20	£80	£250
1875 H	*	£2	£15	£70
1875 H older features	£60	£175	£300	*
1876 H	*	£10	£35	£120
1877 proof only				£6250
1878	*	£2	£10	£75
1879	*	£2	£20	£80
1879 large 9	*	£1	£12	£90
1880	*	£2	£25	£95
1881	*	£5	£20	£75
1881 H	*	£2	£20	£75
1882 H	*	£2	£20	£75
1883	*	£5	£35	£110
1884	*	*	£12	£50
1885	*	*	£12	£50
1886	*	*	£12	£50
1887	*	*	£20	£75
1888	*	*	£12	£50
1890	*	*	£12	£55
1891	*	*	£12	£55
1892	*	£9	£35	£120
1893	*	*	£10	£60
1894	*	*	£12	£70
1895	*	£15	£60	£200
1895 OH	*	*	£3	£25
1896		*	£5	£30
1897 bright finish	*	*	£3	£30
1897 black finish higher horizon	*	*	£2	£30
1898	*	*	£3	£30
1899	*	*	£2	£30
1900	*	*	£2	£30
1901	*	*	£2	£15
EDWARD VII				
1902	*	*	£3	£20
1903 low horizon	*	*	£4	£20
1904	*	*	£4	£20
1905	*	*	£4	£20
1906	*	*	£4	£20
1907	*	*	£4	£20
1908	*	*	£4	£20
1909	*	*	£4	£20
1910	*	*	£8	£25
GEORGE V				
1911	*	*	£4	£15
1912	*	*	£4	£15
1913	*	*	£4	£15
1914	*	*	£4	£15
1915	*	*	£4	£15
1916	*	*	£4	£15

MILLED COINAGE

	F	VF	EF	BU
1917	*	*	£4	£10
1918 black finish	*	*	£6	£20
1919 bright finish	*	*	£3	£9
1919	*	*	£3	£10
1920	*	*	£3	£10
1921	*	*	£3	£10
1922	*	*	£3	£10
1923	*	*	£3	£10
1924	*	*	£3	£10
1925	*	*	£3	£10
1926 mod eff	*	*	£2	£8
1927	*	*	£2	£6
1928	*	*	*	£3
1929	*	*	*	£3
1930	*	*	*	£3
1931	*	*	*	£3
1932	*	*	*	£3
1933	*	*	*	£3
1934	*	*	*	£5
1935	*	*	£1	£7
1936	*	*	*	£2

GEORGE VI

	F	VF	EF	BU
1937	*	*	*	£2
1937 proof	*	*	*	£7
1938	*	*	*	£7
1939	*	*	*	£3
1940	*	*	*	£3
1941	*	*	*	£3
1942	*	*	*	£3
1943	*	*	*	£3
1944	*	*	*	£3
1945	*	*	*	£3
1946	*	*	*	£3
1947	*	*	*	£3
1948	*	*	*	£3
1949	*	*	*	£3
1950	*	*	*	£3
1950 proof	*	*	*	£7
1951	*	*	*	£3
1951 proof	*	*	*	£7
1952	*	*	*	£3

ELIZABETH II

	F	VF	EF	BU
1953	*	*	*	£2
1954	*	*	*	£2
1955	*	*	*	£2
1956	*	*	*	£4

■ FRACTIONS OF FARTHINGS

Copper Half-Farthings

GEORGE IV

	F	VF	EF	BU
1828 Britannia breaks legend	£5	£20	£100	£300
1828 Britannia below legend	£8	£35	£110	£350
1830 trident breaks legend	£5	£25	£100	£295
1830 trident to base of legend	£20	£60	£225	*

	F	VF	EF	BU
WILLIAM IV				
1837	£40	£125	£325	*
VICTORIA				
1839	*	£6	£40	£125
1842	*	£6	£40	£125
1843	*	*	£15	£70
1844	*	*	£15	£70
1844 E/N	£3	£12	£75	£250
1847	*	£5	£20	£85
1851	*	£5	£40	£125
1852	*	£5	£40	£125
1853	*	£8	£45	£140
1853 proof				£675
1854	*	£20	£80	£250
1856	*	£20	£80	£250
1856 large date	£40	£95	£300	*
1868 bronze proof	*			£500
1868 copper-nickel proof	*			£600

Copper Third-Farthings

GEORGE IV

	F	VF	EF	BU
1827	*	£10	£55	£165

WILLIAM IV

	F	VF	EF	BU
1835	*	£12	£85	£225

VICTORIA

	F	VF	EF	BU
1844	*	£25	£85	£325
1844 RE for REG	£25	£60	£325	*

Bronze Third-Farthings

VICTORIA

	F	VF	EF	BU
1866	*	*	£15	£60
1868	*	*	£15	£60
1876	*	*	£15	£65
1878	*	*	£15	£60
1881	*	*	£15	£65
1884	*	*	£10	£60
1885	*	*	£10	£60

EDWARD VII

	F	VF	EF	BU
1902	*	*	£8	£28

GEORGE V

	F	VF	EF	BU
1913	*	*	£8	£28

Copper Quarter-Farthings

VICTORIA

	F	VF	EF	BU
1839	£8	£15	£40	£125
1851	£8	£15	£40	£145
1852	£8	£15	£40	£110
1853	£8	£18	£50	£125
1853 proof	*	*	*	£625
1868 bronze-proof	*	*	*	£475
1868 copper-nickel proof	*	*	*	£600

BRITISH COINS MARKET VALUES 2022 **129**

Knightsbridge Coins

Wanted To Purchase Or For Auction

UNA AND THE LION £5

GEORGE IV 1826 £5

VICTORIA 1887 PROOF £5

VICTORIA 1893 PROOF £5

Single Pieces or Complete Sets, Purchased or for Auction

Generous Advances Available

The Best Commission Rates

For enquiries and to consign please contact:

Knightsbridge Coins

43 Duke Street, St James's, London SW1Y 6DD
Tel: +44 (0)207 930 7597 | Fax: +44 (0)207 839 5500
www.knightsbridgecoins.com | info@knightsbridgecoins.com

MAUNDY SETS

These sets are given out by the monarch each year on Maundy Thursday, the day before Good Friday. The number of recipients and the amount they receive matches the sovereign's age that year. Maundy coins are newly minted every year, and are legal tender. The first recorded occasion when the sovereign distributed alms at a Maundy service was in 1210, when King John did so at Knaresborough. Extremely Fine prices are for evenly matched sets.

CHARLES II	F	VF	EF
Undated	£200	£325	£750
1670	£190	£350	£725
1671	£190	£325	£700
1672	£180	£300	£650
1673	£190	£325	£600
1674	£170	£295	£625
1675	£170	£290	£625
1676	£190	£325	£650
1677	£190	£300	£650
1678	£250	£395	£825
1679	£195	£325	£675
1680	£170	£300	£650
1681	£195	£350	£650
1682	£190	£325	£600
1683	£190	£325	£650
1684	£220	£390	£750

JAMES II	F	VF	EF
1686	£195	£395	£800
1687	£195	£395	£800
1688	£195	£395	£800

WILLIAM AND MARY	F	VF	EF
1689	£525	£1000	*
1691	£385	£700	£1500
1692	£375	£625	£1450
1693	£350	£600	£1500
1694	£350	£575	£1100

WILLIAM III	F	VF	EF
1698	£200	£400	£800
1699	£450	£700	£1500
1700	£200	£400	£850
1701	£195	£385	£775

ANNE	F	VF	EF
1703	£195	£350	£700
1705	£195	£350	£650
1706	£180	£325	£625
1708	£300	£650	*
1709	£225	£380	£850
1710	£230	£380	£800
1713	£195	£350	£675

GEORGE I	F	VF	EF
1723	£195	£300	£685
1727	£185	£325	£700

GEORGE II	F	VF	EF
1729	£150	£245	£500
1731	£150	£245	£500
1732	£150	£245	£500
1735	£150	£245	£500
1737	£150	£245	£500
1739	£150	£250	£500
1740	£150	£250	£500
1743	£170	£275	£575
1746	£150	£240	£475
1760	£150	£240	£425

GEORGE III	F	VF	EF
1763	*	£225	£400
1763 proof	*	*	£15000
1766	*	£225	£400
1772	*	£235	£425
1780	*	£250	£450
1784	*	£225	£400
1786	*	£225	£400
1792 wire type	*	£300	£550
1795	*	£180	£300
1800	*	£180	£300

	F	VF	EF	Unc
1817	*	£120	£245	£400
1818	*	£120	£245	£400
1820	*	£120	£245	£400

ABOVE: George III Maundy set, 1818

GEORGE IV	F	VF	EF	Unc
1822	*	*	£225	£350
1823	*	*	£225	£350
1824	*	*	£225	£350
1825	*	*	£225	£350
1826	*	*	£225	£350
1827	*	*	£225	£350
1828	*	*	£225	£350
1829	*	*	£225	£350
1830	*	*	£225	£350

WILLIAM IV	F	VF	EF	Unc
1831	*	*	£225	£395
1831 proof	*	*	*	£1500
1831 gold proof	*	*	*	£38000
1832	*	*	£225	£400
1833	*	*	£225	£400

MAUNDY SETS

	F	VF	EF	Unc
1834	*	*	£225	£400
1835	*	*	£225	£400
1836	*	*	£225	£400
1837	*	*	£250	£425

VICTORIA

	EF	Unc
1838	£220	£450
1838 proof	*	£2500
1838 gold proof	*	£27500
1839	£250	£425
1839 proof	£600	£1500
1840	£265	£400
1841	£250	£565
1842	£240	£525
1843	£220	£400
1844	£225	£450
1845	£200	£400
1846	£375	£675
1847	£500	£825
1848	£485	£725
1849	£285	£475
1850	£200	£395
1851	£220	£400
1852	£500	£800
1853	£500	£975
1853 proof	*	£2250
1854	£210	£375
1855	£210	£325
1856	£185	£395
1857	£200	£325
1858	£185	£325
1859	£185	£325
1860	£185	£325
1861	£185	£325
1862	£200	£350
1863	£225	£400
1864	£185	£325
1865	£185	£325
1866	£185	£325
1867	£185	£325
1868	£185	£325
1869	£225	£365
1870	£175	£275
1871	£165	£275
1872	£165	£275
1873	£165	£275
1874	£165	£275
1875	£165	£275
1876	£165	£275
1877	£165	£275
1878	£165	£275
1879	£165	£275
1880	£165	£275
1881	£150	£275
1882	£150	£275
1883	£150	£275
1884	£150	£275
1885	£150	£275
1886	£150	£275
1887	£150	£285
1888 JH	£140	£210
1889	£140	£210
1890	£140	£210
1891	£140	£210
1892	£140	£210
1893 OH	£110	£165
1894	£120	£185
1895	£110	£165
1896	£110	£165
1897	£110	£165
1898	£110	£165
1899	£110	£165
1900	£110	£165
1901	£110	£165

EDWARD VII

	EF	Unc
1902	£100	£160
1902 matt proof	*	£250
1903–08	£100	£135
1909–10	£170	£250

GEORGE V

	EF	Unc
1911	£140	£275
1911 proof	*	£250
1912–36	£140	£225

GEORGE VI

	EF	Unc
1937	£120	£195
1938–52	£140	£225

ELIZABETH II

	EF	Unc
1953	*	£1000
1953 proof gold	ext. rare	
1953 matt proof	ext. rare	
1954–69	*	£190
1970–99	*	£200
2000	*	£200
2001	*	£200
2002	*	£200
2002 gold from set	*	£2000
2003	*	£200
2004	*	£200
2005	*	£200
2006	*	£200
2007	*	£225
2008	*	£550
2009	*	£485
2010	*	£475
2011	*	£475
2012	*	£450
2013	*	£575
2014	*	£600
2015	*	£575
2016	*	£600
2017	*	£595
2018	*	£675
2019	*	£725
2020	*	£700
2021	*	£750

DECIMAL COINAGE

■ BRITANNIAS

A United Kingdom gold bullion coin, introduced in the autumn of 1987, which contains one ounce of 22ct gold and has a face value of £100. There are also ½ ounce, ¼ ounce and 1/10 ounce versions, with face values of £50, £25 and £10 respectively. The ½ and ¼ oz are issued only in sets. All are legal tender.

The coins bear a portrait of the Queen on the obverse and the figure of Britannia on the reverse.

BV means bullion value. At the time of going to press gold is around £1000 per troy ounce and platinum is around £1100 per troy ounce.

1987–2005 1oz, proof	*
1987–2005 1/10 oz, proof	*
1987–2005 ½ oz, proof	*
1987–2005 ¼ oz, proof	*

To commemorate the 10th anniversary of the first Britannia issue, new reverse designs were introduced for the gold coins. A series of four silver coins with denominations from £2 to 20 pence was also issued. The silver coins were issued only in proof condition in 1997.

1997 1oz, ¼oz and 1/10oz issued individually; all coins issued in 4-coin sets
1997 1oz, ¼ oz silver coins issued individually; all coins issued in 4-coin sets
1998 gold and silver coins issued with new portrait of HM the Queen and first reverse design
2001 new reverse designs introduced
For all issues from 2011 see the Royal Mint website.

■ FIVE POUNDS
Crown sized.

1990 Queen Mother's 90th birthday, gold, proof	BV
1990 silver, proof	£30
1990 cu-ni, BU	£6
1990 cu-ni, specimen	£7
1993 40th Anniversary of the Coronation, gold, proof	BV
1993 silver, proof	£30
1993 cu-ni, specimen	£8
1993 cu-ni, BU	£5
1993 cu-ni, proof, originally issued in a Royal Mint set	£8
1996 Queen's 70th Birthday, gold, proof	BV
1996 silver, proof	£30
1996 cu-ni, BU	£7
1996 cu-ni, proof, originally issued in a Royal Mint set	£7
1996 cu-ni, specimen	£8
1997 Golden Wedding, gold, proof	BV
1997 silver, proof	£30
1997 cu-ni, BU	£7
1997 cu-ni, proof, originally issued in a Royal Mint set	£7
1997 cu-ni, specimen	£9
1998 Prince Charles 50th Birthday, gold, proof	BV
1998 silver, proof	£60
1998 cu-ni, BU	£7
1998 cu-ni, proof, originally issued in a Royal Mint set	£10
1998 cu-ni, specimen	£8
1999 Diana Memorial, gold, proof	BV
1999 silver, proof	£40
1999 cu-ni, proof, originally issued in a Royal Mint set	£10
1999 cu-ni, BU	£7
1999 cu-ni, specimen	£8
1999 Millennium, gold, proof	BV
1999 silver, proof	£40
1999 cu-ni, BU	£6
1999 cu-ni, specimen	£8
2000 gold, proof	BV
2000 silver with 22 carat gold, proof	£40
2000 cu-ni, BU	£6
2000 cu-ni, specimen	£13
2000 cu-ni, proof, originally issued in a Royal Mint set	£12
2000 cu-ni, specimen, Dome mintmark	£15
2000 silver, proof	£55
2000 Queen Mother commemorative, gold, proof	BV
2000 silver, proof	£40
2000 silver piedfort	£55
2000 cu-ni, BU	£6
2000 cu-ni, proof, originally issued in a Royal Mint set	£7
2001 Victorian Era anniversary, gold, proof	BV
2001 gold, proof with reverse frosting	BV
2001 silver, proof	£45
2001 silver, proof with reverse frosting	£90
2001 cu-ni, BU	£6
2001 cu-ni, proof, originally issued in a Royal Mint set	£10
2001 cu-ni, specimen	£8
2002 Golden Jubilee, gold proof	BV
2002 silver, proof	£50
2002 cu-ni, BU	£5
2002 cu-ni, proof, originally issued in a Royal Mint set	£9
2002 cu-ni, specimen	£8
2002 Queen Mother memorial, gold, proof	BV
2002 silver, proof	£35
2002 cu-ni, BU	£7
2002 cu-ni proof, originally issued in a Royal Mint set	£12
2003 Coronation commemorative, gold proof	BV
2003 silver, proof	£35
2003 cu-ni, BU	£6
2003 cu-ni, proof, originally issued in a Royal Mint set	£8
2003 cu-ni, specimen	£9
2004 Entente Cordiale, gold, proof	BV
2004 platinum, piedfort, proof	BV
2004 silver piedfort, proof	£100
2004 silver, proof	£45
2004 Entente Cordiale, cu-ni, proof	£14
2004 specimen	£10
2004 BU	£5
2005 Trafalgar, gold, proof	BV
2005 silver piedfort, proof	£110
2005 silver, proof	£40
2005 cu-ni, proof, originally issued in a Royal Mint set	£8
2005 specimen	£8
2005 BU	£5
2005 Nelson, gold, proof	BV
2005 platinum, piedfort, proof	BV
2005 silver piedfort, proof	£110
2005 silver, proof	£45

DECIMAL COINAGE

2005 cu–ni, proof, originally issued in a Royal Mint set	£8
2005 BU	£5
2005 specimen	£8
2006 Queen's 80th Birthday, gold, proof	BV
2006 platinum, piedfort, proof	BV
2006 silver piedfort, proof	£65
2006 silver, proof	£35
2006 cu–ni, proof, originally issued in a Royal Mint set	£8
2006 specimen	£8
2006 BU	£5
2007 Diamond Wedding, gold, proof	BV
2007 silver piedfort, proof	£95
2007 silver, proof	£45
2007 cu–ni, proof, originally issued in a Royal Mint set	£12
2008 Elizabeth I, platinum, piedfort, proof	BV
2008 gold, proof	BV
2008 silver piedfort, proof	£85
2008 silver, proof	£45
2008 BU	£5
2009 Henry VIII, gold, proof	BV
2009 silver piedfort, proof	£80
2009 silver, proof	£45
2009 Countdown to London gold proof	BV
2009 silver piedfort, proof	£90
2010 Restoration of Monarchy gold proof	BV
2010 silver, proof	£40
2010 Countdown to London silver, piedforf, proof	£100
2010 silver, proof	£40
2010 BU	£5

■ TWO POUNDS

1986 Commonwealth Games, proof gold	BV
1986 silver, proof	£20
1986 silver unc	£15
1986 proof, nickel brass, originally issued in a Royal Mint set	£5
1986 specimen	£4
1986 unc	£3
1989 Bill of Rights, silver piedfort, proof, originally issued in a Royal Mint set	£60
1989 silver, proof	£35
1989 proof, nickel brass, originally issued in a Royal Mint set	£7
1989 specimen	£4
1989 unc	£3
1989 Claim of Rights, silver piedfort proof, originally issued in a Royal Mint set	£60
1989 silver, proof	£35
1989 proof, nickel brass, originally issued in a Royal Mint set	£7
1989 specimen	£4
1989 unc	£3
1994 Bank of England, gold, proof	BV
1994 gold 'mule', proof	BV
1994 silver piedfort, proof	£40
1994 silver, proof	£30
1994 proof, nickel brass, originally issued in a Royal Mint set	£5
1994 specimen	£4
1994 in folder, BU	£3
1995 50th Anniversary of end of Second World War, gold, proof	BV
1995 silver piedfort, proof	£40
1995 silver, proof	£30
1995 proof, nickel brass, originally issued in a Royal Mint set	£5
1995 specimen	£4
1995 BU	£3
1995 50th Anniversary of United Nations, gold, proof	BV
1995 silver piedfort, proof	£40
1995 silver, proof	£30
1995 specimen	£4
1995 BU	£3
1996 European Football, gold, proof	BV
1996 silver piedfort, proof	£40
1996 silver, proof	£30
1996 proof, nickel brass, originally issued in a Royal Mint set	£5
1996 specimen	£4
1996 BU	£3
1997 Iron Age, bimetal, gold, proof	BV
1997 silver piedfort, proof	£40
1997 silver, proof	£30
1997 proof, originally issued in a Royal Mint set	£5
1997 specimen	£4
1997 BU	£3
1997 Britannia chariot, proof, 1 oz fine silver	£35
1998 bimetal, silver, proof	£30
1998 silver piedfort	£60
1998 proof, originally issued in a Royal Mint set	£6
1998 in folder, BU	£6
1998 Britannia standing, proof, 1 oz fine silver	£25
1998 unc	£10
1999 Rugby World Cup, gold, proof	BV
1999 silver piedfort, proof	£70
1999 silver, proof	£35
1999 proof, originally issued in a Royal Mint set	£5
1999 BU	£3
2000 bimetal, silver, proof, originally issued in a Royal Mint set	£30
2000 proof, originally issued in a Royal Mint set	£5
2000 Britannia standing, unc, 1 oz fine silver	£25
2001 Marconi commemorative, gold, proof	BV
2001 silver piedfort, proof	£70
2001 silver, proof	£35
2001 with reverse frosting, silver, proof	£40
2001 proof, originally issued in a Royal Mint set	£7
2001 specimen	£5
2001 BU	£3
2002 Iron Age, gold proof	BV
2002 Commonwealth Games, gold, proof, four different reverses	*
2002 Commonwealth Games, silver, proof, four different reverses	*
2002 Commonwealth Games, piedfort, four different reverses	*
2002 Commonwealth Games, BU, four different reverses	*
2002 Britannia standing, unc, 1 oz fine silver	£10
2003 DNA gold bi-metal proof	BV
2003 silver piedfort, proof	£70
2003 silver, proof	£35

BRITISH COINS MARKET VALUES 2022

DECIMAL COINAGE

2003 specimen	£5
2003 proof, originally issued in a Royal Mint set	£6
2003 BU	£3
2003 Britannia helmeted, silver, proof	£35
2003 silver	£12
2004 Locomotive, gold, proof	BV
2004 silver piedfort, proof	£60
2004 silver, proof	£35
2004 BU, silver	£22
2004 proof, originally issued in a Royal Mail set	£6
2004 specimen	£6
2004 BU	£3
2004 Britannia standing, proof, 1 oz fine silver	£25
2004 unc	£22
2005 400th Gunpowder Plot gold, proof	BV
2005 silver piedfort, proof	£70
2005 silver, proof	£30
2005 proof, originally issued in a Royal Mint set	£6
2005 specimen	£5
2005 BU	£3
2005 World War II, gold proof	BV
2005 silver, proof, piedfort	£70
2005 silver, proof	£30
2005 specimen	£5
2005 BU	£3
2005 Britannia seated, silver, proof	£30
2005 silver, unc	£14
2006 Brunel the Man, gold, proof	BV
2006 silver, proof, piedfort	£80
2006 silver, proof	£30
2006 proof, originally issued in a Royal Mint set	£7
2006 specimen	£8
2006 BU	£3
2006 Britannia seated, silver, proof	£35
2007 Abolition of the Slave Trade, gold, proof	BV
2007 silver, proof	£35
2007 Act of Union, silver, proof	£35
2007 Britannia, silver	£22
2007 BU	£3
2008 Olympiad London, gold, proof	BV
2008 silver, proof, piedfort	£70
2008 silver, proof	£30
2008 specimen	£8
2008 BU	£3
2009 Brunel, gold, proof	BV
2009 Paddington London, gold, proof	BV
2009 Brunel, piedfort, silver proof	£75
2009 Darwin, piedfort silver proof	£70
2009 silver, proof	£40
2009 Burns, silver proof	£35
2009 Darwin, silver proof	£35
2009 BU	face
2009 Burns, cu-ni, BU	£3
2009 Darwin, cu-ni, BU	£3
2010 Nightingale, gold proof	BV
2010 silver, proof	£40
2010 Nightingale, silver proof	£35
2010 Nightingale, piedfort silver proof	£70
2010 BU	face
2010 Nightingale, cu-ni, BU	face

■ ONE POUND

1983	£3
1983 specimen	£4
1983 proof, originally issued in a Royal Mint set	£4
1983 silver, proof	£20
1983 silver, proof, piedfort	£50
1984 Scottish reverse	£3
1984 specimen	£4
1984 proof, originally issued in a Royal Mint set	£4
1984 silver, proof	£20
1984 silver, proof, piedfort	£45
1985 new portrait, Welsh reverse	£4
1985 specimen	£4
1985 proof, originally issued in a Royal Mint set	£4
1985 silver, proof	£20
1985 silver, proof, piedfort	£45
1986 Northern Ireland reverse	£5
1986 specimen	£4
1986 proof, originally issued in a Royal Mint set	£4
1986 silver, proof	£20
1986 silver, proof, piedfort	£4
1987 English reverse	£4
1987 specimen	£4
1987 proof, originally issued in a Royal Mint set	£4
1987 silver, proof	£20
1987 silver, proof, piedfort	£45
1988 Royal coat of arms reverse	£5
1988 specimen	£4
1988 proof, originally issued in a Royal Mint set	£4
1988 silver, proof	£25
1988 silver, proof, piedfort	£40
1989 Scottish reverse as 1984	£4
1989 proof, originally issued in a Royal Mint set	£4
1989 silver, proof	£20
1990 Welsh reverse as 1985	£5
1990 proof, originally issued in a Royal Mint set	£4
1990 silver, proof	£20
1991 Northern Ireland reverse as 1986	£4
1991 proof, originally issued in a Royal Mint set	£4
1991 silver, proof	£20
1992 English reverse as 1987	£4
1992 proof, originally issued in a Royal Mint set	£4
1992 silver, proof	£20
1993 Royal coat of arms reverse as 1983	£3
1993 proof, originally issued in a Royal Mint set	£4
1993 silver, proof	£20
1993 silver, proof, piedfort	£35
1994 Scottish Lion	£4
1994 specimen	£4
1994 proof, originally issued in a Royal Mint set	£5
1994 silver, proof	£20
1994 silver, proof, piedfort	£40
1995 Welsh dragon	£4
1995 specimen, English version	£4
1995 specimen, Welsh version	£7
1995 proof, originally issued in a Royal Mint set	£5
1995 silver, proof	£20

DECIMAL COINAGE

1995 silver, proof, piedfort	£70
1996 Northern Ireland Celtic Ring	£4
1996 specimen	£4
1996 proof, originally issued in a Royal Mint set	£5
1995 silver, proof	£20
1995 silver, proof, piedfort	£50
1997 English Lions	£5
1997 specimen	£4
1997 proof, originally issued in a Royal Mint set	£5
1997 silver, proof	£20
1997 silver, proof, piedfort	£50
1998 Royal coat of arms reverse as 1983	£4
1998 proof, originally issued in a Royal Mint set	£5
1998 silver, proof	£20
1998 silver, proof, piedfort	£40
1999 Scottish Lion reverse as 1984	£3
1999 specimen	£4
1999 proof, originally issued in a Royal Mint set	£5
1999 silver, proof	£20
1999 with reverse frosting	£20
1999 silver, proof, piedfort	£35
2000 Welsh Dragon reverse as 1995	£3
2000 proof, originally issued in a Royal Mint set	£5
2000 silver, proof	£20
2000 silver, proof, with reverse frosting	£20
2000 silver, proof, piedfort	£30
2001 Northern Ireland reverse as 1996	£4
2001 proof, originally issued in a Royal Mint set	£5
2001 silver, proof	£20
2001 silver, proof, with reverse frosting	£35
2001 silver, proof, piedfort	£35
2002 English design, reverse as 1997	£4
2002 gold proof, originally issued in a Royal Mint set	BV
2002 proof, originally issued in a Royal Mint set	£5
2002 silver, proof	£20
2002 silver, proof, with reverse frosting	£20
2002 silver, proof, piedfort	£35
2003 Royal Arms	£4
2003 proof, originally issued in a Royal Mint set	£8
2003 silver, proof	£20
2003 silver, proof, piedfort	£35
2003 Forth Rail Bridge, 'pattern', silver, proof, originally issued in a Royal Mint set	*
2004 Dragon, 'pattern', silver, proof, originally issued in a Royal Mint set	*
2005 gold proof, originally issued in a Royal Mint set	BV
2004 Unicorn, 'pattern', silver, proof, originally issued in a Royal Mint set	*
2004 Stag, 'pattern', silver, proof, originally issued in a Royal Mint set	*
2004 Lion, 'pattern', silver, proof, originally issued in a Royal Mint set	*
2004 Forth Rail Bridge	£3
2004 specimen	£5
2004 proof, originally issued in a Royal Mint set	£8
2004 silver, proof	£20
2004 silver, proof, piedfort	£35
2004 gold, proof	BV
2005 Menai Bridge	£4
2005 specimen	£5
2005 proof, originally issued in a Royal Mint set	£8
2005 silver, proof	£20
2005 silver, proof, piedfort	£35
2005 gold, proof	BV
2006 Egyptian Arch	£4
2006 specimen	£5
2006 proof, originally issued in a Royal Mint set	£8
2006 silver, proof	£20
2006 silver, proof, piedfort	£35
2006 gold, proof	BV
2007 Millennium Bridge, gold proof	BV
2007 silver, proof, piedfort	£35
2007 silver, proof	£20
2007 proof	£10
2007 BU	£4
2008 Forth, Menai, Egyptian Arch and Millennium Bridges, gold proof, originally issued in a Royal Mint set	BV
2008 Royal Arms, gold, proof	BV
2008 silver, proof, piedfort	£35
2008 silver, proof	£20
2008 proof	£7
2008 BU	£4
2009 Royal Arms, gold, proof	BV
2009 silver, proof, piedfort	£35
2009 silver, proof	£20
2009 proof	£6
2009 BU	£5
2010 Royal Arms, gold, proof	BV
2010 silver, proof, piedfort	£35
2010 silver, proof	£20
2010 proof	£6
2010 BU	£4
2010 London, gold, proof	BV
2010 silver, proof, piedfort	£35
2010 silver, proof	£20
2010 proof	£6
2010 BU	£4
2010 Belfast, gold, proof	BV
2010 silver, proof, piedfort	£35
2010 silver, proof	£20
2010 proof	£6
2010 BU	£3

Note: edge inscriptions on £2 and £1 are either upright or inverted in relation to the obverse.

■ FIFTY PENCE

1969 unc	£2
1970 unc	£3
1971 proof, originally issued in a Royal Mint set	£3
1972 proof, originally issued in a Royal Mint set	£4
1973 EEC proof, originally issued in a Royal Mint set	£3
1973 silver, proof, VIP	ext. rare
1973 unc	£1
1974 proof, originally issued in a Royal Mint set	£3
1975 proof, originally issued in a Royal Mint set	£3
1976 proof, originally issued in a Royal Mint set	£2
1976 unc	£1
1977 proof, originally issued in a Royal Mint set	£2
1977 unc	£1
1978 proof	£2

DECIMAL COINAGE

1978 unc	£1
1979 proof, originally issued in a Royal Mint set	£2
1979 unc	£1
1980 proof, originally issued in a Royal Mint set	£2
1980 unc	£1
1981 proof, originally issued in a Royal Mint set	£2
1981 unc	£1
1982 proof, originally issued in a Royal Mint set	£2
1982 unc	£1
1983 proof, originally issued in a Royal Mint set	£2
1983 unc	£1
1984 proof, originally issued in a Royal Mint set	£2
1984 unc	£3
1985 proof, originally issued in a Royal Mint set	£2
1985 unc	£4
1986 proof, originally issued in a Royal Mint set	£2
1986 unc	£2
1987 proof, originally issued in a Royal Mint set	£3
1987 unc	£2
1988 proof, originally issued in a Royal Mint set	£3
1988 unc	£2
1989 proof, originally issued in a Royal Mint set	£2
1989 unc	£3
1990 proof, originally issued in a Royal Mint set	£4
1990 unc	£3
1991 proof, originally issued in a Royal Mint set	£4
1991 unc	£2
1992 proof	£4
1992 unc	£2
1992 European Community	£5
1992 specimen	£2
1992 proof, originally issued in a Royal Mint set	£7
1992 silver, proof	£20
1992 silver, proof, piedfort	£35
1992 gold, proof	BV
1993 proof	£3
1993 unc	£3
1994 Normandy Landings	£2
1994 specimen	£2
1994 proof, originally issued in a Royal Mint set	£4
1994 silver, proof	£25
1994 silver, proof, piedfort	£45
1994 gold, proof	£650
1995 proof	£3
1995 unc	£2
1996 proof	£3
1996 unc	£2
1996 silver, proof	£15
1997 unc	£2
1997 proof	£3
1997 silver, proof	£2
1997 new size (27.3mm diameter), unc	£2
1997 proof, originally issued in a Royal Mint set	£4
1997 silver, proof	£18
1997 silver, proof, piedfort	£35
1998 proof, originally issued in a Royal Mint set	£2
1998 unc	£1
1998 European Presidency	£2
1998 specimen	£2
1998 silver, proof	£20
1998 silver, proof, piedfort	£35
1998 gold, proof	£650
1998 NHS, unc	£2
1998 proof, originally issued in a Royal Mint set	£2
1999 silver, proof	£25
1999 silver piedfort	£35
1999 gold, proof	£650
1999 proof, originally issued in a Royal Mint set	£2
1999 unc	face
2000 proof, originally issued in a Royal Mint set	£2
2000 unc	face
2000 silver, proof	£15
2000 Library Commemorative, unc	£2
2000 specimen	£5
2000 proof, originally issued in a Royal Mint set	£2
2000 silver, proof	£25
2000 silver, proof, piedfort	£35
2000 gold, proof	£650
2002 gold proof, originally issued in a Royal Mint set	£650
2003 Suffragette, unc	£1
2003 proof, originally issued in a Royal Mint set	£4
2003 specimen	£3
2003 silver, proof	£20
2003 silver, proof, piedfort	£35
2003 gold, proof	£650
2004 Roger Bannister, unc	£1
2004 specimen	£4
2004 proof, originally issued in a Royal Mint set	£4
2004 silver, proof	£20
2004 silver, proof piedfort	£25
2005 Samuel Johnson, unc	£1
2005 proof, originally issued in a Royal Mint set	£4
2005 silver, proof	£4
2005 silver, proof, piedfort	£35
2005 gold proof	£550
2006 Victoria Cross, unc	£1
2006 proof, originally issued in a Royal Mint set	£4
2006 specimen	£3
2006 silver, proof	£20
2006 silver, proof, piedfort	£35
2006 gold, proof	£650
2007 Scouting Centenary, gold, proof	£650
2007 silver, proof	£25
2007 silver piedfort, proof	£45
2008 issued in sets only	*
2009 gold, proof	£550
2009 silver, proof	£25
2009 unc	£1
2010 England, gold, proof	£650
2010 silver piedfort, proof	£45
2010 silver, proof	£32
2010 Northern Ireland, gold, proof	£650
2010 silver piedfort, proof	£45
2010 silver, proof	£25
2010 Shield, silver proof	£25

■ TWENTY-FIVE PENCE (crown)

1972 Silver Wedding	£1
1972 proof, originally issued in a Royal Mint set	£4

138 BRITISH COINS MARKET VALUES 2022

DECIMAL COINAGE

1972 silver, proof	£20
1977 Jubilee	£1
1977 proof, originally issued in a Royal Mint set	£4
1977 specimen	£2
1977 silver, proof	£20
1980 Queen Mother 80th Birthday	£1
1980 specimen	£2
1980 silver, proof	£25
1981 Royal Wedding	£1
1981 specimen	£3
1981 silver, proof	£25

■ TWENTY PENCE

1982–2010 unc	£1.50
1982–2010 BU	£3
1982–2010 proof, originally issued in a Royal Mint set	£3
1982 silver, proof, piedfort	£28
2000 silver, proof, originally issued in a Royal Mint set	*
2002 gold proof, originally issued in a Royal Mint set	£325
2008, 2008 new rev. gold proofs	£325
2008, 2008 new rev. platinum proofs	£750
2006–2010 silver, proof	£20
2009 error, obverse of 2008, no date	£45

■ TEN PENCE

1968–1981 new pence from	£1
1972 & 1981 proof, originally issued in a Royal Mint set	£2
1982–1984 pence, unc & proof, originally issued in a Royal Mint set	£2
1985–1992 unc & proof, originally issued in a Royal Mint set	£2
1992–1997 new size: 24.5mm diameter, 1993 & 1994 issued in sets only from	£1
1992–1997 proof, originally issued in a Royal Mint set	£2
1992 silver, proof	£10
1992 silver, proof, piedfort	£20
1996 silver, proof	£10
1998–2007, 1998, 1999 & 2007 issued in sets only	face
1998–2010 proof, originally issued in a Royal Mint set	£2
2002 gold proof, originally issued in a Royal Mint set	£300
2008 gold proof	£325
2008 new reverse, gold proof	£325
2008 platinum proof	£500
2008 new reverse, platinum proof	£500
2008 new reverse, silver piedfort proof	£30
2006–2010 silver, proof	£15

■ FIVE PENCE

1968–81, 1972–74, 1976 & 1981 issued in sets only	£0.25
1971–1981 proof, originally issued in a Royal Mint set	£1
1982–1984 proof, unc, originally issued in a Royal Mint set	£1
1985–1990, 1985, 1996 & 1990 issued in sets only	face
1985–1990 proof, originally issued in a Royal Mint set	£2
1990–1997	face
1990–1997 proof, originally issued in a Royal Mint set	£2
1990 silver, proof, originally issued in a Royal Mint set	£10
1990 silver, proof piedfort	£20

1996 silver, proof	£10
1998–2008, 2007–8 issued in sets only	face
1998–2010 proof, originally issued in a Royal Mint set	£3
2000 silver, proof	*
2002 gold proof, originally issued in a Royal Mint set	£300
2008 gold proof	£200
2008 new reverse, gold proof	£200
2008 platinum proof	£275
2008 new reverse, platinum proof	£275
2008 new reverse, silver piedfort proof	£20
2006–2010 silver, proof	£14

■ TWO PENCE

1971–1981, 1972 & 1974 issued in sets only	face
1971–1981 proof, originally issued in a Royal Mint set	£1
1982–1984 new reverse	face
1983, mule, old reverse issued in sets	£400
1982–1984 proof, originally issued in a Royal Mint set	£1
1985–1992 1992 issued in sets only	face
1985–1992 proof, originally issued in a Royal Mint set	£1
1992–1997	face
1993–1997 proof, originally issued in a Royal Mint set	£1
1996, 2000, 2006, 2008 silver proof	£13
2002 gold proof, originally issued in a Royal Mint set	£450
1998–2010	face
1998–2010 proof originally issued in a Royal Mint set	£1
2008 gold proof	£450
2008 new reverse, gold proof	£450
2008 platinum proof	£520
2008 new reverse, platinum proof	£520
2008 new reverse, silver piedfort proof	£30
2006–2010 silver proof	£12

■ ONE PENNY

1971–1981, 1972 issued in sets only from	£1
1971–1981 proof, originally issued in a Royal Mint set	£1
1982–1984 new reverse, proof, unc, originally issued in a Royal Mint set	£1
1985–1992, 1992 issued in sets only	face
1985–1992 proof, originally issued in a Royal Mint set	£1
1992–1997	face
1993–1997 proof, originally issued in a Royal Mint set	£1
1996 silver, proof, originally issued in a Royal Mint set	£12
2002 gold proof, originally issued in a Royal Mint set	£220
2008 gold proof	£220
2008 new reverse, gold proof	£220
2008 platinum proof	£260
2008 new reverse, platinum proof	£260
2008 new reverse, silver piedfort proof	£20
1998–2010	face
1998–2010 proof, originally issued in a Royal Mint set	£1

■ HALF PENNY

1971–1981	£0.10
1971–1981 proof, originally issued in a Royal Mint set	£1
1982–1984 new reverse	face
1982–1984 proof, originally issued in a Royal Mint set	£1

BRITISH COINS MARKET VALUES 2022

PROOF & SPECIMEN SETS

Proof or specimen sets have been issued since 1887 by the Royal Mint. Before then sets were issued privately by the engraver.

Some sets are of currency coins, easily distinguishable from proofs, which have a vastly superior finish. The two 1887 sets frequently come on to the market, hence their place in this list.

The 1953 'plastic' set, though made up of currency coins, is official and was issued in a plastic packet, hence the name. Sets are proof sets unless stated.

GEORGE IV	**FDC**
1826 new issue, £5-farthing (11 coins) from	£130000
WILLIAM IV	
1831 Coronation, £2-farthing (14 coins) from	£80000
VICTORIA	
1839 young head, 'Una and the Lion'	
£5, sovereign-farthing (15 coins) from	£350000
1853 sovereign-half farthing,	
inc Gothic crown (16 coins) from	£100000
1887 Jubilee head, £5-threepence	
('full set': 11 coins) from	£40000
1887 currency set, unofficial	£4500
1887 crown-threepence ('short set': 7 coins)	£4500
1887 currency set, unofficial	£500
1893 old head, £5-threepence	
('full set': 10 coins) from	£45000
1893 crown-threepence ('short set': 6 coins)	£7500
EDWARD VII	
1902 Coronation, £5-Maundy penny,	
matt proofs (13 coins)	£6500
1902 sovereign-Maundy penny, matt proofs (11 coins)	£2200
GEORGE V	
1911 Coronation, £5-Maundy penny (12 coins)	£17500
1911 sovereign-Maundy penny (10 coins)	£3500
1911 halfcrown-Maundy penny (8 coins)	£1450
1927 new types, crown-threepence (6 coins)	£800
GEORGE VI	
1937 Coronation, gold set, £5-half sovereign (4 coins)	£13000
1937 silver and bronze set, crown-farthing	
including Maundy money (15 coins)	£425
1950 mid-century, halfcrown-farthing (9 coins)	£150
1951 Festival of Britain, crown-farthing (10 coins)	£200
ELIZABETH II	
1953 Coronation, crown-farthing (10 coins)	£100
1953 currency, official, known as the 'plastic' set,	
halfcrown-farthing (9 coins)	£20
Specimen decimal set, 1968 10p, 5p;	
1971 2p, 1p, ½p in blue wallet (5 coins)	£1
1970 last £sd coins, (issued 1971-73),	
halfcrown-halfpenny (8 coins)	£18
1971 decimal (issued 1973),	
50p, 10p, 5p, 2p, 1p, ½p (6 coins)	£12
1972 decimal 50p, Silver Wedding	
25p, 10p, 5p, 2p, 1p, ½p (7 coins)	£17
1973-76 decimal, 50p-½p (6 coins)	£13
1977 decimal 50p-½p and Jubilee crown (7 coins)	£13
1978 decimal, 50p-½p (6 coins)	£13
1979 decimal, 50p-½p (6 coins)	£13
1980 decimal, 50p-½p (6 coins)	£13
1980 gold, £5, £2, sovereign, half sovereign (4 coins)	BV
1981 commemorative, £5, sovereign,	
Royal Wedding silver crown, 50p-½p (9 coins)	£1900
1981 commemorative, sovereign and	
Royal Wedding silver crown (2 coins)	£350
1981 decimal, 50p-½p (6 coins)	£13
1982 gold, £5, £2, sovereign, half sovereign (4 coins)	BV
1982 decimal, 50p-½p including 20p (7 coins)	£13
1982 uncirculated decimal,	
50p-½p including 20p (7 coins)	£6
1983 gold, £2, sovereign, half sovereign (3 coins)	BV
1983 decimal, £1-½p (8 coins)	£15
1983 uncirculated decimal, £1-½ p (8 coins)	£13
1984 gold, £5, sovereign, half sovereign (3 coins)	BV
1984 decimal, £1 Scottish rev-½p (8 coins)	£16
1984 uncirculated decimal, £1	
Scottish rev-½p (8 coins)	£10
1985 gold, new portrait, £5, £2,	
sovereign, half sovereign (4 coins)	BV
1985 decimal, £1 Welsh	
rev-1p (7 coins) in deluxe case	£20
1985 in standard case	£13
1985 uncirculated decimal, £1 Welsh rev-1p (7 coins)	£10
1986 gold, Commonwealth Games,	
£2, sovereign, half sovereign (3 coins)	BV
1986 decimal, Commonwealth Games £2,	
Northern Ireland £1-1p	
(8 coins) in deluxe case	£25
1986 in standard case	£19
1986 uncirculated decimal, in folder	£10
1987 gold Britannia, £100-£10 (4 coins)	BV
1987 decimal, £25, £10 (2 coins)	BV
1987 gold, £2, sovereign, half sovereign (3 coins)	BV
1987 decimal, £1 English rev-1p (7 coins) in deluxe case	£25
1987 in standard case	£17
1987 uncirculated decimal, in folder	£8
1988 gold Britannia, £100-£10 (4 coins)	BV
1988 £25, £10 (2 coins)	BV
1988 £2, sovereign, half sovereign (3 coins)	BV
1988 £1 Royal Arms rev-1p (7 coins) in deluxe case	£24
1988 in standard case	£14
1988 uncirculated decimal, in folder	£9
1989 gold Britannia, £100-£10 (4 coins)	BV
1989 £25, £10 (2 coins)	BV
1989 gold 500th anniversary of the sovereign,	
£5, £2, sovereign, half sovereign (4 coins)	£4500
1989 gold 500th anniversary of the sovereign,	
£2, sovereign, half sovereign (3 coins)	£2350
1989 decimal, Bill of Rights £2, Claim of Right	
£2, £1 Scottish rev, 50p-1p (9 coins) in deluxe case	£35
1989 in standard case	£23

142 BRITISH COINS MARKET VALUES 2022

PROOF & SPECIMEN

1989 silver, Bill of Rights £2, Claim of Right £2 (2 coins)	**£50**
1989 silver piedfort, £2 as above (2 coins)	**£80**
1989 uncirculated, decimal, £2, in folder (2 coins)	**£12**
1989 uncirculated decimal, in folder, £1 Scottish rev-1p (7 coins)	**£18**
1990 gold Britannia, £100–£10 (4 coins)	**BV**
1990 gold, £5, £2, sovereign, half sovereign (4 coins)	**BV**
1990 £2, sovereign, half sovereign (3 coins)	**BV**
1990 silver, 5p, large and small size (2 coins)	**£28**
1990 decimal, £1 Welsh rev-1p including large and small 5p (8 coins) in deluxe case	**£30**
1990 in standard case	**£20**
1990 uncirculated decimal, in folder, £1 Welsh rev as 1985-1p including large and small 5p (8 coins)	**£17**
1991 gold Britannia, £100–£10 (4 coins)	**BV**
1991 gold, £5, £2, sovereign, half sovereign (4 coins)	**BV**
1991 £2, sovereign, half sovereign (3 coins)	**BV**
1991 decimal, £1–1p (7 coins) in deluxe case	**£34**
1991 in standard case	**£25**
1991 uncirculated decimal, in folder,	**£16**
1992 gold Britannia, £100–£10 (4 coins)	**BV**
1992 gold, £5, £2, sovereign, half sovereign (4 coins)	**BV**
1992 £2, sovereign, half sovereign (3 coins)	**BV**
1992 silver, ten pence, large and small size (2 coins)	**£30**
1992 decimal, £1 English rev-1p including two 50p, new 10p (9 coins) in deluxe case	**£30**
1992 in standard case	**£26**
1992 uncirculated decimal, in folder	**£17**
1993 gold Britannia, £100–£10 (4 coins)	**BV**
1993 gold, £5, £2, sovereign, half sovereign (4 coins)	**BV**
1993 £2, sovereign, half sovereign (3 coins)	**BV**
1993 Coronation Anniversary £5, £1–1p (8 coins), in deluxe case	**£37**
1993 in standard case	**£30**
1993 uncirculated decimal, with two 50p, no £5 (8 coins)	**£20**
1994 gold Britannia, £100–£10 (4 coins)	**BV**
1994 gold, Bank of England, £5, £2 sovereign, half sovereign (4 coins)	**BV**
1994 £2 Bank of England, sovereign, half sovereign (3 coins)	**BV**
1994 decimal, £2 Bank of England, £1 Scottish rev, 50p D Day–1p (8 coins) in deluxe case	**£34**
1994 in standard case	**£28**
1994 uncirculated decimal, 1994	**£11**
1995 gold Britannia, £100–£10 (4 coins)	**BV**
1996 gold, £5, £2 Peace, sovereign, half sovereign (4 coins)	**BV**
1996 gold, £2 Peace, sovereign, half sovereign (3 coins)	**BV**
1996 decimal, £2 Peace, £1 Welsh rev-1p (8 coins), deluxe case	**£35**
1996 in standard case	**£28**
1996 uncirculated decimal	**£10**
1996 gold Britannia, £100–£10 (4 coins)	**BV**
1996 gold, £5, £2, sovereign, half sovereign (4 coins)	**BV**
1996 gold, £2, sovereign, half sovereign (3 coins)	**BV**
1996 silver decimal, £1–1p (7 coins)	**£85**
1996 decimal, £5 60th Birthday, £2 Football, £1 Northern Irish rev-1p in deluxe case (9 coins)	**£30**
1996 in standard case	**£28**
1997 gold Britannia, £100–£10 (4 coins)	**BV**
1996 uncirculated decimal, £2–1p (8 coins)	**£8**
1997 gold, £5, £2 bimetal, sovereign, half sovereign (4 coins)	**BV**
1997 £2 bimetal, sovereign, half sovereign (3 coins)	**BV**
1997 silver Britannia, £2-20p	**£100**
1997 decimal, 50p, large and small size	**£55**
1997 Golden Wedding £5, £2 bimetal, £1 English rev-1p with new 50p in deluxe case	**£33**
1997 in standard case	**£28**
1997 uncirculated decimal, £2 bimetal, £1 English rev-1p with new 50p (9 coins)	**£9**
1998 gold Britannia, £100–£10 (4 coins)	**BV**
1998 silver Britannia, £2-20p	**£100**
1998 gold, £5–half sovereign	**BV**
1998 £2–half sovereign	**BV**
1998 decimal, Prince Charles, £5–1p in deluxe case	**£35**
1998 in standard case	**£27**
1998 uncirculated, as above, £2–1p (9 coins)	**£11**
1998 silver, EU and NHS 50p (2 coins)	**£40**
1999 gold Britannia, £100–£10 (4 coins)	**BV**
1999 £5, £2 Rugby World Cup, sovereign, half sovereign	**BV**
1999 £2 Rugby World Cup, sovereign, half sovereign	**BV**
1999 decimal, Diana £5–1p in deluxe case	**£35**
1999 in standard case	**£28**
1999 uncirculated, £2–1p (8 coins)	**£11**
2000 gold Britannia, £100–£10 (4 coins)	**BV**
2000 gold, £5 half sovereign	**BV**
2000 £2–half sovereign	**BV**
2000 decimal, £5–1p Maundy coins (13 coins)	**£250**
2000 executive (10 coins)	**£55**
2000 deluxe (10 coins)	**£32**
2000 standard (10 coins)	**£24**
2001 gold Britannia, £100–£10 (4 coins)	**BV**
2001 gold, £5, £2 Marconi Commemorative, sovereign, half sovereign (4 coins)	**£2700**
2001 £2 Marconi commemorative, sovereign, half sovereign (3 coins)	**BV**
2001 silver Britannia, new reverse designs, £2-20p	**£80**
2001 decimal, executive (10 coins)	**£45**
2001 deluxe (10 coins)	**£32**
2001 gift (10 coins)	**£32**
2001 standard (10 coins)	**£27**
2001 uncirculated, as above but no £5 (9 coins)	**£12**
2002 gold, £5–half sovereign, new reverse design	**BV**
2002 £2–half sovereign, new reverse design	**BV**
2002 Golden Jubilee £5, £2 bimetal, £1 (English rev)–1p plus Maundy coins (13 coins)	**£8000**
2002 Commonwealth Games £2, four reverses: England, Northern Ireland, Scotland and Wales	**BV**
2002 silver, Commonwealth Games, four reverses: £2 England, Northern Ireland, Scotland and Wales	**£98**
2002 gold Britannia, £100–£10 (4 coins)	**BV**
2002 silver piedfort, Commonwealth Games £2, four reverses: England, Northern Ireland, Scotland and Wales	**£195**
2002 decimal, Executive, Golden Jubilee £5,	

PROOF & SPECIMEN

£2 bimetal, £1 English rev-1p (9 coins)	£58
2002 deluxe (9 coins)	£37
2002 gift (9 coins)	£32
2002 standard (9 coins)	£25
2002 uncirculated, 2002, £2 bimetal, £1 English rev-1p (8 coins)	£14
2002 uncirculated, Commonwealth Games £2, reverses: England, Northern Ireland, Scotland and Wales	£12
2003 gold, £5-half sovereign	BV
2003 £2 DNA-half sovereign	BV
2003 pattern set gold pounds (4 coins)	BV
2003 pattern set silver pounds (4 coins)	£80
2003 gold Britannia £100-£10 (4 coins)	BV
2003 silver Britannia £2-20p	£75
Gold set, mixed dates £100 (4 coins)	BV
Silver set, mixed dates £2 (4 coins)	£40
Silver set, mixed dates £2 (4 coins)	£40
Silver set, £5 (2 coins) different types	£50
2003 Silver set, £5-50p Coronation-Suffragette (5 coins)	£140
2003 decimal, executive (11 coins)	£55
2003 deluxe (11 coins)	£37
2003 standard (11 coins)	£28
2003 uncirculated (10 coins)	£11
2004 gold £5-half sovereign (4 coins)	BV
2004 gold, £2-half sovereign (3 coins)	BV
2004 pattern set, gold pounds (4 coins)	BV
2004 pattern set, silver pounds (4 coins)	£80
2004 silver set, £5-50p Entente Cordiale-Bannister (5 coins)	£125
2004 silver piedfort set, £2-50p Penydarren engine-Bannister (3 coins)	£120
2004 gold Britannia, £100-£10 (4 coins)	BV
2004 £50-£10	BV
2004 uncirculated set, 'new coin pack' (10 coins)	£9
2004 deluxe (10 coins)	£23
2004 executive (10 coins)	£42
2004 standard (10 coins)	£18
2005 gold, £5-half sovereign (4 coins)	BV
2005 £2-half sovereign (3 coins)	BV
2005 silver piedfort set, £2-50p Gunpowder Plot-Johnson's Dictionary (4 coins)	£140
2005 silver piedfort set, £5 (2 coins)	£110
2005 decimal, 2005, Executive (12 coins)	£65
2005 deluxe (12 coins)	£40
2005 standard (12 coins)	£30
2005 uncirculated (10 coins)	£12
2005 gold Britannia, £100-£10 (4 coins)	BV
2005 £50-£10 (3 coins)	BV
2005 silver Britannia, £2-20p (4 coins)	£80
2006 gold, £5-half sovereign (4)	BV
2006 £2-half sovereign (3 coins)	BV
2006 gold Britannia, £100-£10 (4 coins)	BV
2006 silver Britannia £2 gold plated, 5 different (5 coins)	£225
2006 gold, Brunel £2 (2 coins)	BV
2006 Victoria Cross 50p (3 coins)	BV
2006 silver, 80th Birthday (13 coins)	£275
2006 silver Britannia (5 coins)	£275
2006 Brunel £2 (2 coins)	£60
2006 silver piedfort, Brunel £2 (2 coins)	£80
2006 silver, 50p, Victoria Cross & Wounded Soldier (2 coins)	£50
2006 silver piedfort, 50 pence (2 coins)	£50
2006 silver piedfort, £5-50p 80th Birthday-Wounded Soldier (6 coins)	£275
2006 executive (13 coins)	£70
2006 deluxe (13 coins)	£45
2006 standard (13 coins)	£35
2007 gold, £5-half sovereign (4 coins)	BV
2007 £2-half sovereign (3 coins)	BV
2007 'Bridge' series (4 coins)	BV
2007 sovereign and half sovereign (2 coins)	BV
2007 platinum Britannia, £100-£10 (4 coins)	BV
2007 silver 'Bridge' series (4 coins)	£115
2007 decimal executive (12 coins)	£79
2007 deluxe (12 coins)	£50
2007 standard (12 coins)	£39
2007 uncirculated (9 coins)	£14
2008 gold Britannia, £100-£10 (4 coins)	BV
2008 gold, £5-half sovereign (4 coins)	BV
2008 gold £2-half sovereign (3 coins)	BV
2008 gold, sovereign and half sovereign (2 coins)	BV
2008 platinum Britannia, £100-£10 (4 coins)	BV
2008 platinum Royal Shield (7 coins)	BV
2008 platinum Emblems of Britain (7 coins)	BV
2008 platinum double set (14 coins)	BV
2008 gold Royal shield (7 coins)	BV
2008 gold Emblems of Britain (7 coins)	BV
2008 gold double set (14 coins)	BV
2008 silver Britannia, £100-£10 (4 coins)	BV
2008 silver Piedfort Royal Shield (6 coins)	£200
2008 silver Royal Shields (6 coins)	£149
2008 silver Emblems of Britain (6 coins)	£149
2008 silver double set (12 coins)	£275
2008 Family (5 coins)	£150
2008 commemorative piedfort (4)	£200
2008 decimal Royal Shields (6 coins)	BV
2008 decimal executive (11 coins)	£60
2008 deluxe (11 coins)	£40
2008 standard (11 coins)	£30
2008 uncirculated (9 coins)	£15
2008 uncirculated Emblems of Britain (9 coins)	£9
2008 Royal Shields (6 coins)	£30
2008 standard royal shields (6 coins)	£9
2008 double set (12 coins)	£18
2009 gold Britannia, £100-£10 (4 coins)	BV
2009 gold, £5-half sovereign (4 coins)	BV
2009 gold £2-half sovereign (3 coins)	BV
2009 silver Britannia, £2-20p	£100
2009 gold, sovereign and half sovereign (2 coins)	BV
2009 silver 50th Anniversary Mini (4 coins)	£150
2009 silver piedfort collection (4 coins)	£225
2009 silver family collection (6 coins)	£150
2009 silver set (12 coins)	£225
2009 decimal executive (12 coins)	£60
2009 deluxe (12 coins)	£40
2009 standard (12 coins)	£32
2009 uncirculated (11 coins)	£16

Sets beyond 2009 are not listed in this guide.

SCOTTISH COINS

■ MINTS IN OPERATION IN SCOTLAND

Map of Scotland showing mint locations. H = A HOARD

Mint towns shown on map: FORRES, INVERNESS, ABERDEEN, MONTROSE, FORFAR, DUNDEE, PERTH (H), ST ANDREWS, STIRLING, LINLITHGOW, KINGHORN (H), DUMBARTON, DUNBAR, EDINBURGH, BERWICK, RENFREW, GLASGOW, KELSO, ROXBURGH, JEDBURGH, BAMBOROUGH, AYR, CROSSRAGUEL ABBEY (H), DUMFRIES, CORBRIDGE, CARLISLE

The mints of the first coinage of Alexander III were the greatest number working together in Scotland, and therefore this area attracts collectors of the different mint issues.

For his reign, we give a price for issues of each mint town, but not for any other reign. From the reign of Mary, all Scottish coins were struck at Edinburgh.

MINT TOWN	KING
Aberdeen	Alexander III, David II, Robert III, James I, II, III
Ayr	Alexander III
Bamborough	Henry
Berwick	David I, Malcolm IV, William I, Alexander II, III, Robert Bruce, James III
Carlisle	David I, Henry
Corbridge	Henry
Dumbarton	Robert III
Dumfries	Alexander III
Dunbar	William I?, Alexander III
Dundee	William I?, Alexander III
Dunfermline	William I
Forfar	Alexander III
Forres	Alexander III
Glasgow	Alexander III
Inverness	Alexander III
Jedburgh	Malcolm IV
Kelso	Alexander II
Kinghorn	Alexander III
Lanark	Alexander III
Linlithgow	James I, II
Montrose	Alexander III
Perth	William I, Alexander III, Robert II–James II
Renfrew	Alexander III
Roxburgh	Alexander III
St Andrews	Alexander III
Stirling	Alexander III, James I, II, Mary Stuart

SCOTTISH COINS

Prices are for the commonest coins in each case.
For further details see *The Scottish Coinage*, by I Stewart (Spink, 1967, reprint 1975) and *Coins of Scotland, Ireland and The Islands* (Spink 2003).

DAVID I 1124–53

	F	VF
Silver Pennies	£1250	£3000

Four different groups; struck at the mints of Berwick, Carlisle, Roxborough and Edinburgh.

HENRY 1136–52
Earl of Huntingdon and Northumberland

	F	VF
Silver Pennies	£3000	£7000

Three types; struck at the mints of Corbridge, Carlisle and Bamborough.

MALCOLM IV 1153–65

	F	VF
Silver Pennies	£5750	£12500

Five types; struck at the mints of Roxburgh and Berwick.

ABOVE: William the Lion Penny, Edinburgh

WILLIAM THE LION 1165–1214

	F	VF
Silver Pennies	£225	£650

Three issues; struck at the mints of Roxburgh, Berwick, Edinburgh, Dun (Dunfermline?), Perth.

ALEXANDER II 1214–49

	F	VF
Silver Pennies	£875	£2500

Mints of Berwick and Roxburgh, varieties of bust.

ABOVE: Alexander III first coinage Penny

ALEXANDER III 1249–86
Transitional coinage 1249–50

Pennies	£500	*

First coinage silver Pennies 1250–80

Aberdeen	£200	£450
Ayr	£225	£500
Berwick	£140	£250
'DUN'	£275	£565
Edinburgh	£175	£350
Forfar	£485	£925
Fres	£400	£875
Glasgow	£225	£450
Inverness	£365	£750
Kinghorn	£525	£1350

	F	VF
Lanark	£350	£825
Montrose	£875	£1950
Perth	£140	£295
Renfrew	£775	£1875
Roxburgh	£140	£295
St Andrews	£350	£750
Stirling	£195	£495
'WILANERTER'	£600	£1475

ABOVE: Alexander III second coinage Halfpenny

Second coinage c1280

Silver Pennies	£45	£125
Halfpennies	£125	£350
Farthings	£350	£750

Many types and varieties.

JOHN BALLIOL 1292–6
First coinage, rough surface issue

Silver Pennies	£175	£485
Halfpennies	£400	£875

Second coinage, smooth surface issue

Silver Pennies	£145	£425
Halfpennies	£250	£600
Farthing	£1750	*

ROBERT BRUCE 1306–29

Silver Pennies	£825	£1950
Halfpennies	£1250	£3500
Farthings	£1750	£4000

Probably all struck at Berwick.

ABOVE: David II Halfgroat

DAVID II 1329–71

Gold Nobles		ext. rare
Silver Groats	£195	£495
Halfgroats	£195	£495
Pennies	£85	£200
Halfpennies	£450	£1100
Farthings	£775	£1850

Three issues, but these denominations were not struck for all issues. Edinburgh and Aberdeen mints.

SCOTTISH COINS

	F	VF
ROBERT II 1371–90		
Silver Groats	£185	£465
Halfgroats	£165	£485
Pennies	£135	£400
Halfpennies	£185	£475

Some varieties. Struck at Dundee, Edinburgh and Perth.

ROBERT III 1390–1406
	F	VF
Gold Lion or Crowns	£2650	£5000
Demy-lions or Halfcrowns	£1350	£3500
Silver groats	£135	£350
Halfgroats	£185	£500
Pennies	£395	£925
Halfpennies	£400	£850

Three issues, many varieties. Struck at mints of Edinburgh, Aberdeen, Perth and Dumbarton.

ABOVE: James I Demy

JAMES I 1406–37
	F	VF
Gold Demies	£1750	£4000
Half-demies	£1850	£4500
Silver Groats	£225	£600
Billon Pennies	£250	£750
Billon Halfpennies	£500	£1500

Mints: Aberdeen, Edinburgh, Inverness, Linlithgow, Perth and Stirling.

JAMES II 1437–60
	F	VF
Gold Demies from	£1750	£3350
Lions from	£2950	£6500
Half lions	£3650	£7500
Silver Groats	£250	£700
Halfgroats	£850	£1750
Billon Pennies	£400	£1000

Two issues, many varieties. Mints: Aberdeen, Edinburgh, Linlithgow, Perth, Roxburgh and Stirling.

ECCLESIASTICAL ISSUES c1452–80
	F	VF
Bishop Kennedy copper Pennies	£140	£365
Copper Farthings	£295	£800

Different types and varieties.

JAMES III 1460–88
		F	VF
Gold Riders	from	£3750	£7500
Half-riders		£4000	£8250
Quarter-riders		£5250	*
Unicorns		£3750	£8750
Silver Groats	from	£500	£975

ABOVE: James IIII Groat

		F	VF
Halfgroats	from	£825	£2750
Pennies	from	£400	£850
Billon Placks	from	£100	£275
Half-Placks	from	£140	£395
Pennies	from	£185	£500
Halfpennies		ext.rare	
Copper Farthings	from	£500	*

Many varieties. Mints: Aberdeen, Berwick and Edinburgh.

ABOVE: James IV Unicorn

JAMES IV 1488–1513
		F	VF
Gold Unicorns		£2500	£5250
Half-unicorns		£1850	£4250
Lions or Crowns		£4250	£10500
Half-lions		£4750	£11500
Pattern Angel			unique
Silver Groats	from	£625	£1625
Halfgroats		£685	£1825
Pennies, light coinage		ext. rare	*
Billon Placks		£40	£100
Half-placks		£125	£400
Pennies		£70	£165

Different types and varieties. Mint: Edinburgh.

ABOVE: James V 1540 'Bonnet' piece

BRITISH COINS MARKET VALUES 2022 **147**

SCOTTISH COINS

JAMES V 1513–42		F	VF
Gold Unicorns		£3000	£6750
Half-unicorns		£3750	£7950
Crowns		£1950	£4000
'Bonnet' pieces or Ducats		£5000	£12000
Two-thirds ducats		£3750	£8750
One-third ducats		£5250	*
Silver Groats	from	£400	£900
One-third groats		£265	£650

ABOVE: James V Groat

Billon Placks	£25	£85
Bawbees	£25	£80
Half-bawbees	£75	£225
Quarter-bawbees		unique

Different issues and varieties. Mint: Edinburgh.

MARY 1542–67

First period 1542–58

Gold Crown	£3250	£7500
Twenty Shillings	£4250	£9250
Lions or Forty-four Shillings	£3000	£7000

ABOVE: Mary three pound piece or ryal

Half-lions or Twenty-two shillings	£1950	£5000
Ryals or Three Pound pieces, 1555, 1557, 1558	£8850	£18000
Half-ryals 1555, 1557, 1558	£9000	£19250
Portrait Testoons, 1553	£7000	*
Non-portrait Testoons, 1555–58	£350	£850
Half-testoons, 1555–58	£295	£725
Billon Bawbees	£45	£125
Half-bawbees	£65	£175
Pennies, facing bust	£225	£650
No bust 1556	£165	£495
Lions, 1555, 1558	£30	£125
Placks, 1557	£45	£125

	F	VF
Second period, Francis and Mary, 1558–60		
Gold Ducats or Sixty shillings		ext. rare
Non-portrait Testoons, 1558–61	£350	£850
Half-testoons, 1558–60	£275	£625
Twelvepenny groats, Nonsunt, 1558–9	£75	£225
Lions, 1559–60	£30	£95

Third period, widowhood, 1560–5

Gold Crown 1561		ext. rare
Portrait Testoons, 1561–2	£3250	£8000
Half-testoons, 1561–2	£3250	£8000

Fourth period, Henry and Mary, 1565–7

Portrait Ryals, 1565		ext. rare
Non-portrait Ryals, 1565–7	£700	£1875

ABOVE: Mary and Henry Darnley 1566 Ryal

Two-third ryals, 1565–7	£495	£1375
Two-third ryals, undated	£1650	£4000
One-third ryals, 1565–6	£600	£1500
Testoon, 1565		ext. rare

Fifth period, 2nd widowhood, 1567

Non-portrait Ryals, 1567	£700	£1925
Two-thirds ryal, 1567	£600	£1750
One-thirds ryals, 1566–7	£625	£1725

Mints: Edinburgh, Stirling (but only for some bawbees).

JAMES VI

Before English accession 1567–1603

First coinage 1567–71

Ryals 1567–71	£485	£1375
Two-third ryals	£375	£825
One-third ryals	£400	£950

Second coinage 1571–80

Gold Twenty Pounds pieces	£38000	£75000
Silver half merks or nobles, 1572–77, 1580	£135	£365
Quarter merks or half nobles	£110	£310

148 BRITISH COINS MARKET VALUES 2022

SCOTTISH COINS

	F	VF
Two merks, 1578–80	£2850	£6500
Merks, 1579–80	£3500	*

Third coinage 1580–81
	F	VF
Gold Ducats, 1580	£8000	£22500
Sixteen shillings, 1581	£300	£7250
Eight shillings, 1581	£2250	£5250
Four shillings, 1581	£3500	*
Two shillings, 1581		ext. rare

Fourth coinage 1582–88
	F	VF
Gold Lion Nobles	£13500	ext. rare
Two-third lion nobles	£11000	£27500
One-third lion nobles	£8750	£22500
Silver Forty shillings, 1582	£7500	£19500
Thirty shillings, 1582–86	£525	£1850
Twenty shillings, 1582–85	£485	£1500
Ten shillings, 1582–84	£295	£1100

ABOVE: James VI 1582 Ten Shillings

Fifth coinage 1588
	F	VF
Gold Thistle nobles	£5000	£12500

Sixth coinage 1591–93
	F	VF
Gold Hat pieces, 1591–93	£7250	£16500
Silver Balance half-merks, 1591–93	£350	£750
Balance quarter merks, 1591	£675	£1500

Seventh coinage 1594–1601
	F	VF
Gold Riders	£1500	£4000
Half Riders	£1550	£4000
Silver Ten Shillings, 1593–95, 1598–1601	£135	£375
Five shillings, 1593–5, 1598–1601	£135	£375

ABOVE: James VI seventh coinage 1593 Five shillings

	F	VF
Thirty-pence pieces 1595–6, 1598–9, 1601	£150	£375
Twelve-pence piece 1594–6	£135	£275

ABOVE: James VI 1603 Sword and Sceptre piece

Eighth coinage 1601–4
	F	VF
Gold Sword and Sceptre pieces	£775	£2000
Half sword and sceptre pieces	£575	£1375
Silver Thistle-merks, 1601–4	£100	£425
Half thistle-merks	£75	£225
Quarter thistle-merks	£65	£200
Eighth thistle-merks, 1601–3	£45	£125

Billon and copper issues
	F	VF
Billon Placks or Eightpenny groats	£20	£90
Half-placks	£135	£400
Hardheads	£40	£150
Saltire Placks	£200	£525
Copper Twopence 1597	£95	£325
Penny 1597	£600	*

After English accession 1603–25
	F	VF
Gold Units	£1100	£2750
Double Crowns	£1650	£4250
Britain Crowns	£700	£1650
Halfcrowns	£575	£1375
Thistle Crowns	£400	£1000
Silver Sixty shillings	£500	£1475
Thirty shillings	£125	£325
Twelve shillings	£135	£400
Six shillings	£500	£1650
Two shillings	£40	£110
One shilling	£65	£165
Sixpences	*	*
Copper Twopences	£20	£60
Pennies	£135	£375

CHARLES I 1625–49
First coinage 1625–36
	F	VF
Gold Units	£1500	£3850
Double Crowns	£3000	£7000
Britain Crowns	ext. rare	
Milled Angel	ext. rare	
Silver Sixty shillings	£875	£2950
Thirty shillings	£150	£450
Twelve shillings	£285	£725
Six shillings	£395	£1250
Two shillings	£65	£165
One shilling	£85	£250

BRITISH COINS MARKET VALUES 2022 149

SCOTTISH COINS

Second coinage 1636	F	VF
Half-merks	£70	£175
Forty-pence pieces	£70	£175
Twenty-pence pieces	£65	£150

Third coinage 1637–42		
Gold Units	£2500	£6000
Half-units	£1150	£4250
Britain Crowns	£1650	£4250
Britain Halfcrowns	£825	£1825
Silver Sixty shillings	£725	£2000
Thirty shillings	£125	£325

ABOVE: Charles I third coinage Briot's issue twelve shillings

Twelve shillings	£110	£300
Six shillings	£90	£225
Half-merks	£90	£225
Forty-pence piece	£35	£100
Twenty-pence piece	£30	£80
Three shillings	£65	£175
Two shillings	£50	£125
Copper twopences, lion	£20	£50
Pennies	£300	*
Twopences, CR crowned	£15	£35
Twopences, Stirling turners	£15	£35

CHARLES II 1660–85
First coinage

Silver Four merks, 1664 thistle above bust	£850	£3000
1664 thistle below bust	£875	£2750
1665	£4000	*
1670	£900	£2250
1673	£800	£2750
1674 F below bust	£800	£2750
1675	£800	£2750
Two merks, 1664 thistle above bust	£485	£1425
1664 thistle below bust	£485	£1425
1670	£485	£1425
1673	£485	£1425
1673 F below bust	ext.rare	
1674	£485	£1425
1674 F below bust	£500	£1750
1675	£385	£1350
Merks, 1664	£110	£375
1665	£125	£485
1666	£275	£750

ABOVE: Charles II first coinage 1669 Merk

	F	VF
1668	£265	£700
1669	£80	£300
1670	£80	£300
1671	£80	£325
1672	£90	£325
1673	£80	£300
1674	£150	£495
1674 F below bust	£120	£375
1675 F below bust	£120	£375
1675	£225	£625
Half-merks, 1664	£175	£500
1665	£250	£675
1666	£295	£700
1667	£225	£700
1668	£225	£725
1669	£90	£350
1670	£90	£350
1671	£100	£325
1672	£100	£325
1673	£120	£400
1675 F below bust	£110	£375
1675	£140	£475

ABOVE: Charles II second coinage 1676 Dollar

Second coinage

Silver Dollars, 1676	£550	£1750
1679	£585	£1800
1680	£725	£2350
1681	£585	£1800
1682	£425	£1650
Half-dollars, 1675	£450	£1325
1676	£525	£1650

150 BRITISH COINS MARKET VALUES 2022

SCOTTISH COINS

	F	VF
1681	£450	£1425
Quarter-dollars, 1675	£135	£475
1676	£120	£350
1677	£120	£375
1678	£125	£450
1679	£135	£475
1680	£120	£375
1681	£120	£375
1682	£125	£425
Eighth-dollars, 1676	£85	£300
1677	£85	£300
1678/7	£175	£575
1679	£250	£600
1680	£80	£275
1682	£250	£600
Sixteenth-dollars, 1677	£65	£225
1678/7	£75	£275
1679/7	£100	£375
1680	£225	£575
1681	£70	£275
Copper twopence, CR crowned	£20	£70
Bawbees, 1677–9	£75	£275
Turners, 1677–9	£50	£150

JAMES VII 1685–9

Silver sixty shillings, 1688, proof only	FDC	£3000
Gold proof only	FDC	£90000

Struck in 1828, not contemporary.

	F	VF
Silver forty shillings, 1687	£350	£1000
1688	£250	£1000
Ten shillings, 1687	£135	£500
1688	£225	£700

WILLIAM AND MARY 1689–94

	F	VF
Sixty shillings, 1691	£650	£2000
1692	£650	£1950
Forty shillings, 1689	£250	£850
1690	£250	£695
1691	£200	£595
1692	£175	£550
1693	£175	£550
1694	£250	£695
Twenty shillings, 1693	£485	£1425
1694	£600	£1625
Ten shillings, 1689	*	*
1690	£275	£750
1691	£150	£495
1692	£150	£495
1694	£240	£675
Five shillings, 1691	£175	£425
1694	£175	£425
Copper Bawbees, 1691–4	£110	£425
Bodles, 1691–4	£35	£120

WILLIAM II 1694–1702

	F	VF
Gold Pistole 1701	£6000	£12500
Half-pistole, 1701	£4500	£10000

	F	VF
Silver sixty shillings, 1699	*	*
Forty shillings, 1695	£195	£500
1696	£200	£525
1697	£250	£600
1698	£250	£625
1699	£250	£625
1700	ext. rare	
Twenty shillings, 1695	£225	£725
1696	£195	£725
1697	£325	£1000
1698	£175	£725
1698/7	£225	£700
1699	£375	£1150

ABOVE: William III 1696 Ten shillings

	F	VF
Ten shillings, 1695	£165	£425
1696	£165	£425
1697	£175	£585
1698	£175	£485
1699	£185	£500
Five shillings, 1695	£100	£275
1696	£90	£250
1697	£90	£250
1699	£90	£250
1700	£90	£250
1701	£110	£400
1702	£125	£400
Copper Bawbees, 1695–7	£85	£375
Bodles, 1695–7	£50	£160

ANNE 1702–14
Pre-Union 1702–7

	F	VF
Ten shillings, 1705	£150	£425
1706	£150	£400
Five shillings, 1705	£60	£165
1706	£60	£165

JAMES VIII 1688–1766 The Old Pretender

Gold Guinea 1716	FDC	£15000
Silver	FDC	£1650
Bronze	FDC	£1350
Crown 1709		unique
Crown 1716, silver	FDC	£3500
Gold		ext. rare
Bronze		ext. rare

The 1716-dated pieces were struck in 1828 from the original dies.

BRITISH COINS MARKET VALUES 2022   **151**

QUIZ
What Kind of Collector are You?

START HERE

COLLECTOR: GENERAL? | ADVANCED? | SPECIALIST?

BUDGET: MODEST? | MEDIUM? | SIGNIFICANT?

YES ← Unit Prices? Per Stamp

NO

Learn about **Top-UpTwenty**, On-line Instant-Purchase Price-Drop Selling-System e-mail updates

Consider **Approvals** but Take Auction 1st £55 Free Offer

Up to 20,000 lot NO Buyers Premium £2M **World Auctions**

Try **Approvals** Est 62 years – 1st £25 Free

Collect **Classic GB** 1840-1940 – send wants list

Take **World Mixtures** 1st 500 Free Trial

Join 2000+ Regular Bidders in 52 different Countries – Unique, All Lots Guaranteed Reducing Estimate **Auctions** + **£55 Free Trial Offer** when you win £75+ – **It's easy to Request your FREE Catalogue Now**

It's Easy to Select Yours Now at UPA

152

De-Mystifying Philately – QUIZ

SELLING

YES → Continuing Collecting?

– Cash / Part exchange/vendor options

NO

Quality Sought – naturally

Contact Andrew Now or another member of his specialist Team to discuss the market/selling options:
andrew@upastampauctions.co.uk
☎ **01451 861111**

'money spent in the wrong way soon mounts up ...'

Successful and enjoyable collecting depends upon understanding the relationship of your budget to your interest.

Offers and services can be confusing can't they, and money spent in the wrong way soon mounts up.

In philately, sometimes it is hard to decide which way to go. Your passion may exceed your resource, so just what may be best for you?

Often, it is not what you collect but how you collect

This is the reason why my team and I have devised this quick and easy philatelic route-map QUIZ which does not ask you what you collect – but helps you to determine by your answers just which type of collecting service may best suit you ...

Presently you may find few philatelic companies other than UPA which can offer you integrated philatelic selling systems, but obviously once you determine which philatelic services best suit your collecting interest – you may have a clearer idea of which way is best to go – depending upon your levels of specialism and philatelic budget, of course

Check out our Philatelic QUIZ right now and see for yourself. To select your choice, visit our website or call my team

Dedicated to De-mystifying Philately

Andrew

Andrew McGavin,
Veteran Philatelic Auctioneer
Philatelic Expert & Author
Managing Director
Universal Philatelic Auctions (UPA)

Visit: www.UPAstampauctions.co.uk

Fax: 01451 861297 ~ info@upastampauctions.co.uk ~ T: 01451 861111
Participate in this Philatelic Route-Map to Enjoyable Collecting.
Find UPA also on-line at www.top-uptwenty.co.uk   BCMV 2022
New Instant-Purchase Price-Drop Selling-System

IRISH COINS

■ HAMMERED ISSUES 995–1661

Most of the Irish coins of this period are in fairly poor condition and it is difficult to find specimens in VF condition or better.

For more details see *The Guide Book to the Coinage of Ireland AD 995 to the Present Day* by Anthony Dowle or Spink's *Coins of Scotland, Ireland & the Islands* by Patrick Finn (Spink 2002) and *Irish Coin Values* by Patrick Finn (Spink 1979). Prices are for the commonest coins in each case.

HIBERNO-NORSE OF DUBLIN 995–1150

This series runs from Phase I to Phase VII and prices quoted are for the commonest type of each phase.

		F	VF
Silver Pennies, imitative of English coins, many types and varieties			
Phase 1	from	£500	£1700
Phase 2	from	£425	£750
Phase 3	from	£250	£500
Phase 4	from	£425	£975
Phase 5	from	£500	£1525
Phase 6	from	£500	£975
Phase 7	from	£900	£2650

ABOVE: Hiberno-Norse phase II Penny

ABOVE: Hiberno-Norse phase IV Penny

JOHN AS LORD OF IRELAND c1185–1199

		F	VF
Silver Halfpennies, profile portrait		£2850	*
Facing head		£200	£485
Farthings		£725	£1900

Different types, varieties, mints and moneyers.

JOHN DE COURCY LORD OF ULSTER 1177–1205

		F	VF
Silver Halfpenny			unique
Farthings	from	£1850	£4500

Different types, varieties, mints and moneyers.

JOHN AS KING OF ENGLAND AND LORD OF IRELAND c1199–1216

Rex/Triangle types

		F	VF
Silver Pennies	from	£70	£150
Halfpennies		£110	£325
Farthings		£950	£2250

Different types, varieties, mints and moneyers.

HENRY III 1216–1272

		F	VF
Silver Pennies, c 1251–1254	from	£65	£175

Dublin only, moneyers DAVI and RICHARD, many varieties.

ABOVE: Edward I Waterford Penny

EDWARD I 1272–1307

First coinage, 1276–79

	F	VF
Pennies	£1500	£4250

Second coinage, 1279–1302

	F	VF
Silver Pennies from	£50	£140
Halfpennies	£75	£225

ABOVE: Edward I Farthing Dublin

	F	VF
Farthings	£135	£375

Dublin, Waterford and Cork, many different issues.

EDWARD III 1327–1377

	F	VF
Silver Halfpennies Dublin mint	£3250	*
Silver Farthing Dublin mint	£3000	*

HENRY VI 1422–1461

	F	VF
Silver Pennies, Dublin mint	£4250	*

ABOVE: Edward IV untitled crown type Groat

154 BRITISH COINS MARKET VALUES 2022

IRISH COINS

EDWARD IV 1461–1483

		F	VF
Silver untitled crown Groats	from	£1250	£3500
Pennies		£1500	*
Halfpenny		ext. rare	
Cross on rose/sun Groats		£3250	£9250
Pennies		£1500	£4250
Titled crown Groats		£2750	£6750
Halfgroats		£3000	*
Pennies		£2250	*
Cross & pellets Groats		£325	£700
Halfgroats		£100	£250
Halfpenny		£500	£1500
Bust/rose-sun Double Groats		£3000	£8000
Groats		£2500	£6250
Halfgroats		£2500	*
Pennies		£1850	*
Copper crown/cross Farthing		£1500	£3250
Half-farthings		£1625	£3500

PATRICIUS/SALVATOR 1463–65

	F	VF
Silver Farthing	£1750	£3850
Three crowns/sun Half-farthings	£1500	£3750

HENRY VI Restored 1470–1471

Groats	ext. rare

EDWARD IV Second reign 1471–83

		F	VF
'English style' Groats	from	£300	£700
Halfgroats		£750	£1825
Pennies		£60	£225
Halfpenny		£525	£1500
Ungoverned mints, c. 1470–77			
Groats	from	£650	£1750
Halfgroats		£1500	£3500
Pennies		£285	£750
Suns and roses/rose on cross coinage			
Groat		£750	£2000
Pennies		£350	£1500

This is an abbreviated listing of the issues of Edward IV which are numerous. There are also many varieties and different mints.

EDWARD V April–June 1483

	F	VF
Groats	£750	£1825
Pennies	£1100	£3000

ABOVE: Richard III 'three crowns' Groat

RICHARD III 1483–1485

		F	VF
Silver bust/rose-cross Groats	from	£2350	£4950
Halfgroats		unique	
Pennies		£3000	£7250
Cross and pellet pennies		£1650	£4000
Three-crown Groats		£800	£1975

Different mints and varieties.

ABOVE: Henry VII early 'three crowns' groat

ABOVE: Henry VII facing bust Groat, Dublin

HENRY VII 1485–1509
Early issues

	F	VF
Three-crown Groats	£225	£585
Halfgroats	£350	£925
Pennies	£875	£2250
Halfpennies	£1750	*

Later issues

	F	VF
Facing bust Groats	£250	£675
Halfgroats	£1000	£3000
Pennies	£1100	£2950
Crowned H Pennies	£2000	*

Many varieties. Mints: mainly Dublin, Waterford issues are extremely rare.

LAMBERT SIMNEL, Pretender 1487

	F	VF
Three-crown Groats	£1850	£5250

Different mints and varieties.

HENRY VIII 1509–1547

	F	VF
Silver 'harp' Groats	£250	£465
Halfgroats	£1500	£3000

These harped coins carry crowned initials, such as HA (Henry and Anne Boleyn), HI (Henry and Jane Seymour), HK (Henry and Katherine Howard) or HR (Henricus Rex).

Posthumous issues

	F	VF
Portrait Groats current for 6 pence	£200	£725
Halfgroats current for 3 pence	£250	£825
Pennies current for 3 halfpence	£550	£1650
Halfpennies current for 3 farthings	£925	£2750

IRISH COINS

ABOVE: Henry VIII posthumous portrait Groat

Different busts and mintmarks.

EDWARD VI 1547–1553
	F	VF
Base Shillings 1552 (MDLII)	£925	£3000
Contemporary copy	£50	£225

ABOVE: Mary 1553 Shilling

MARY 1553–1558
	F	VF
Shillings 1553 (MDLIII)	£975	£3850
1554 (MDLIIII)	£3000	£7250
Groats		ext. rare
Halfgroats		ext. rare
Pennies		ext. rare

Several varieties of the shillings and groats.

PHILIP AND MARY 1554–1558
	F	VF
Base Shillings	£425	£1750
Groats	£100	£495

Several minor varieties.

ELIZABETH I 1558–1603
	F	VF
Base portrait Shillings	£475	£1650
Groats	£120	£575
Fine silver portrait Shillings 1561	£450	£1350
Groats	£475	£1650
Base shillings arms–harp	£175	£625
Sixpences	£90	£400
Threepences	£500	*
Pennies	£30	£100
Halfpennies	£50	£175

JAMES I 1603–1625
	F	VF
Silver shillings	£125	£525
Sixpences	£90	£375

Different issues, busts and mintmarks.

Siege money of the Irish Rebellion 1642–1649

Siege coins are rather irregular in size and shape.

CHARLES I 1625–1649
Kilkenny Money 1642
	F	VF
Copper Halfpennies F	£450	£1500
Copper Farthings F	£625	*

Inchiquin Money 1642–1646
The only gold coins struck in Ireland. *from*
Gold Double Pistole		ext. rare
Gold Pistole F	£65000	*
Silver Crowns	£3750	£6850
Halfcrowns	£3250	£5500
Shillings	£2500	£7000
	F	VF
Ninepences	£6500	*
Sixpences	£5750	*
Groats F	£6000	£13000
Threepences		ext. rare

Three issues and many varieties.

Ormonde Money 1643
		F	VF
Crowns F	from	£650	£1425
Halfcrowns F		£485	£975
Shillings		£225	£500
Sixpences F		£175	£450
Groats F		£200	£400
Threepences		£175	£450
Halfgroats F		£700	£1500

Many varieties.

ABOVE: Ormonde Money Halfcrown

156 BRITISH COINS MARKET VALUES 2022

ABOVE: Ormonde Money Sixpence

Rebel Money 1643
Crowns	£4250	£13000
Halfcrowns	£4500	£13750

Town Pieces 1645–1647
Bandon
Copper Farthings F	£975	*

Kinsale
Copper Farthings F	£500	*

Youghal
Copper Farthings F	£500	£1750
Brass Twopences		ext. rare
Pewter Threepences		ext. rare

Cork
	F	VF
Silver Shillings F	£6000	£14000
Sixpences F	£1100	£2750
Copper Halfpennies	£1500	*
Copper Farthings F	£1350	*
Elizabeth I Shillings countermarked CORKE F		ext. rare

ABOVE: Cork 1647 Sixpence

'Blacksmith's' Money 1649
Based on English Tower Halfcrown.
Halfcrown, varieties	£875	£2500

Dublin Money 1649
Crowns	£5250	£12500
Halfcrowns	£3750	£8750

■ CHARLES II TO GEORGE IV

All the issues of this series except Bank of Ireland tokens were struck in base metal.

The series features a large number of varieties, but there is space here for only the main types and best-known variants. A number of rare proofs have also been omitted.

Except for the 'gunmoney' of James II, Irish copper coins are hard to find in the top grades, especially the so-called 'Voce Populi' issues and specimens of Wood's coinage.

We have listed some of the 'gunmoney' of James II in only three grades – Fair, Fine and VF. The majority of these hastily produced coins were not well struck and many pieces with little substantial wear are, arguably, not Extremely Fine.

Dating of gunmoney: in the calendar used up to 1723, the legal or civil year started on March 25 in Great Britain and Ireland, so December 1689 came before, not after January, February and March 1689. Coins dated March 1689 and March 1690 were struck in the same month.

CHARLES II	Fair	F	VF	EF
Armstrong issues 1660–1661				
Copper Farthings	£15	£30	£150	*
St Patrick's coinage				
Halfpennies	£875	£2000	*	*
Star in rev legend	£1100	*	*	*
Farthings	£150	£475	*	*
Stars in rev legend	£200	£600	*	*
Cloud around St Patrick	£225	£700	*	*
Martlet below king	£200	£600	*	*
Annulet below king	£200	£600	*	*

ABOVE: Charles II St Patrick's Farthing

Regal coinage	Fair	F	VF	EF
Halfpennies, 1680, large letters, small cross	£15	£50	£250	*
1680 pellets	£15	£50	£250	*
1681 large letters	£15	£50	£250	*
1681 small letters	£50	£185	*	*
1682 large letters	£15	£50	£250	*
1682 small letters	£15	£50	£250	£1500
1683	£15	£50	£250	£1500
1684	£25	£95	£400	*

JAMES II				
Regular coinage				
Halfpennies, 1685	£20	£65	£275	*
1686	£20	£65	£275	*
1687	£125	£450	*	*
1688	£20	£85	£300	*

Emergency coinage, 'Gunmoney'				
Crowns, 1690	£50	£100	£265	£750
1690 horseman, sword to E of REX	£125	£225	£550	£1350

IRISH COINS

BRITISH COINS MARKET VALUES 2022 157

ABOVE: James II 1690 'Gunmoney' Crown

Large Halfcrowns,				
1689 July	£15	£60	£195	£500
1689 August	£10	£40	£165	£425
1689 September	£8	£35	£150	£450
1689 October	£8	£35	£150	£450
1689 November	£10	£40	£125	£450
	Fair	F	VF	EF
1689 December	£10	£40	£150	£450
1689 January	£10	£40	£150	£400
1689 February	£8	£35	£150	£450
1689 March	£8	£35	£150	£450
1690 March	£8	£35	£150	£450
1690 April	£8	£35	£150	£450
1690 May	£10	£40	£150	£400
Small Halfcrowns,				
1690 April	£20	£75	£375	£895
1690 May	£10	£30	£170	£450
1690 June	£10	£35	£195	£450
1690 July	£10	£35	£165	£500
1690 August	£12	£40	£175	£685
1690 September	*	*	*	*
1690 October	£35	£110	£485	*
Large Shillings, 1689 July	£8	£25	£95	£300
1689 August	£6	£20	£80	£275
1689 September	£6	£20	£70	£275
1689 October	£8	£25	£95	£300
1689 November	£6	£20	£75	£275
1689 December	£6	£20	£70	£265
1689 January	£6	£20	£70	£265
1689 February	£6	£20	£70	£265
1689 March	£7	£20	£70	£275
1690 March	£8	£25	£70	£275
1690 April	£8	£25	£90	£300
Small Shillings,1690 April	£10	£30	£125	£350
1690 May	£7	£20	£90	£300
1690 June	£7	£20	£80	£300
1690 July	*	*	*	*
1690 August	*	*	*	*
1690 September	£125	£300	*	*

Sixpences, 1689 June	£10	£40	£120	£325
1689 July	£8	£35	£110	£275
1689 August	£8	£35	£110	£275
1689 September	£10	£40	£135	£575
1689 October	*	*	*	*
1689 November	£8	£35	£110	£300
1689 December	£8	£35	£110	£275
1689 January	£10	£40	£120	£300
1689 February	£8	£35	£110	£300
1689 March	*	*	*	*
1690 March	*	*	*	*
1690 April	*	*	*	*
1690 May	£15	£50	£150	*
1690 June	*	*	*	*
1690 October	*	*	*	*

Pewter Money

Crowns	£900	£2500	£4950	*
Groats	£750	£1650	*	*
Pennies large bust	£500	£1500	*	*
Small bust	£475	£975	*	*
Halfpennies large bust	£125	£350	£900	*
Halfpennies small bust	£90	£295	£750	£2500

ABOVE: Limerick Money Halfpenny

Limerick Money	Fair	F	VF	EF
Halfpennies	£20	£65	£225	£525
Farthings reversed N	£35	£90	£295	*
Normal N	£45	£100	£300	*

WILLIAM AND MARY

Halfpennies, 1692	£9	£40	£225	*
1693	£9	£40	£225	*
1694	£12	£50	£225	*

WILLIAM III

Halfpennies, 1696 draped bust	£15	£65	£285	£1500
Halfpennies 1696 crude undraped bust	£40	£250	£700	*

GEORGE I

Wood's coinage

Halfpennies, 1722 harp left	£18	£65	£385	£1325
1722 harp right	£12	£35	£200	£675
1723	£10	£30	£135	£550
1723 obv Rs altered Bs	£12	£35	£135	£550
1723 no stop after date	£12	£35	£135	£550
1723/2	£10	£35	£150	£600

IRISH COINS

1723 star in rev legend	*	*	*	*
1723 no stop before HIBERNIA	£10	£30	£135	£600
1724 head divided rev legend	£10	£30	£165	£685
1724 legend continuous over head	£15	£40	£175	*
Farthings 1722 harp left	£100	£400	£1350	*
1723 D: G:	£45	£125	£500	£2000
1723 DEI GRATIA	£10	£35	£135	£485
1724	£12	£50	£165	£625

GEORGE II

Halfpennies, 1736	*	£10	£50	£375
1737	*	£10	£50	£375
1738	£1	£12	£70	£450
1741	*	£10	£50	£375
1742	*	£10	£50	£375
1743	£2	£15	£60	£425
1744	£1	£12	£60	£475
1744/3	£2	£15	£60	£425
1746	£1	£12	£60	£425
1747	*	£10	£70	£425
1748	£2	£12	£65	£475
1749	*	£10	£50	£375
	Fair	F	VF	EF
1750	*	£10	£45	£400
1751	*	£10	£45	£400
1752	*	£10	£45	£400
1753	*	£12	£50	£400
1760	*	£10	£40	£350
Farthings, 1737	£1	£12	£65	£450
1738	*	£10	£50	£400
1744	*	£10	£45	£400
1760	*	£8	£40	£300

Voce populi coinage

Halfpennies, 1760, Type 1	£35	£150	£425	*
Type 2	£5	£175	£350	*
Type 3	£75	£175	£400	*
Type 4	£60	£150	£325	*
Type 5	£60	£150	£300	*
Type 6	£60	£150	£300	£1450
Type 7	£60	£160	£350	£1575
Type 8	£60	£150	£300	*
Type 9	£75	£175	£400	*
Type 9, P before head	£25	£100	£300	£1450
Type 9, P under head	£25	£100	£300	£1450
Farthings, 1760, Type 1 loop to truncation	£75	£250	£1250	£3500
Type 2 no loop	*	*	*	*

GEORGE III
London coinage

Halfpennies, 1766	£5	£25	£195	£500
1769	£5	£30	£225	£525
1769 2nd type	£5	£40	£235	£550
1775	£5	£30	£225	£525
1776	£25	£125	£385	*
1781	£5	£20	£160	£450

1782	£5	£20	£160	£400

Soho coinage

Penny 1805	*	£30	£125	£350
Halfpenny 1805	*	£15	£85	£195
Farthing 1806	*	£12	£50	£195

Bank of Ireland token coinage 1804 Six shillings

Bank of Ireland token coinage

Silver Six shillings 1804	£85	£250	£575	£950
Thirty pence 1808	£25	£55	£110	£350
Ten pence 1805	*	£10	£30	£100
Ten pence 1806	*	£10	£30	£100
Ten pence 1813	*	£10	£30	£100
Five pence 1805	*	£10	£25	£85
Five pence 1806	*	£10	£30	£100

GEORGE IV

	F	VF	EF	Unc
Penny 1822	£8	£40	£175	£425
1823	£10	£60	£200	£465
Halfpenny 1822	£5	£15	£110	£265
1823	£5	£15	£125	£275

The best magazine for stamp collectors

www.stampmagazine.co.uk

ABOVE: George IV proof penny, 1822

FREE STATE AND REPUBLIC

Proofs exist for nearly all dates of the modern Irish coinage. However, only a few dates have become available to collectors or dealers and apart from the 1928 proofs, are all very rare. They have therefore been omitted from the list.

TEN SHILLINGS

1966	*	£2	£6	£20
1966 proof	*	*	*	£30

HALFCROWNS

1928	*	£8	£20	£60
1928 proof	*	*	*	£85
1930	*	£30	£225	£465
1931	£8	£30	£200	£425
1933	*	£25	£175	£500
1934	*	£20	£100	£300
1937	£35	£100	£725	£1950
1938	*	*	*	*
1939	*	£5	£25	£80
1940	*	£6	£20	£95
1941	*	£6	£25	£85
1942	*	£4	£20	£75
1943	£70	£150	£850	£2750
1951	*	*	£6	£40
1954	*	*	£7	£45
1955	*	*	£5	£25
1959	*	*	£4	£20
1961	*	*	£5	£15
1961 mule normal obv/pre-1939 rev	£8	£20	£300	£725
1962	*	*	*	£5
1963	*	*	*	£10
1964	*	*	*	£5
1966	*	*	*	£10
1967	*	*	*	£3

FLORINS

	F	VF	EF	Unc
1928	*	£5	£18	£40
1928 proof	*	*	*	£60
1930	*	£15	£145	£425
1931	£5	£35	£185	£425
1933	£8	£18	£185	£425
1934	£12	£60	£385	£1000
1935	*	£10	£125	£325
1937	£5	£18	£185	£365
1939	*	£4	£10	£50
1940	*	£5	£12	£50
1941	*	£5	£20	£85
1942	*	£5	£12	£60
1943	£3850	£8000	£15000	£30000
1951	*	*	£3	£25
1954	*	*	£3	£20
1955	*	*	£3	£20
1959	*	*	£3	£20
1961	*	*	£6	£40
1962	*	*	£3	£18
1963	*	*	£3	£18
1964	*	*	*	£5
1965	*	*	*	£5
1966	*	*	*	£5
1968	*	*	*	£5

SHILLINGS

1928	*	£3	£8	£30
1928 proof	*	*	*	£45
1930	£7	£20	£145	£425
1931	*	£15	£65	£275
1933	£5	£10	£80	£265
1935	*	£5	£40	£135
1937	£10	£25	£400	£1000
1939	*	£3	£8	£35
1940	*	£3	£12	£40
1941	*	£5	£15	£45
1942	*	£5	£8	£28
1951	*	*	£3	£20
1954	*	*	£3	£15
1955	*	*	£3	£18
1959	*	*	£6	£25
1962	*	*	*	£5
1963	*	*	*	£4
1964	*	*	*	£5
1966	*	*	*	£4
1968	*	*	*	£4

SIXPENCES

1928	*	*	£3	£25
1928 proof	*	*	*	£30
1934	*	*	£12	£100
1935	*	£3	£18	£165
1939	*	*	£5	£35
1940	*	*	£5	£25
1942	*	*	£5	£25
1945	*	£8	£40	£200
1946	£5	£12	£85	£475
1947	*	£6	£25	£135

IRISH COINS

	F	VF	EF	Unc		F	VF	EF	Unc
1948	*	£2	£8	£35	1950	*	*	£3	£15
1949	*	*	£5	£30	1952	*	*	£2	£7
1950	*	£15	£35	£185	1962	*	*	£2	£3
1952	*	*	£4	£20	1963	*	*	*	£2
1953	*	*	£5	£22	1964	*	*	*	£2
1955	*	*	£4	£18	1965	*	*	*	£1
1956	*	*	£3	£12	1966	*	*	*	£1
1958	*	*	£5	£40	1967	*	*	*	£1
1959	*	*	£2	£7	1968	*	*	*	£1
1960	*	*	£2	£7					
1961	*	*	£2	£7	**HALFPENNIES**				
1962	*	*	£3	£30	1928	*	*	£4	£20
1964	*	*	*	£3	1928 proof	*	*	*	£25
1965	*	*	*	£3	1933	*	£20	£100	£450
1966	*	*	*	£3	1935	*	£10	£80	£285
1967	*	*	*	£3	1937	*	*	£12	£40
1968	*	*	*	£2	1939	*	£10	£45	£195
1969	*	*	*	£3	1940	*	£10	£65	£225
					1941	*	*	£5	£25
THREEPENCES					1942	*	*	£2	£20
1928	*	*	£3	£18	1943	*	*	£5	£25
1928 proof	*	*	£3	£25	1946	*	*	£15	£85
1933	*	£5	£60	£250	1949	*	*	£3	£18
1934	*	£3	£15	£65	1953	*	*	*	£4
1935	*	£5	£25	£175	1964	*	*	*	£2
1939	*	£5	£60	£195	1965	*	*	*	£2
1940	*	*	£10	£40	1966	*	*	*	£2
1942	*	*	£5	£35	1967	*	*	*	£1
1943	*	*	£8	£75					
1946	*	*	£5	£30	**FARTHINGS**				
1948	*	£2	£15	£80	1928	*	*	£3	£12
1949	*	*	£5	£30	1928 proof	*	*	*	£20
1950	*	*	£2	£6	1930	*	*	£5	£18
1953	*	*	£2	£5	1931	£1	£3	£8	£30
1956	*	*	*	£4	1932	£1	£3	£10	£35
1961	*	*	*	£3	1933	*	£2	£5	£25
1962	*	*	*	£3	1935	*	£5	£12	£45
1963	*	*	*	£3	1936	*	£6	£15	£50
1964	*	*	*	£3	1937	*	£2	£5	£20
1965	*	*	*	£3	1939	*	*	£3	£12
1966	*	*	*	£3	1940	*	£3	£6	£35
1967	*	*	*	*	1941	*	*	£3	£7
1968	*	*	*	*	1943	*	*	£3	£7
					1944	*	*	£3	£7
PENNIES					1946	*	*	£3	£7
1928	*	*	£6	£25	1949	*	*	£5	£10
1928 proof	*	*	*	£35	1953	*	*	£3	£7
1931	*	£2	£25	£80	1959	*	*	£1	£4
1933	*	£3	£40	£150	1966	*	*	£2	£6
1935	*	*	£15	£45					
1937	*	*	£25	£80	**DECIMAL COINAGE**				
1938 (possibly unique)	*	*	*	£37500	50p, 10p, 5p, 2p, 1p, ½p, all face value only.				
1940	*	£15	£145	£600					
1941	*	*	£6	£30	**SETS**				
1942	*	*	£3	£15	1928 in card case	*	*	FDC	£275
1943	*	*	£5	£20	1928 in leather case	*	*	FDC	£400
1946	*	*	£3	£15	1966 unc set	*	*	*	£10
1948	*	*	£3	£15	1971 specimen set in folder	*	*	*	£5
1949	*	*	£3	£15	1971 proof set	—	*	*	£9

SELLING IRISH COINS *where they sell best...*

Hiberno Norse Phase 1 'helmet' silver penny. *Sold for £10,000 at Whyte's*

Bronze Age Irish "ring money". *Sold for £2,800 at Whyte's*

James II "Gunmoney" halfcrown (large), 1690 Apr. very rare silver proof. *Sold for £9,500 at Whyte's*

Twenty pence trial 1985. *Sold for £5,500 at Whyte's*

Florin, 1943. Fine/very good. *Sold for £7,000 at Whyte's*

All Whyte's auctions are broadcast live on the internet with free on-line bidding at www.whytes.ie
Contact Ian Whyte iw@whytes.ie for advice and valuations.

WHYTE'S
WHERE IRISH COLLECTIBLES ARE TRULY VALUED

PSRA Licensed Auctioneer No. 001759

38 Molesworth Street Dublin 2 D02 KF80 Ireland 00 3531 676 2888 whytes.ie whytes.com whytes.eu

---

IRELAND
WORLD'S LARGEST STOCK
dentonirishcoins.com
Coins, Tokens, Medals 995AD - 2002

C.J. DENTON
124 Crofton Road, Orpington, Kent, BR6 8HZ
dentoncoins@outlook.com (01689 873690)

SOVEREIGN RARITIES LTD

For the rarest historic coins, and the most exciting modern issues.

17-19 MADDOX STREET, LONDON, W1S 2QH
INFO@SOVR.CO.UK   TEL: +44 (0)20 3019 1185
WWW.SOVR.CO.UK

Keep up with all the latest Post & Go news in the pages of Stamp Magazine

LONDON COINS
DEALERS AND AUCTIONEERS

FREE VALUATIONS AND APPRAISALS

- English Milled Coins
- British Hammered Coins
- World Coins
- Roman and Ancient Coins
- Proof Sets
- Royal Mint Issues
- Paper Money
- Medals
- Gold Coins, Sovereigns, Guineas and Krugerrands
- Tokens
- Bonds and Shares

Free Catalogues

'How To Sell Your Coins' Information Pack

See our website for our stock of choice English coins
www.londoncoins.co.uk

Email: info@londoncoins.co.uk
Tel: 01474 871464

FOUR AUCTIONS EVERY YEAR

THE ANGLO-GALLIC SERIES

Anyone interested in studying this series should obtain *The Anglo-Gallic Coins* by E R D Elias, who neatly summarised the series: 'All Kings of England in the period 1154–1453 had interests in France. They were Dukes or Lords of Aquitaine, Counts of Poitou or Ponthieu, Lords of Issoudun or they were even or pretended to be, Kings of France itself, and, in those various capacities, struck coins.

These coins, together with the French coins of their sons, and of their English vassals, are called Anglo-Gallic coins'.

See our table for the English kings' French titles.

KINGS OF ENGLAND AND FRANCE 1154–1453

ENGLAND	FRANCE
Henry II 1154–89 Duke of Normandy and Count of Anjou, Maine and Touraine. By marrying Eleanor of Aquitaine in 1152, he became Duke of Aquitaine and Count of Poitou. He relinquished Aquitaine and Poitou to his son Richard in 1168. In 1185 he forced Richard to surrender Aquitaine and Poitou to Eleanor who governed between 1199–1204.	Louis VII 1137–80 Philip II 1180–1223
Richard I the Lionheart 1189–99 Formally installed as Duke of Aquitaine and Count of Poitou in 1172.	
John 1199–1216 He lost all parts of the Angevin Empire except Aquitaine and part of Poitou.	
Henry III 1216–72 In 1252 he ceded Aquitaine to his son Edward.	Louis VIII 1223–26 Louis IX 1226–70 Philip III 1270–85
Edward I 1272–1307 He governed Aquitaine from 1252. In 1279 he became Count of Ponthieu. In 1290 the county went to his son Edward.	Philip IV 1285–1314
Edward II 1307–27 He was Count of Ponthieu from 1290. In 1325 he relinquished the county of Ponthieu and the Duchy of Aquitaine to his son Edward.	Louis X 1314–16 Philip V 1316–22 Charles IV 1322–28
Edward III 1327–77 Count of Ponthieu and Duke of Aquitaine from 1325. He lost Ponthieu in 1337 but it was restored in 1360. In 1340 he assumed the title of King of France, which he abandoned again in 1360. He gave Aquitaine to his son, Edward the Black Prince, (b1330–d1376), who was Prince of Aquitaine 1362–1372, although he actually ruled from 1363–1371. In 1369 Edward III reassumed the title King of France.	Philip VI 1328–50 John II 1350–64 Charles V 1364–80
Richard II 1377–99 The son of the Black Prince succeeded his grandfather, Edward III, as King of England and Lord of Aquitaine.	Charles VI 1380–1422
Henry IV 1399–1413 He adopted the same titles as Richard II.	
Henry V 1413–22 From 1417–1420 he used the title King of the French on his 'Royal' French coins. After the Treaty of Troyes in 1420 he styled himself 'heir of France'.	
Henry VI 1422–61 He inherited the title King of the French from his grandfather Charles VI. He lost actual rule in Northern France in 1450 and in Aquitaine in 1453.	Charles VII 1422–61

ANGLO-GALLIC

	F	VF
HENRY II 1152–68		
Denier	£45	£110
Obole	£90	£220
RICHARD THE LIONHEART 1168–99		
Aquitaine		
Denier	£60	£135
Obole	£60	£135
Poitou		
Denier	£45	£100
Obole	£60	£160
Issoudun		
Denier	£275	*
ELEANOR 1199–1204		
Denier	£65	£145
Obole	£325	*
EDWARD I		
During the lifetime of his father 1252–72		
Denier au lion	£30	£90
Obole au lion	£45	£120
After succession to the English throne 1272–1307		
Denier au lion	£60	£150
Obole au lion	£145	*
Denier à la croix longue	£70	£165
Au lćopard, first type	£30	£85
Obole au léopard, first type	£55	£140
Denier à la couronne	£250	*
EDWARD II		
Gros Turonus Regem		ext. rare
Maille blanche		ext. rare
Hibernie	£45	£135
EDWARD III		
Gold coins		
Ecu d'or	£2850	£7250
Florin	£6250	£13000
Léopard d'or, 1st issue		ext. rare
2nd issue	£4500	£8950
3rd issue	£3250	£7000

	F	VF
4th issue	£3250	£7750
Guyennois d'or, 1st type	£7500	*
2nd type	£5250	£11750
3rd type	£3950	£7000
Silver coins		
Gros aquitainique au léopard	£195	£585
Tournois à la croix mi-longue	£350	£900
À la croix longue	£140	£300
Sterling	£90	£260
Demi-sterling	£165	£450
Gros au léopard passant	£575	*
À la couronne	£160	£425
Au châtel aquitainique	£195	£600
Tournois au léopard au-dessus	£85	£260
À la porte	£85	£260
Aquitainique au léopard au-dessous	£260	*
Blanc au léopard sous couronne	£75	£165
Gros au léopard sous couronne	£210	£600
À la couronne avec léopard	£175	£485
Sterling à la tête barbue	£325	£875
Petit gros de Bordeaux		ext. rare
Gros au lion	£150	£425
Demi-gros au lion	£275	*
Guyennois of argent (sterling)	£95	£250
Gros au buste	£1100	*
Demi-gros au buste	£585	£1500
Black coins		
Double à la couronne, 1st type	£110	*
2nd type	£90	£265
3rd type	£185	*
Double au léopard	£70	£175
Sous couronne	£35	£100
Guyennois		ext. rare
Denier au léopard, 2nd type	£35	£100
Obole au léopard, 2nd type		ext. rare
Denier au léopard, 3rd type	£40	£120
4th type	£35	£100
Obole au léopard, 4th type	£40	£120
Denier au lion	£45	£145

Some issues of the 2nd and 3rd type deniers au léopard are very rare to extremely rare and therefore much more valuable.

EDWARD THE BLACK PRINCE 1362–72

ABOVE: Edward lll 2nd issue léopard d'or

ABOVE: Edward the Black Prince chaise d'or of Bordeaux

BRITISH COINS MARKET VALUES 2022 **165**

ANGLO-GALLIC

Gold coins	F	VF
Léopard d'or	£3500	£8750
Guyennois d'or	£3500	£7500
Chaise d'or	£4000	£8500
Pavillon d'or 1st issue	£3950	£8750
2nd issue	£3950	£8750
Demi-pavillon d'or	*	*
Hardi d'or	£4000	£8750

Silver coins		
Gros	£800	£1925
Demi-gros	£110	£300
Sterling	£75	£165
Hardi d'argent	£50	£135

Black coins		
Double guyennois	£120	£295
Denier au lion	£55	£145
Denier	£60	£150

RICHARD II 1377–99

Gold coins		
Hardi d'or	£5000	£10500
Demi-hardi d'or		ext. rare

Silver coins		
Double hardi d'argent	£925	£2750
Hardi d'argent	£55	£165

Black coins		
Denier	£90	£260

HENRY IV 1399–1413

Silver coins		
Double hardi d'argent	£575	£1625
Hardi d'argent	£40	£125
Hardi aux genêts	£185	£575

Black coins		
Denier	£55	£150
Aux genêts	£150	£385

HENRY V 1413–22

Gold coins		
Agnel d'or	£7000	£16500
Salut d'or	£8250	£19750

Silver coins		
Florette, 1st issue	£90	£225
2nd issue	£165	£395
3rd issue	£65	£175
4th issue	£90	£225
Guénar	£425	£985
Gros au léopard	£475	*

Black coins		
Mansiois		ext. rare
Niquet	£60	£180
Denier tournois	£75	£195

HENRY VI 1422–53

Gold coins	F	VF
Salut d'or	£650	£1350
Angelot	£3250	£7500

ABOVE: Henry VI Salut d'or Paris mint

Silver coins		
Grand blanc aux ècus	£75	£225
Petit blanc	£95	£275
Trésin		ext. rare

Black coins		
Denier Paris, 1st issue	£70	£160
2nd issue	£70	£160
Denier tournois	£75	£175
Maille tournois	£75	£175

The prices of the saluts and grands blancs are for mints of Paris, Rouen and Saint Lô; coins of other mints are rare to very rare.

■ PONTHIEU

EDWARD I

Denier	£95	£250
Obole	£85	£215

EDWARD III

Denier	£165	*
Obole	£250	*

■ BERGERAC

HENRY, EARL OF LANCASTER 1347–51

Gros tournois à la croix longue	£925	£1950
À la couronne	£795	*
Au châtel aquitainique	£925	£1950
Tournois au léopard au-dessus	£600	£1375
À la couronne		ext. rare
À fleur-de-lis		ext. rare
Au léopard passant		ext. rare
Double	£1250	*
Denier au léopard	£795	*

HENRY, DUKE OF LANCASTER 1351–61

Gros tournois à la couronne avec léopard	£900	*
Au léopard couchant	£900	*
Sterling à la tête barbue	£795	*
Gros au lion		ext. rare

166 BRITISH COINS MARKET VALUES 2022

STAMP INSURANCE SERVICES
C G I Services Limited
INSURING COLLECTABLES SINCE 1973

LET US INSURE YOUR COLLECTION

REPLACEMENT VALUE, ALL RISKS, NO EXCESS
Includes whilst on display or on exhibition anywhere in Europe, worldwide cover can be arranged

Stamps & Postcards
£6,250   cover for   £30 pa*
£10,000 cover for   £42 pa*

All other Collectables
£5,000   cover for   £35 pa*
£10,000 cover for   £60 pa*
*plus IPT

CIRCULATING PACKETS: CUPS & TROPHIES: AUCTIONS: EXHIBITIONS etc.

SPECIAL SCHEME for SOCIETIES
Includes Public & Employers Liability

PUBLIC LIABILITY for COLLECTOR SOCIETIES
Premiums from £25 pa for £5,000,000 cover

DEALERS COMBINED POLICY

Please write, email or telephone for a quotation and a Prospectus/Proposal form.

C G I Services Limited
29 Bowhay Lane, EXETER EX4 1PE
mail@stampinsurance.co.uk
tel: **01392 433 949**

Authorised & Regulated by the Financial Conduct Authority No.300573

ON SALE NOW!

THE BEST-VALUE GUIDE TO STAMP PRICES

8500 ITEMS LISTED

2022 BRITISH STAMP MARKET VALUES

- EVERY GREAT BRITAIN ISSUE SINCE 1840
- DEFINITIVES, COMMEMORATIVES, BOOKLETS
- OFFICIALS, POSTAGE DUES, SMILERS, POST & GO
- REAL MARKET VALUES, NOT CATALOGUE PRICES

VICTORIA • EDWARD VII • GEORGE V • EDWARD VIII

Order your copy at www.mags-uk.com
Or telephone 01795 662976

BETTER VALUE THAN ANY OTHER PRICE GUIDE

ONLY £15.99

› Fully updated to mid-2021
› Handy, pocket-size format

ISLAND COINAGE

Proofs have been struck for a large number of Channel Islands coins, particularly in the case of Jersey. Except for those included in modern proof sets, most are very rare and in the majority of cases have been omitted from the list.

For further information refer to *The Coins of the British Commonwealth of Nations, Part I, European Territories* by F Pridmore (Spink, 1960). BU prices are for coins with brilliant mint lustre.

■ GUERNSEY

	F	VF	EF	BU
TEN SHILLINGS				
1966	*	*	*	£2.50
THREEPENCE				
1956	*	*	*	£2.50
1959	*	*	*	£2.50
1966 proof	*	*	*	£2.50
EIGHT DOUBLES				
1834	*	£14	£75	£500
1858	*	£14	£75	£400
1864	*	£20	£85	*
1868	*	£15	£70	£195
1874	*	£15	£70	£189
1885 H	*	*	£20	£95
1889 H	*	*	£20	£80
1893 H	*	*	£20	£80
1902 H	*	*	£18	£50
1903 H	*	*	£20	£60
1910 H	*	*	£20	£60
1911 H	*	£20	£50	£120
1914 H	*	*	£15	£50
1918 H	*	*	£15	£50
1920 H	*	*	£8	£30
1934 H	*	*	£8	£30
1934 H 'burnished flan'	*	*	*	£450
1938 H	*	*	*	£15
1945 H	*	*	*	£10
1947 H	*	*	*	£10
1949 H	*	*	*	£10
1956	*	*	*	£7
1956 proof	*	*	*	£10
1959	*	*	*	£3
1966 proof	*	*	*	£3
FOUR DOUBLES				
1830	*	*	£55	£350
1858	*	*	£60	£350
1864	*	£8	£70	£350
1868	*	£8	£60	*
1874	*	*	£50	*
1885 H	*	*	£8	£60
1889 H	*	*	£8	£65
1893 H	*	*	£8	£45
1902 H	*	*	£8	£55
1903 H	*	*	£8	£55

	F	VF	EF	BU
1906 H	*	*	£8	£80
1908 H	*	*	£8	£75
1910 H	*	*	£5	£65
1911 H	*	*	£5	£55
1914 H	*	*	£5	£55
1918 H	*	*	£5	£40
1920 H	*	*	*	£35
1945 H	*	*	*	£18
1949 H	*	*	*	£20
1956	*	*	*	£5
1956 proof	*	*	*	£10
1966 proof	*	*	*	£5
TWO DOUBLES				
1858	*	£35	£140	£370
1868	*	£35	£140	£370
1874	*	£30	£135	£350
1885 H	*	*	£12	£35
1889 H	*	*	£12	£35
1899 H	*	*	£12	£35
1902 H	*	*	£12	£35
1903 H	*	*	£12	£30
1906 H	*	*	£12	£30
1908 H	*	*	£12	£30
1911 H	*	*	£18	£50
1914 H	*	*	£18	£50
1917 H	£30	£55	£140	£300
1918 H	*	*	£12	£30
1920 H	*	*	£12	£30
1929 H	*	*	£5	£12
ONE DOUBLE				
1830	*	*	£20	£75
1868	*	£45	£120	£330
1868/30	*	£45	£120	£330
1885 H	*	*	£3	£20
1889 H	*	*	£3	£20
1893 H	*	*	£3	£20
1899 H	*	*	£3	£20
1902 H	*	*	£3	£20
1903 H	*	*	£3	£20
1911 H	*	*	£3	£20
1911 H new type	*	*	£3	£20
1914 H	*	*	£3	£15
1929 H	*	*	£3	£15
1933 H	*	*	£3	£15
1938 H	*	*	£3	£12
SETS				
1956 proof				£65
1966 proof				£15
1971 proof				£10

For coins after 1971 refer to the *Standard Catalogue of World Coins* published by Krause Publications annually.

www.stampmagazine.co.uk

ISLAND COINAGE

■ JERSEY

CROWN	F	VF	EF	BU
1966	*	*	*	£4
1966 proof	*	*	*	£10

¼ OF A SHILLING

	F	VF	EF	BU
1957	*	*	*	£6
1960 proof only	*	*	*	£85
1964	*	*	*	£4
1966	*	*	*	£4

1/12 OF A SHILLING

	F	VF	EF	BU
1877 H	*	*	£18	£120
1881	*	*	£15	£80
1888	*	*	£15	£70
1894	*	*	£12	£70
1909	*	*	£15	£140
1911	*	*	£10	£70
1913	*	*	£10	£70
1923	*	*	£10	£75
1923 new type	*	*	£12	£70
1926	*	*	£12	£60
1931	*	*	£5	£30
1933	*	*	£5	£30
1935	*	*	£5	£30
1937	*	*	*	£18
'1945' (George VI)	*	*	£5	£12
'1945' (Elizabeth II)	*	*	*	£8
1946	*	*	*	£12
1947	*	*	*	£12
1957	*	*	*	£5
1960	*	*	*	£5
1964	*	*	*	£4
1966	*	*	*	£3
1966 proof	*	*	*	£7

The date 1945 on 1/12 shillings commemorates the year of liberation from German occupation. The coins were struck in 1949, 1950, 1952 and 1954.

1/13 OF A SHILLING

	F	VF	EF	BU
1841	*	*	£75	£420
1844	*	*	£75	£420
1851	*	*	£85	£350
1858	*	*	£70	£300
1861	*	*	£70	£300
1865 proof only	*	*	*	£900
1866	*	*	£40	£160
1870	*	*	£40	£160
1871	*	*	£40	£160

1/24 OF A SHILLING

	F	VF	EF	BU
1877 proof only	*	*	*	£400
1877 H	*	*	£20	£110
1888	*	*	£15	£60
1894	*	*	£15	£60
1909	*	*	£15	£75
1911	*	*	£12	£50
1913	*	*	£12	£50

	F	VF	EF	BU
1923	*	*	£10	£50
1923 new type	*	*	£10	£50
1926	*	*	£12	£55
1931	*	*	£7	£25
1933	*	*	£7	£20
1935	*	*	£7	£15
1937	*	*	£7	£12
1946	*	*	£7	£12
1947	*	*	£7	£12

1/26 OF A SHILLING

	F	VF	EF	BU
1841	*	*	£55	£260
1844	*	*	£60	£290
1851	*	*	£55	£260
1858	*	*	£50	£260
1861	*	*	£45	£220
1866	*	*	£25	£175
1870	*	*	£25	£175
1871	*	*	£25	£175

1/48 OF A SHILLING

	F	VF	EF	BU
1877 proof	*	*	*	£400
1877 H	*	£25	£95	£275

1/52 OF A SHILLING

	F	VF	EF	BU
1841	*	£40	£175	£395
1841 proof	*	*	*	£1300
1861 proof	*	*	*	£1400

Decimal coinage

SETS	BU
1957	£40
1960	£15
1964	£12
1966 four coins, proof	£8
1966 two crowns	£10
1972 Silver Wedding five gold, four silver coins	BV
1972 proof	BV
1972 four silver coins	£50

For coins after 1972 refer to the *Standard Catalogue of World Coins* published by Krause Publications annually.

■ ISLE OF MAN

Contemporary forgeries of earlier Isle of Man coins exist.

Copper and Bronze 1709–1839

ABOVE: James Stanley, 10th Earl of Derby, penny, 1709

ISLAND COINAGE

PENNIES	F	VF	EF	Unc
1709	£50	£120	*	*
1733	£45	£200	£395	*
1733 proof	*	*	£500	*

ABOVE: Proof penny in silver, 1733

	F	VF	EF	Unc
1733 silver	*	£400	£750	£1400
1758	£40	£100	£300	*
1758 proof	*	*	£1000	*
1758 silver	*	*	£2500	*
1786	£15	£50	£200	£485
1786 plain edge proof	*	*	£750	£1600
1798	£15	£60	£250	£600
1798 bronzed proof	*	*	£425	£750
1798 AE gilt proof	*	*	£1250	£2500
1798 silver proof	*	*	£2250	£4000
1813	£15	£60	£250	£600
1813 bronze proof	*	*	£425	£700
1813 gilt proof	*	*	£1250	£2500
1839	*	£15	£75	£250
1839 proof	*	*	*	£1500
1841 proof	*	*	*	£3500
1859 proof	*	*	*	£5000

HALFPENNIES				
1709	£75	£185	*	*
1723	£1250	*	*	*
1723 silver	£1500	*	*	*
1733	£50	£125	£275	£500
1733 proof	*	*	£650	£1000
1733 silver	*	*	£900	£1500
1758	£20	£60	£265	*
1758 proof	*	*	*	£2000
1786	£10	£45	£150	£275
1786 plain edge proof	*	*	£425	£875
1798	£10	£40	£100	£265

ABOVE: Proof halfpenny, 1798

	F	VF	EF	Unc
1798 proof	£10	£30	£275	£400
1798 silver proof	*	*	£1650	£3000
1798 gilt proof	*	*	*	£1500
1813	£10	£30	£225	£350
1813 proof	*	*	£250	£600
1813 gilt proof	*	*	*	£1700
1839	*	*	£45	£225
1839 proof	*	*	*	£3000

FARTHINGS				
1839	£10	£25	£45	£125
1839 proof	*	*	*	£625
1841 proof only	*	*	*	£1750
1860 proof only	*	*	*	£3500
1864 proof only	*	*	*	£4000

AUCTION HIGHLIGHTS

FRANCE 1871
Ballon monté entire to Mexico

Schuyler Rumsey's sale of the stunning Dale Forster collection of *ballon monté* (manned balloon) covers from the Siege of Paris in 1870-71 included this remarkable entire to Mexico City.

Postmarked with the double-circle handstamp of Rue St Lazare, it is franked with both a French Empire (Napoleon III) 80c pink and a French Republic (Cérès) 40c orange, cancelled by a numeral '2' star-of-dots and also tied by a red London transit mark of January 27.

Also tying the 80c to the cover is a large numeral '4' (meaning 4 reales) Mexican postage due handstamp in black.

Carried out of the French capital by the balloon *Vaucanson*, the cover was endorsed 'via St Nazaire ou des Etats Unis' at bottom left. In fact, it was transported by RMSP *Seine* from Southampton to St Thomas in the Danish West Indies, arriving on February 18, and by RMSP *Eider* from there to Vera Cruz, arriving on March 2.

SOLD BY SCHUYLER RUMSEY £34,500

SOLD FOR £34,500

NEW SOUTH WALES 1850
Sydney Views 1d

This unused 1d from the 'Sydney Views' first issue of New South Wales, sold by Abacus, is one of the finest in private hands.

Printed from plate II (with clouds) it is in the dull carmine shade on greyish paper.

The original plate went into service in January 1850. It was re-engraved before being put back into service in August, and in this state is known as plate II.

SOLD BY ABACUS £11,600

UNITED STATES 1979
'CIA Invert' error

Cherrystone's sale offered an example of the most celebrated error in modern US philately, the so-called 'CIA Invert'.

The $1 value, issued in 1979 as part of the Americana definitive series of 1975-81, illustrating a colonial rushlight holder, has the dark brown colour inverted, leaving only the candle and flame the right way up.

An almost complete pane, comprising 100 stamps, was purchased by a CIA employee at the post office in McLean, Virginia, for use on mail from the agency. Having noticed the error, nine employees pooled funds to buy a replacement sheet before selling the errors to a dealer.

A scandal erupted over legal ownership of the stamps, and the CIA demanded the return. Some employees returned their stamps and kept their jobs, while others refused and were sacked.

BRITISH GUIANA 1852
4c black on blue

A highlight of the Corbitts auction was a rarity of British Guiana, the 1852 4c black on deep blue paper.

This example, showing part of a Demerara circular datestamp, had three margins but was missing part of its frame at top right. Mounted on thin card, it came with an Royal Philatelic Society London certificate from 2019.

The 1852 issue, comprising values of 1c and 4c, was the colony's second, after the so-called 'Cottonreels' of 1850-51. It was the first to be printed in Britain, in litho by Waterlow.

SOLD BY CORBITTS £2,700

FRANCE 1871
Captured ballon monté mail

Selling for almost as much as the Mexico cover at Schuyler Rumsey was one of only two known *ballon monté* covers addressed to Cuba.

Franked with a French Empire 80c pink tied by 5 star-of-dots cancellation, it has a double-circle Rue de Bondy postmark of December 12, 1870 and a small red 'PD' boxed handstamp.

Loaded aboard the balloon *Ville de Paris*, it was addressed to Santiago and endorsed in manuscript 'Par les Vapours Transatlantiques' (by the Atlantic steamships).

There is no arrival postmark, however, because this mailbag never made it to the wider world. The balloon was captured by the Prussian forces besieging Paris.

SOLD BY SCHUYLER RUMSEY £32,700

GREAT BRITAIN 1883
1s with inverted watermark

Great Britain's 1883 1s dull green with its Imperial Crown watermark inverted is listed but unpriced in the Stanley Gibbons catalogue.

Only four examples are recorded, and one came up Mayfair's auction, with strong colour and lightly postmarked.

This was the highest value in the so-called 'Lilac & Green' issue of stamps valid for both postage and revenue use. Their colours were chosen because they were the only fugitive inks available, at a time when the authorities were particularly concerned about fraudulent reuse.

SOLD BY MAYFAIR £5,500

OFFER ENDS 30TH SEPT 2022

SPECIAL OFFER FOR BCMV READERS!

Terms & conditions: *Digital downloads are currently available on iPad, iPhone, Android & Kindle Devices. You can also download to an Offline Reader on PC Computers. MyTimeMedia Ltd reserves the right to withdraw this offer at any time without prior notice. **Terms & conditions apply - visit www.mytimemedia.co.uk/terms for full terms & conditions.

FOR PRINT & PRINT + DIGITAL SUBSCRIPTIONS PLEASE VISIT WWW.STAMPMAGAZINE.CO.UK/SUBSCRIBE

STAMP
MAGAZINE

Have you tried STAMP Digital?

ONLY £2.50 PER ISSUE!

JUST £29.99
FOR A WHOLE YEAR!

- Read your magazine with no internet connection
- Keep your issues digitally without needing lots of storage space
- Receive your magazine before it hits the shops – regardless of your location

SUBSCRIBE TODAY!
https://stamp.secureorder.co.uk/STPD/BCMV21D
or call 0344 243 9023 and quote ref BCMV21D

LINES OPEN MON - FRI - 9.00AM - 5.00PM GMT & SAT - 9.30AM - 3.30PM GMT.

Calls are charged at the same rate as standard UK landlines and are included as part of any inclusive or free minutes allowances.

BRITISH PAPER MONEY

As of June 2021 only three out of the four current polymer denominations have been Issued with the Sarah John signature.

Condition is the most important factor in banknote pricing although it's possible to collect an attractive selection in lower grades; some notes are never seen in better than Very Fine.

We have not listed banknotes prior to 1914 as these are scarce and generally only available in grades up to Very Fine.

Serial numbers with the prefix 'No' are referred to as 'dot' if 'No' is followed by a full stop and 'dash' if followed by a dash.

Reference numbers are according to Vincent Duggleby's *English Paper Money*. The 9th edition (Pam West, 2017) is a must for the collector.

■ TREASURY NOTES

JOHN BRADBURY
First issue

			VF	EF
T1	£1	Black on white, prefix large letters A, B or C	£1800	£2600
T2	£1	No full stop after serial letter	£2800	£4500
T3	£1	Six digits	£800	£1250
T4	£1	Large serial number, 'dot' and five digits	£900	£1750
T5	£1	Large serial number, 'dash' and five digits	£900	£1600
T6	£1	Letter, letter, number, number	£1100	£1800
T7	£1	Small typeface serial number		rare
T8	10s	Red on white, six digits	£700	£1200
T9	10s	Prefix 'No'	£520	£820
T10	10s	Red on white, five digits	£950	£1500

Second issue

T12	10s	Red on white, five digits	£420	£700
T13	10s	Six digits	£380	£650
T11	£1	Black on white	£380	£700
T14	£1	Arabic overprint	£4500	£9000
T15	10s	Arabic overprint	£820	£1600

Third issue

T16	£1	Green and brown on white	£140	£280
T17	10s	Black serial no with 'dot'	£540	£850
T18	10s	Black serial no with 'dash'	£510	£830
T19	10s	Red serial no with 'dot'	£2000	*
T20	10s	Red serial no with 'dash'	£430	£750

NORMAN FENWICK WARREN FISHER
First issue

T24	£1	Green and brown on white	£80	£170
T25	10s	Green and brown on white, 'dot'	£250	£450
T26	10s	'Dash'	£220	£400

Second issue

T30	10s	Green and brown on white	£170	£330
T31	£1	'Dot'	£95	£190
T32	£1	Square 'dot'	£190	£360

Third issue, Northern Ireland

T33	10s	Green and brown on white	£210	£480
T34	£1	'Dot'	£120	£210
T35	£1	Square 'dot'	£210	£420

Fractionals

T27	5s	Violet and green on white	£8000	£12000
T28	2s 6d	Olive-green and chocolate	£9500	*
T29	1s	Green and brown on white	£9000	*

■ BANK OF ENGLAND NOTES

CYRIL PATRICK MAHON 1925–29

			VF	EF
B210	10s	Red-brown	£130	£270
B212	£1	Green	£130	£250
B215	£5	Black and white	£450	£800

BASIL GAGE CATTERNS 1929–34

B223	10s	Red-brown:	£70	£120
B225	£1	Green: letter, number, number	£30	£65
B226	£1	Number, number, letter	£100	£220
B228	£5	Black on white	£300	£500

KENNETH OSWALD PEPPIATT 1934–49

B236	10s	Red-brown: number, number, letter 1st period	£35	£70
B238	£1	Green: number, number, letter, 1st issue	£25	£60
B241	£5	Black on white, one straight edge, three deckled	£200	£350
B249	£1	Blue (shades), 2nd issue	£12	£25
B251	10s	Mauve, 2nd period	£35	£70
B255	£5	Straight edges, metal filament, thick paper	£130	£220
B256	10s	Red-brown: number, number, letter, 3rd period	£70	£140
B258	£1	Green: letter, number, number, letter, 3rd issue	£18	£45
B260	£1	Metal filament, 4th issue	£10	£22
B262	10s	Metal filament, 4th period	£30	£70
B264	£5	Straight edges, metal filament, thin paper	£130	£220

Fractionals

B253	5s	Olive-green on pale pink background	from £6000	*
B254	2s 6d	Black on pale blue background	from £6000	*

PERCIVAL SPENCER BEALE 1949–55

B265	10s	Red-brown: number, number, letter	£18	£35
B266	10s	letter, number, number, letter	£12	£25
B268	£1	Green	£5	£15
B270	£5	Black on white	£110	£160

174 BRITISH COINS MARKET VALUES 2022

LESLIE KENNETH O'BRIEN 1955–62

B271	10s	Red-brown: letter, number, number, letter	£6	£15
B272	10s	Replacement	£55	£110
B273	£1	Green	£6	£12
B275	£5	Black on white	£120	£210
B277	£5	Blue, pale green and orange, solid blue symbols reverse	£22	£45
B280	£5	Hollow white £5 symbols reverse	£22	£45

Queen's portrait

			EF	Unc
B281	£1	Letter, number, number	£4	£8
B282	£1	Number, number, letter	£4	£8
B284	£1	Letter, number, number, letter	£16	£30

JASPER QUINTUS HOLLOM 1962–66

B288	£1	Green	£4	£8
B292	£1	Green, letter 'G' reverse	£8	£18
B294	10s	Red-brown: number, number, letter	£4	£8
B295	10s	Red-brown: number, number, letter	£4	£8
BB297	£5	Blue	£25	£60
B299	£10	Multicoloured brown	£35	£70

JOHN STANDISH FFORDE 1966–70

B301	£1	Green	£5	£12
B303	£1	'G' variety	£8	£15
B309	10s	Red-brown: number, number, letter	£4	£8
B310	10s	Letter, number, number, letter	£4	£8
B311	10s	Letter, number, number	£8	£14
B312	£5	Blue: letter, number, number	£25	£60
B314	£5	Number, number, letter	£25	£60
B316	£10	Multicoloured brown	£35	£70
B318	£20	Multicoloured purple	£320	£460

JOHN BRANGWYN PAGE 1970–80

B322	£1	Green: letter, letter, number, number	£3	£6
B324	£5	Blue	£30	£65
B326	£10	Multicoloured	£35	£65
B328	£20	Multicoloured purple	£45	£90
B330	£10	Letter, number, number	£25	£45
B332	£5	Multicoloured: letter, number, number, 1st series	£14	£30
B334	£5	L on reverse, signifies lithographic printing	£14	£30

DAVID HENRY FITZROY SOMERSET 1980–88

B341	£1	Green	£3	£6
B343	£5	Multicoloured: letter, letter, number, number	£10	£25
B346	£10	Multicoloured: letter, letter, number, number	£32	£80
B350	£20	Multicoloured purple	£50	£110
B352	£50	Olive green, brown, grey	£85	£140

GEORGE MALCOLM GILL 1988–91

B353	£5	Blue	£10	£25
B354	£10	Brown	£20	£40
B355	£20	Multicoloured purple	£65	£130
B356	£50	Olive green, brown, grey	£120	£250
B357	£5	Turquoise, Series E	£12	£25
B358	£20	Multicoloured purple	£45	£90

GRAHAM EDWARD ALFRED KENTFIELD 1991–1998

B360	£10	Multicoloured brown	£40	£80
B361	£50	Olive green, brown, grey	£95	£180
B362	£5	Turquoise	£20	£45
B363	£5	Multicoloured letter, letter, number, number	£12	£25
B364	£5	Multicoloured blue	£10	£20
B366	£10	Orange brown	£18	£35
B369	£10	Orange brown	£16	£35
B371	£20	Multicoloured purple	£45	£95
B374	£20	Multicoloured purple	£40	£90
B377	£50	Red	£70	£120

MERLYN VIVIENNE LOWTHER 1999–2004

B380	£5	Turquoise	£10	£20
B382	£10	Orange brown	£25	£45
B384	£20	Multicoloured purple	£60	£100
B385	£50	Red	£70	£120
B386	£20	Multicoloured purple	£25	£40
B388	£10	Orange And 'Co'	£16	£32
B390	£10	Orange The 'Co'	£16	£30
B393	£5	Turquoise	£8	£18
B395	£5	Turquoise	£8	£15

ANDREW JOHN BAILEY 2004–2011

B398	£5	Turquoise	£8	£15
B400	£10	Orange brown	£12	£18
B402	£20	Purple	£25	£40
B404	£50	Red	£70	£110
B405	£20	Purple, Adam Smith reverse	£25	£35

CHRIS SALMON 2011–2014

B407	£5	Turquoise	£6	£10
B408	£10	Orange brown	£12	£20
B409	£20	Purple	£25	£35
B410	£50	Red, Boulton, Watt reverse	£55	£85

VICTORIA CLELAND 2014–2018

B411	£10	Orange brown	£12	£18
B412	£20	Purple	£28	£40
B413	£50	Red, Boulton, Watt reverse	£60	£75
B414	£5	Polymer, Churchill		£8
B415	£10	Polymer, Jane Austen		£14

No paper £5 notes were issued with Cleland signature

SARAH JOHN 2018–

B416	£20	Polymer, Turner	face	£8
B417	£10	Polymer, Jane Austen	face	£14
B418	£50	Polymer, Alan Turing	face	£65

Missed an issue?

If you've missed an issue of Stamp Magazine, you can order it online, subject to availability

JUST £4.99 plus p&p

ALSO AVAILABLE

- **Stamp Magazine branded binders**
- **British Stamp Market Values**
- **dozens of other hobby magazines**

Order online: www.mags-uk.com
Order by telephone: 01795 662976

SOVEREIGN RARITIES LTD

For the rarest historic coins, and the most exciting modern issues.

17-19 MADDOX STREET, LONDON, W1S 2QH
INFO@SOVR.COM   TEL: +44 (0)20 3019 1185

WWW.SOVR.CO.UK

RP COINS
Dealers in Coins, Accessories and Numismatic Literature.

Check the website for our extensive range of stock and if you don't see what you are looking for – please ask.
PO Box 367, Manchester, M25 9ZH   Phone: 07802 713444
www.rpcoins.co.uk   Email: sales@rpcoins.co.uk

ABC Coins and Tokens

We stock a large selection of Scottish coins, tokens and communion tokens and also offer a wide range of hammered and milled British and World coins, tokens and numismatic books.

Always interested in purchasing new material

Contact David at:
Alnwick British & Colonial Coins & Tokens
P.O. Box 52, Alnwick, Northumberland
NE66 1YE, United Kingdom

Website: www.abccoinsandtokens.com
E-mail: enquiries@abccoinsandtokens.com
Telephone: 01665 603851

DAUWALDERS

WE BUY AND SELL QUALITY BRITISH COINS

SHOP OPEN 6 DAYS EACH WEEK

01722 412100
www.dauwalders.co.uk
42 Fisherton Street, Salisbury SP2 7RB

ADVERTISING INDEX

A.D.HAMILTON	140
ABC COINS	177
AMR COINS	33
ANTHONY HALSE	53
ARROWFILE	37
B& G COINS	15
C.J. DENTON	162
CHARLES RILEY	63
COLIN COOKE	27
COLLECTORS FORUM	63
DAUWALDERS	177
DAVISSONS	16
DIX ,NOONAN, WEBB	12
DORSET COIN CO.	15
DRAKE STERLING NUMISMATICS	130
GUERNSEY POST OFFICE	85
HALLS HAMMERED COINS	83
HERITAGE AUCTIONS	9
HISTORY IN COINS	130
H.W. WOOD	42
KNIGHTSBRIDGE COINS	131
LONDON COIN CO.	107, 163
LONDON & MIDLAND COIN FAIRS	16
MARK RASMUSSEN	5
MALCOLM BORD (GOLD COIN EXCHANGE)	71
MERSEYSIDE COLLECTORS CENTRE	140
MIDDLESEX COINS	140
MORTON & EDEN LTD	IFC
PAUL DAVIES	48
PETER MORRIS	48
PHILATELIC HERITAGE	23
R.INGRAM	17
ROYAL GOLD	67
RP COINS	177
SILBURY COINS	53
SOVEREIGN RARITIES	21, 106, 140, 162, 177
ST JAMES 'S AUCTIONS	4, 47, 141, OBC
STAMP INSURANCE SERVICES	167
TOM HART	106
UPA	152, 153
WARWICK & WARWICK	IBC
WHYTES	162
YORK COINS	53